ADVANCES IN
HUMAN ECOLOGY

Volume 2 • 1993

EDITORIAL ADVISORS

ADVANCES IN
HUMAN ECOLOGY

Editor: LEE FREESE
Department of Sociology
Washington State University

*PUBLISHED IN ASSOCIATION WITH THE
SOCIETY FOR HUMAN ECOLOGY*

VOLUME 2 • 1993

 JAI PRESS INC.

Greenwich, Connecticut   *London, England*

CONTENTS

LIST OF CONTRIBUTORS

Kenneth E. Bailey

Department of Sociology
University of California, Los Angeles

Curtis E. Beus

Department of Rural Sociology
Texas A&M University

A.R. Maryanski

Department of Sociology
University of California, Riverside

Emilio F. Moran

Department of Anthropology
Indiana University

Marvin E. Olsen

Department of Sociology
Michigan State University

Jonathan H. Turner

Department of Sociology
University of California, Riverside

Carlo C. Yaeger

Human Ecology Group
Swiss Federal Institute of Technology

PREFACE

EDITORIAL POLICY

This series publishes original theoretical, empirical, and review papers on scientific human ecology. Human ecology is interpreted to include structural and functional patterns and changes in human social organization and sociocultural behavior as these may be affected by, interdependent with, or identical to changes in ecosystemic, evolutionary, or ethological processes, factors, or mechanisms. Three degrees of scope are included in this interpretation: (1) the adaptation of sociocultural forces to bioecological forces; (2) the interactions between sociocultural and bioecological forces; (3) and the integration of sociocultural with bioecological forces.

The goal of the series is to promote the growth of human ecology as a transdisciplinary problem solving paradigm. Contributions are solicited without regard for particular theoretical, methodological, or disciplinary orthodoxies, and may range across ecological anthropology, socioecology, sociobiology, biosociology, environmental sociology, ecological economics, ecological demography, ecological geography, and other relevant fields of specialization. The editor will be especially receptive to contributions that promote the growth of general scientific theory in human ecology. No single volume will represent the full range the series is intended to cover.

CONTENTS OF VOLUME 2

The contributors to this volume are based in anthropology, economics, and sociology. Their contributions reach well beyond their disciplinary bases.

The volume begins with several theoretical papers that address evolutionary and ecological foundations for sociology's most fundamental subject: social organization. Jonathan H. Turner and A.R. Maryanski review and critique various efforts to supply biological foundations for social organization, as an introduction to their own analysis of biological foundations. They base their analysis on an application of evolutionary theory to the available fossil and archaeological record, in order to describe selection pressures for increasing hominid social organization. Marvin E. Olsen follows this with two complementary papers that sketch some general ecological and evolutionary properties of human social organization. In the first paper, Olsen analyzes what he takes to be the critical components that constitute socioecological organization: tools, resources, energy, and power. With the concept of power Olsen is able to link socioecological with sociocultural organization—one of his principal aims.

In the second paper, Olsen develops his results from the previous paper to explore an ecologically based theory of human macrosocial evolution, using a framework of self-organizing systems. In both papers (fully completed before his untimely death in 1992) Olsen develops, extends, and advances prior theoretical work done independently by Richard Adams and the editor. Curtis E. Beus, aware of Olsen's work, suggests that it together with the work of Adams, the editor, W.R. Catton, Jr., and R.E. Dunlap can be integrated with the POET model of Otis D. Duncan, which sought to incorporate bioecological components into the analysis of human social organization. Mostly, however, Beus devotes his effort to showing why such theory has not previously been developed much within sociology which, historically, has had the largest concentration of human ecologists.

Kenneth E. Bailey's paper attempts a fuller development of Duncan's POET model. It does this by explicitly considering the human ecological significance of the physical theory of nonequilibrium thermodynamics. The point is to establish that thermodynamic entropy is connected to social entropy. Bailey produces an extension of Duncan's model by way of social entropy theory. Carlo C. Jaeger focusses on one facet of human social organization: its economics. Jaeger takes as his point of departure the problem of greenhouse emissions, and tries to establish that high levels of emissions need not be an inevitable consequence of economic growth. Jaeger's equations describe conditions by which economic growth may become decoupled from physical growth over the course of sufficient generations, during which environmental policy can accommodate sustainable development and quantitative growth, and after which standards of living can be maintained and enhanced through qualitative growth.

The concluding papers, both rich in substance, are noteworthy for their distinctive methodologies. Emilio F. Moran undertakes to identify criteria that provide a minimum basis in terms of which data sets, obtained about human sociocultural functioning within different ecosystems, can be compared. Moran's criteria are developed from conditions found among current Amazonian populations, with intended application to other populations and other human ecological conditions. A. R. Maryanski, as she did in Volume 1, adapts the methodology of social network analysis to develop some evolutionary-ecological hypotheses about the form of the first hominid societies. Maryanski does this by examining contemporary primate social networks, reasoning that human social patterns must be connected to these by evolutionary descent. She finds that male-female bonds with a patrifocal emphasis would have been the most suitable candidates for natural selection under the savanna-like conditions of early human evolution. Taken together, the papers by Moran and Maryanski illustrate well the wide range of methodologies that studies of human ecology can employ when using an anthropological perspective.

Lee Freese
Editor

This volume is dedicated

to the memory of

Marvin E. Olsen

THE BIOLOGY OF
HUMAN ORGANIZATION

Jonathan H. Turner and A. R. Maryanski

ABSTRACT

The resurrection of the evolutionary paradigm in the social sciences has ushered in a variety of biological perspectives—from the strict propositions of sociobiology that stress the importance of genes alone for understanding human behavior to the new coevolutionary approaches that emphasize in varying degrees the importance of both genes and culture. This paper reviews the impact of evolutionary thinking on the field of sociology. It concludes that while reductionistic approaches have failed to make an impact on the field, coevolutionary approaches have been more successful and offer promise in understanding human organization. In addition, this paper summarizes a more basic historical/network perspective that can complement coevolutionary approaches by using data available from the fossil and archaeological records along with primate data to reconstruct the biological basis of human organization.

In the early decades of the last century, the titular founder of sociology, Auguste Comte, proclaimed that while "biology has hitherto been the guide and

Advances in Human Ecology, Volume 2, pages 1-33.
Copyright © 1993 by JAI Press Inc.
All rights of reproduction in any form reserved.
ISBN: 1-55938-558-8

1

preparation for sociology . . ., sociology will in the future . . . (provide) the ultimate systematization of biology" (Comte [1830-1842]1896). There is a certain irony in these confident words, uttered over 150 years ago, for now some are making the opposite assertion: biology will provide for the ultimate systematization of sociology. Indeed, one of the popularizers of the term sociobiology, Edward O. Wilson (1975, p. 4), was moved to assert that "it may not be too much to say that sociology and the other sciences, as well as the humanities, are the last branches of biology waiting to be included in the modern synthesis."

While the term *sociobiology* has been discarded by some in favor of alternative labels—biosociology, evolutionary biology, behavioral biology, evolutionary ecology, behavioral ecology, and so on—the basic goal of many such approaches is to explain human behavior and patterns of social organization in terms of biological processes, particularly those operating at the genic level (for overviews see Caplan 1978; Barash 1982; Freeman 1979; Bell and Bell 1989; Gray 1985; Chagnon and Irons 1979; van den Berghe 1990; Dickemann 1985). Such reductionism is viewed with great suspicion, if not outright derision, by mainstream sociologists; and so, hard-core sociobiology has not swept over the field. Yet, in rejecting or ignoring sociobiological arguments, sociological theorists have, we contend, ignored an important dimension of human organization. For humans are animals with an evolutionary history that has certainly influenced behavior and social organization. Too much sociology "brackets out" this fact and, as a result, sociology's theoretical formulations remain not only incomplete, but also somewhat mistaken about the nature of humans as an animal.

This paper will briefly review the basic tenets of hard-core sociobiology, emphasizing that sociologists are wise to be suspicious of this extreme approach for introducing biological forces into sociological explanations. We will also review other alternatives to hard core sociobiology, ranging from close kindred such as behavioral ecology to such real alternatives as coevolutionary strategies. We will then propose an alternative and much simpler strategy which can help "bring biology back into" explanations of human behavior and organization in ways that capture the flavor of sociobiology without its extremes, while at the same time, providing a supplement to coevolutionary approaches. This alternative takes us back to the older "instinct" theories of early social theory, but places it on a much sounder theoretical and empirical foundation.

HARD-CORE SOCIOBIOLOGY

Sociobiology, like all biological theories, builds upon Darwin's (and Wallace's) basic arguments about natural selection: Members of species reveal variations in their physical and behavioral traits; those traits best suited to securing resources in an environment will enable members to survive and reproduce, whereas those traits unsuited for securing resources in an environment will inhibit survival and reproduction; therefore, the environment "naturally selects" those members better able to survive and reproduce, while "selecting out" those unable to do so. Two major problems with the early Darwinian model is that it could not explain why conspecifics reveal variations in their traits or how these traits are inherited by surviving offspring. The rediscovery of Gregor Mendel's ideas on genetics in 1900 corrected for this problem and set the stage for the emergence of sociobiology (see Darwin [1859]1958; Mendel [1866]1948).

Curiously, genetics and Darwinian theory were not initially viewed as compatible, and in fact, "mutation theory" was seen as an alternative to natural selection as the basic explanatory mechanism of evolution (De Vries 1909-1910; Dennert 1904; Allen 1969). It was R.A. Fisher (1930) who forged the connection between genetics and natural selection by demonstrating that large mutations will almost always be harmful and doomed to extinction, thereby removing them from the gene pool of a species. Instead, small mutations that provide slight advantages in adaptation are the creative force in evolution, but such is the case only in concert with the directive force of selection to favor these small mutations. Fisher further argued that the "fitness" of a population to adapt and survive in an environment is a function of its degree of genetic variation. Those gene pools with high degrees of variation will provide a greater range of options for natural selection to work on, thereby increasing the "mean fitness" of a population to survive. The significance of Fisher's work is that it conceptually linked notions of fitness, selection, and genetic variation; and in so doing, provided the core ideas undergirding sociobiology. Fisher even went so far as to speculate on the relevance of these ideas for human social organization, setting forth a future path of inquiry for sociobiologists.

The transition to full-blown sociobiology came with George C. Williams' (1966) argument that the unit of selection is the gene. Genes, temporarily "housed" in organisms, which promote "fitness" or reproductive advantage will be retained in the gene pool. Williams went on to emphasize that "group selection" arguments (e.g., Wynne-Edwards 1962, 1986) are inappropriate: Genes are the only units of selection. And for Williams, the characteristics of groups—altruism, reciprocity, exchange, friendship, and the like—are the result of selection at the genic level for those traits in individual organisms promoting groupness, *if* groupness promotes fitness (or the capacity to pass on genetic material) in a given environment.

W.O. Hamilton (1963, 1964) took this line of reasoning further by introducing the notion of "inclusive fitness" which argues the following: Cooperation occurs among relatives because natural selection operates to promote "kin selection" in which those who share genes will interact and cooperate since such activities promote each other's fitness, or capacity to pass on their genes. And, the more genetic material relatives share, the more they will cooperate, since such cooperation keeps their genetic material in the gene pool. What might be seen as altruism, then, is a simple matter of self-interest: to maximize the genetic material that stays in the gene pool. The "goal" of genes, then, is to reproduce themselves; and it is "rational" for them to help maintain those bodies with similar genetic endowments. Genes do not "think," of course, but blind natural selection has operated in the past to promote behaviors in organisms, such as altruism, that increase fitness by maximizing the preservation of certain sets of genes in the pool.

The immediate problem in this argument is how to explain cooperation among nonrelatives or those who do not share genetic material. Robert Trivers (1971) introduced the notion of reciprocal altruism to account for this phenomenon: Natural selection can operate to produce organisms that will incur the "costs" of helping nonrelatives because at some later time these individuals will help them, thereby increasing their fitness. And, organisms that "cheat" and do not reciprocate will be selected out, because others will shun those who fail to return acts of kindness. Thus, once again altruism is disguised as selfishness on the part of individuals trying to maximize their fitness, or enhance their genes in the pool.

These are the core arguments of sociobiology: Genes seek to increase their numbers in the gene pool; those behaviors of organisms temporarily housing genes that promote fitness (i.e., the capacity to pass on genes) will be selected; and hence, social behaviors and patterns of organization among humans are to be explained in terms of their capacity to maximize fitness of genes. This argument has been modelled in a variety of ways, most notably in terms of game theory (Maynard-Smith 1974, 1978), but even here the argument is the same: The payoff of the game for its players, the genes, is fitness, with players adopting varying strategies to maximize fitness.

Several sociologists (e.g., van den Berghe 1981, 1986; van den Berghe and Barash 1977; Lopreato 1984) have adopted this sociobiological argument, although there is usually a caveat that culture is also involved. Indeed, some sociobiologists are now talking in terms of coevolution at the genic and cultural levels. But the basic features of society—favoritism of kin, or in Pierre van den Berghe's (1986) terms, "nepotism"; reciprocity and exchange; and even coercion—are the result of genes trying to maximize fitness.

The logic of a strict sociobiological explanation goes something like the following: Structure x exists in all human societies; it must, therefore, meet the needs of genes for inclusive fitness; structure x meets these needs in the following way (a story is now constructed, ad hoc, to explain how structure x allows genes to maximize inclusive fitness); and this relation between structure x and maximization of fitness is the result of "blind" natural selection processes (usually unspecified) in the distant past. These kinds of explanations tend to be illegitimate teleologies: The end-state or consequence of the structure—that is, fitness—is what causes the structure to exist. Such explanations also tend to be tautologies: Structure x exists; structure x must, therefore, promote fitness; otherwise structure x would not exist. To avoid these problems, which we should note plagued functional analysis (Turner and Maryanski 1979), it is necessary to provide a precise description of how selection processes worked to produce a given behavioral tendency or structure. But when one *begins* with the assumption of maximizing fitness, historical or empirical descriptions of particular selection processes are generally abandoned in favor of ad hoc scenarios about how fitness was maximized by a given behavior or structure. Such scenarios are easy to construct, and the end result is that sociobiological explanations often become pseudo-explanations that merely confirm unsubstantiated assumptions which, we should add, sound rather like those in modern rational choice theories.

Ironically, sociobiological explanations disconnect statements about the biological basis of human social organization from the actual history of the selection processes that supposedly produced this biological basis. In the place of such historical descriptions are unsubstantiated utilitarian-sounding assertions about genes, fitness, and maximization. In this respect, sociobiological explanations are much like the older "instinct theories" that posited, sometimes implicitly and at other times explicitly, lists of human instincts for such states as group affiliation, gregariousness, territoriality, aggression, hierarchy, and other instinctual behaviors. Sociobiology is superior to this older approach because at least it posits a mechanism—maximization of fitness by natural selection—but much like instinct theories, it is not clear just how and through what specific historical process a given behavioral tendency came to exist for a particular species. Indeed, whatever the species and whatever the trait, there is only one explanation: maximization of fitness. At times, of course, the history of selection processes producing particular traits cannot be known, but at other times it is possible to construct in broad contours a description of the selection forces operating to produce a given species and its distinguishing traits. In constructing the history of a species, explanation occurs in terms of the synthetic theory of evolution, but without the extra conceptual baggage of sociobiology.

The assumptions of sociobiology, even when advocated by sociologists, have not persuaded many in the social sciences, although one finds hard core analysis in anthropology (Chagnon and Irons 1979; Gray 1985; Dyson-Hudson and Little 1983) and psychology (Daly and Wilson 1978). As a consequence of this negative reaction, the assumptions of early, hard core sociobiology are now being repackaged in an increasing variety of alternatives.

BEHAVIORAL ECOLOGY

One direction in which sociobiology assumptions have been carried is behavioral ecology (e.g., Krebs and Davies 1987). As with Williams (1966) and later Dawkins (1976), behavioral ecologists are likely to regard organisms as temporary vehicles or survival machines in which genes survive and are replicated. Thus, the selection of genes is mediated through phenotypes; and those individual phenotypes that can survive in an environment are likely to keep their genes in the pool. The behavioral responses of organisms are part of the phenotype; and those responses that facilitate survival to the specific conditions of an environment are what enable genes to survive. Behavioral ecologists do not assert that there is a perfect match between genes and behavior; rather, behaviors are a complex mix of genetic influences and adjustments (read: learning) to the environment. Moreover, since clusters of genes at varying points on a chromosome or on different chromosomes produce most behavioral responses, such as foraging, mating preferences, and migration patterns, the relationship between genetic codes and behavior is complex. And, for some behavioral ecologists, this genic complexity is further compounded by learned adaptive components of behavior that are only influenced (as opposed to directed) by these clusters of genes. Yet, differences in behaviors within a species are, behavioral ecologists tend to argue, the result of genetic differences; and as variations in behavioral responses lead to differential rates of reproductive success, clusters of genes are either removed or retained in the gene pool.

The ecology of individual organisms is thus the stage on which behaviors are performed; and in Krebs' and Davies' words (1987, p. 22), evolution is "the process which selects individuals whose behaviour results in greatest success in the struggle to contribute genes to the population's gene pool." Hence, behavioral ecology seeks to understand how specific behaviors within ecological niches contribute to an animal's survival and reproductive success— that is, to its fitness.

Much behavioral ecology retains the basic assumption of hard core sociobiology. The genes of animals are selfish in that they seek to survive under given ecological conditions and to pass on as much genetic material as is possible. Then the vocabulary of modern-day economics is often added: Behaviors have "costs" and "benefits" in an environment; and animals are designed by natural selection to maximize "net benefit," defined as the amount of genetic material passed on to future generations, less the short term costs in lost genetic material from various behaviors. For some behaviors, however, optimality models do not work because the best behavioral strategy that maximizes "net benefit" is contingent on what other animals do; and so, to deal with this complication, game theory is imported from economics to explain the development of an evolutionary stable strategy or ESS (Maynard-Smith

1974, 1978) which, when adopted by most members of the population, cannot be beaten (extinguished) by any other strategy.

Thus, the array of animal behaviors—mate selection, foraging, cooperation, migration, fighting, rituals, and so on—are strategies that are employed to maximize an evolutionary payoff: fitness. Animals must act selfishly because their behaviors are influenced by genes trying to maximize their survival in the gene pool. And so, even "altruistic" and "cooperative" behaviors are an evolutionary stable strategy (ESS) that, under certain ecological conditions, function to maximize payoffs or "net benefits" to organisms and their selfish genes. Behavioral ecology thus sustains many extreme assumptions of hard core sociobiology, while importing some equally narrow assumptions from modern-day economics. While the verdict is not in on this marriage, its utility (pun intended) for understanding culturally-mediated behaviors is questionable. It is for this reason that coevolutionary and dual inheritance approaches have emerged in recent years.

COEVOLUTIONARY THEORIES

Even early sociobiologists recognized that genes may not be the only replicators driving the evolution of smart animals. For example, Richard Dawkins (1976) hedges his bets in the last chapter of *The Selfish Gene*, as have many contemporary sociobiologists in recent years. Dawkins posits a "new replicator" that he terms *memes*. The basic tenets of sociobiology—genic selection, inclusive fitness, and reciprocal altruism as these produce strategies and "survival machines" for genes—can explain how humans came to exist, but culture begins to supplement and supplant biology as the major replicating mechanism. Memes are those new cultural units that exist inside brains and that, via socialization, are passed on and preserved in a "meme pool." Dawkins recognizes that meme evolution will now begin to accelerate, for "once genes have provided their survival machines with brains which are capable of rapid imitation, the memes will automatically take over." And it might even be possible for memes to rebel against their creators, the selfish genes. Similarly, other biologically oriented social scientists have begun to talk in terms of "coevolution," operating at both the genetic and cultural levels.

Coevolutionary approaches all emphasize that evolution involves Darwin's emphasis on descent with modification, in which a set of elements is related by inheritance. In coevolutionary approaches this process of inheritance operates at both the biological and sociocultural levels; and so, biological and sociocultural evolution are guided by similar evolutionary processes. Yet, the isomorphism with biological forces varies in different coevolutionary approaches. For some (e.g., Durham 1991), biological evolution is but one type of a more general evolutionary process that also includes cultural evolution, whereas for others (e.g., Boyd and Richerson 1985, 1990), biological processes can provide the conceptual leads for developing distinctive models for understanding the evolution of traits in sociocultural systems. There are also differences in how much the biological and cultural inheritance systems influence each other. For some who remain sympathetic with sociobiology (e.g., Alexander 1979; Lumsden and Wilson 1981, 1982, 1983), much sociocultural inheritance is circumscribed by biology. For others much less committed to sociobiology (e.g., Boyd and Richerson 1985), the two systems of inheritance, the genetic systems of biology and the traits of sociocultural systems, are distinctive, although understandable with similar models emphasizing variation and selection processes. For still others (Durham 1991), the two systems of inheritance often interact. Let us briefly review the range of conceptualization in such coevolutionary models, beginning with those most connected to sociobiology and moving toward those least committed to sociobiology or behavioral ecology.

Alexander's Approach

Richard Alexander (1979) offered one of the earliest coevolutionary theories that invokes an analogy to the forces of evolution. For Alexander, "traits of culture" are learned by individuals, and these traits change in the direction of increasing the level of adaptation of their carriers to an environment. Cultural change operates in a manner parallel to biological change: There is "inheritance" through learning; there is "mutation" through invention; there is "selection" of cultural traits promoting adaptation; there is "drift" by accidents that lead some traits to disappear and by "isolation" that enable human populations separated by barriers to develop distinctive traits; and there is "flow" as populations come together mixing various cultural traits.

For Alexander, these processes operate to maintain a "link" between genetic and cultural "instructions." But this link is biased toward assumptions reminiscent of hard core sociobiology: Genic selection has already produced individuals who find certain cultural traits reinforcing, and so as people learn, adopt and use cultural traits, they do so in terms of genic constraints. Thus, culture is not so much a "replicator . . . but a vehicle of the genetic replicators" (1979, pp. 78-79). Coevolution in Alexander's eyes is, thereby, as reductionist as earlier hard core sociobiology.

The Lumsden-Wilson Approach

E.O. Wilson has, over the years, modified his early hard core approach when considering humans. He has, fortunately, abandoned the extreme notion of biogramers for each of the basic structures organizing humans (Wilson 1978), and along with Charles Lumsden (Lumsden and Wilson 1981, 1982, 1983;

Lumsden and Gushurst 1985), Wilson has moved to a more coevolutionary approach. The basic unit of culture is what Lumsden and Wilson term a *culturgen*. Culturgens are "an array of transmissible behaviors, mentifacts, and artifacts" within a population. These culturgens are processed through "epigenetic rules" that are genetically determined ways that the mind is organized or "hard wired" which, as a consequence, affect the probability that individuals will adopt and use various culturgens. It is possible, therefore, to construct "bias curves" representing the distribution, adoption, and usage of various culturgens; and these curves will be biased by epigenetic rules. These rules determine the distribution of culturgens by influencing individual choices that are then translated (through unspecified processes) into societal patterns.

These societal patterns and individual genotypes determine an individual's inclusive fitness which, under the influence of selection, can change genotypes, epigenetic rules and, hence, the culturgens that will be adopted and used. While this model is an improvement on Wilson's earlier efforts, it still reduces coevolution to genetic forces, mediated by epigenetic rules; and in so doing, it does not adequately deal with those processes of sociocultural evolution that operate independently of epigenetic rules.

The Pulliam and Dunford Approach

H. Ronald Pulliam and Christopher Dunford (1980, p. 8) begin with the recognition that with "the advent of social learning, the evolution of behavior begins to run on two tracks, genetic and cultural, which are interdependent but nevertheless separable." Cultural transmission occurs through learning, whereas a genetic trait "spreads in the population because it enhances fitness." The critical question is whether or not cultural traits also spread because they enhance fitness. For Pulliam and Dunford, cultural traits are "ideas," and they persist or die out depending upon the nature and number of their carriers (individuals) and the extent to which the ideas held by these carriers can be learned by others. Thus, cultural evolution is tied to selection among the carriers of ideas. Cultural ideas are selected out when their carriers do not pass on their ideas, whereas others are retained when these carriers can pass on to others their ideas.

Yet, Pulliam and Dunford do not carry their analogy to biological evolution very far. They do not draw out the full analogy between individuals as temporary vessels or carriers of cultural codes vs. individuals as "survival machines" for selfish genes. Nor do they develop a detailed theory of those processes, analogous to the forces of biological evolution, that change the relative frequencies of cultural ideas in a population. And finally, they do not specify the connection between genic and cultural selection. Other theories have, however, sought to fill in some of these gaps.

The Cavalli-Sforza and Feldman Approach

Another early cultural trait approach has been developed by Luigi Cavalli-Sforza and Marcus Feldman (1981; Cavalli-Sforza, Feldman, Chen, and Dornbusch 1982). The units of cultural transmission are "cultural traits" that are learned and, in their terms, are transmitted by nongenetic mechanisms like imprinting, conditioning, and instruction. For Cavalli-Sforza and Feldman, the central question is, what forces change the relative frequencies of traits over time in human populations? The answer revolves around the balances among several evolutionary forces: "Mutation," which in cultural evolution is purposive (innovation) and random (copy error), while being less inert than in genic evolution; "cultural drift," which is the movement of cultural traits among populations; "cultural selections," which are the decisions by individuals to use and adopt traits; and "natural selection" which, in the context of their theory, is the differential survival of "trait carriers" (not genotypes).

By calculating the net effects of these evolutionary forces, coupled with various modes of transmission of traits (vertical, horizontal, oblique, and mixes among these), it is possible to construct "transmission coefficients" that can make predictions about whether or not specific traits will be transmitted to others. Thus, the structure of transmission—that is, the relative importance of vertical (e.g., parent to children), horizontal (e.g., peer to peer), or oblique (nonparental elders to children)—determines the frequencies of cultural traits among a population. This kind of reasoning has been increasingly adopted in coevolutionary approaches.

The Boyd and Richerson Approach

Robert Boyd and Peter Richerson (1976, 1983, 1985, 1990) were first to use the term *dual inheritance*, and to forge a more detailed set of models to explain cultural transmissions. For Boyd and Richerson, humans acquire a great deal of adaptive information from others through imitation and learning; and so, cultural transmission involves the passing on of traits from generation to generation. And, since culture is transmitted, it can be studied using the same Darwinian *methods* used to study genetic evolution (Boyd and Richerson 1992). But this system of inheritance is distinctive in the sense that culture allows for acquired or learned variations to be transmitted; and yet, the fundamental processes—variation and selection of adaptive variants—are operative in both cultural and biological evolution. But unlike many coevolutionary theories, the "forces" of cultural inheritance do not always maximize fitness. There are "indirect biases" in which one cultural trait is used as an indicator of others which are viewed by some as useful traits and then transmitted via imitation (e.g., the imitation of behavioral styles of the wealthy by the less affluent); and there is a "frequency dependent bias" in which people imitate and learn those traits most frequently available, regardless of their fitness value. Yet, Boyd and Richerson recognize that people do not acquire cultural traits at random; they pick and choose what to imitate and learn. Cultural inheritance thus reveals "biased transmissions" in which people select what to imitate, and learn what seems most useful and adaptive. In this sense biased transmission is analogous to natural selection: Individuals choose from those available cultural variants that which is most likely to facilitate their adaptation to their environment. Finally, there is "guided variation," which are the "rules" guiding which cultural variations are selected for imitation and learning. These rules can, perhaps, have a genetic basis (thereby linking this process to those in sociobiology and evolutionary psychology), or they can be cultural in nature and, hence, the product of past transmissions.

These "forces"—guided variation, biased transmission, frequency bias, and indirect bias—of cultural transmission operate like those in biological evolution, with selection among existing variants. But there are important differences: Transmission is through imitation and learning; conscious decision making is involved; and acquired variations can be transmitted. There is, then, a universe of dual-inheritance—one cultural, the other biological—that can be analyzed in terms of similar methods of Darwinian evolution, but whose substance differs in significant respects.

Durham's Approach

For William Durham (1991, 1992), the basic issues in the analysis of coevolution are the processes by which cultural systems change through time and the relationship of these changes in cultural ideas to the genetic system of inheritance. The answers revolve around a series of common evolutionary processes:

- units of culture or "memes" (Dawkins 1976) that organize information to regulate phenotypes of behavior;
- alternative variants of memes termed "holomemes";
- "allomemes" which are the subsets of holomemes actually used to guide behavior in an environment;
- "nonconveyance forces" that influence the extent of variation among allomemes, including "innovations" (the analogue of mutation), "migrations" (the analogue of gene flow), and "cultural drift" (the analogue of genetic drift);
- "conveyance forces" (some of which are analogous to natural selection) influencing the transmission and relative frequency of allomemes;
- "cultural fitness" of allomemes, or the "overall suitability" of cultural memes for "replication" and "use" by a population;

- "cultural selection" or the "differential social transmissions of cultural variants through human decision making," preference, or imposition (by social structures of power and other forms of constraint).

The analysis of cultural evolution thus involves efforts to understand the relative frequencies and rates of transmission of memes in the "cultural meme pool," although Durham does not quite phrase the matter in these terms. Instead for Durham, there is an "ideational" or "cultural" space that influences, to varying degrees, the "phenotypic space"; and when changes in the elements of this phenotypic space are influenced by culture independently of changes in genotypes, then this change is "pure" cultural evolution. At other times changes in phenotypic space are confounded with changes in genotypes and are, therefore, a case of biocultural evolution. Thus, coevolution for Durham involves a simultaneous analysis of the common evolutionary processes operating at the genic and memic levels, along with an effort to determine the relative effects of the forces of genetic and memic evolution on phenotypes among members of a population. While there are important differences between biological and cultural evolution—especially those revolving around the forces of influencing variation and selection (e.g., choice, learning, power), the processes can be analyzed in roughly equivalent ways, because there is a pan evolutionary process across the biological and sociocultural realms. This equivalence and the isomorphisms it implies provide a useful way to assess the relative effects of biological and cultural evolution.

ON THE ORIGINS OF HUMANS

Implications For Theorizing About The Biology of Social Organization

As this cursory review of more recent efforts to incorporate biological thinking into the analysis of human social organization underscores, there is a broad range of opinion on just how to proceed. Sociobiology and behavioral ecology, as well as additional variants like evolutionary psychology (e.g., Daly and Wilson 1988a, 1988b), emphasize that evolutionary processes have produced a species with certain biological predispositions to behave and, hence, to organize in certain ways revolving around genic fitness. There is an appeal to this kind of thinking—one that goes back to older "instinct" theories about human nature. For it is important to know what, if any, biological forces constrain human behavior and social organization. The problem with the old as well as the new sociobiological versions of such approaches is that they have an ad hoc quality, because few details are given about the selection pressures in the sixty-five million year history of the primate order.

Coevolutionary approaches have an appeal that resonates with early functional theorizing: to see the organic and sociocultural realms as operating in terms of common and, in some approaches, interdependent evolutionary processes. While this approach appears promising, just how far the adoption of Darwinian evolutionary concepts and models to sociocultural processes will go remains an open question. Yet, those coevolutionary models most removed from sociobiology and behavioral ecology—for example, Durham (1991) and Boyd and Richerson (1985)—do not offer a picture of "human nature" and its effects on social organization. Instead, the effect of biology on culture is usually modeled for a specific trait or set of memes. While this is prudent, especially in comparison with the extreme assumptions of hard core sociobiology, it does not provide a broader picture of how humans' biological evolution now shapes the basic nature of human organization—a point of emphasis which, despite all of the problems, made older instinct theories as well as present-day sociobiological theories sociologically intriguing.

One way to reconnect biology to social structure without the extremes of sociobiology is to consider a more empirical approach. Instead of starting with sweeping assertions about the maximization of fitness and then constructing a story to fit such presuppositions, we might begin by turning to the fossil and archaeological record to construct a historical picture of primate evolution in Darwinian terms, and ask how this account can help us to understand human social organization. This approach takes what is interesting in sociobiology— the way biological forces impinge upon social organization—without the extremes. Such a delineative exercise can supplement coevolutionary approaches, to the extent that humans' primate legacy sets up certain genetically-based biases in people's choices about what memes and traits they will select and choose from among existing variations, or what types of sociocultural traits they will create and construct. This descriptive approach loses the precision of most models of sociobiology and coevolution, but what it lacks in elegance it makes up for in interest and congruence with humans' long-term evolutionary history.

An Abridged Evolutionary Account of Human Evolution

A first step in bringing biology back into sociology is to begin by viewing humans as members of the primate order who, while sharing a common evolutionary history with other existing primates, at some point in time diverged into the hominid line leading to humans. As obvious as this statement is, it permits us to consider the biological bases of human organization in a far more sober way and with far more detail and plausibility than most sociobiological approaches. Its advantages over hard-core sociobiology include the following: First, it uses the historical record, as best this can be documented, to uncover what actually occurred as natural selection worked on variations and small mutations. Second, it utilizes the accumulated data on living primates, rather than ad hoc scenarios, to develop inferences about humans' most basic behavioral, interactional, and organizational propensities. Third, it avoids reductionism and, as a consequence, allows for the operation of selection processes that operate at times independently of selection at the genic level. Fourth, it is unburdened with the unsubstantiated utilitarian assumptions of sociobiology, and instead it employs only the most basic ideas of evolutionary biology—variation, natural selection, and speciation—to explain the biological basis of human organization. Fifth, it complements coevolutionary approaches in arguing that there are basic biological pressures behind the selection or choice of sociocultural traits by human populations. While the procedure for applying this approach includes the use of such methodical techniques as social network analysis and the historical/ comparative method in concert with the fossil and archaeological records, the following synopsis on hominoid (i.e., ape and human) evolutionary history will hopefully serve to sketch this approach and to highlight its potential value for providing insights into the biological foundations of human organization.

Differentiation of Hominoids and Monkeys

Most of the biological characteristics that distinguish primates from other mammalian orders are the result of adaptation to an arboreal niche where natural selection operated in a number of interconnected levels—anatomical, neurological, behavioral, and organizational. Certain characters at all these levels—distinctive teeth and skeleton, comparatively large hemispheric brains, expansion of the neocortex right on top of the older limbic system, prehensile hands for dexterity and grasping, stereoscopic color vision, visual dominance over the other senses, reduced olfactory sense, and enhanced capacity for learning—are common to all higher primates (i.e., anthropoids—monkeys, apes and humans), while separating them from all lower primates (i.e., prosimians). For our purposes, it is the differences between hominoids (i.e., apes, and humans) and monkeys that are particularly significant.

Anatomical Differences. A major morphological distinction between monkeys and hominoids revolves around locomotor differences. The limb bones of monkeys reflect an adaptation in the ancestral line to quadrupedal locomotion with an emphasis on the hind limbs for propulsion, whereas the limb bones of hominoids reflect an original adaptation with an emphasis on the front limbs for propulsion of the body through space. That is, in the ancestral lineage, hominoids evolved a movement pattern with very efficient, mobile grasping forelimbs in order to suspend themselves entirely by two limbs and, when necessary, to perform hand-over-hand movements with the trunk held vertical (for discussions see Tattersall, Delson, and Van Couvering 1988; Rodman and Cant 1984; Napier and Napier 1985). The fossil and archeological records suggest that this rare locomotion strategy evolved in the Miocene epoch when competition forced early hominoids to seek out novel foraging zones such as the terminal branches of trees; and, thus, hominoids' anatomy differs dramatically from that of monkeys in such features as hands, wrists, trunk, tail, and shoulders[1] (see Andrews 1981; Temerin and Cant 1983; Ciochon and Corruccini 1983). In turn, this rare and marginal niche seemingly produced significant differences in the organization and neuroanatomy of hominoids and monkeys.

Neurological Differences. At the neurological level, ancestors in the hominoid lineage developed considerably more fissuration of the cortical surface of the brain, creating a significant expansion of the neocortex relative to monkeys (Campbell 1974, p. 262; Steklis and Erwin 1988). All hominoids are equipped with an arm-hanging "brachiator adaptation"—that is, propulsion dominated by the front limbs (Hunt 1991). Seemingly, when survival depends upon reaching and grabbing in a three dimensional area, selection favored the "brachiator adaptation" along with the storing of memories about the relative size, distance, touch, and strength of branches and a general recognition of size, form, weight, and what lies under the surface of objects. As a result of this expansion, the cortical association areas in hominoids (relative to monkeys) were further elaborated for processing sensory information especially through the dominant visual system (see Maryanski and Turner [1992], for a detailed analysis of the primate brain). Further, reliance on the integration of sensory information in the association zones of the neocortex led to an increase in the size of the cortical areas of the brain and a reorganization of the older limbic system. These neurological milestones are seemingly reflected in living hominoids: Only apes reveal the same asymmetry as humans in the left hemisphere of the neocortex, where the length and height of the Sylvian fissure are greater on the left than on the right (Heilbroner and Holloway 1989, p. 210). Since this area is where the language functions of humans (i.e., Broca's and Wernicke's areas) are located, it is reasonable to speculate, as we will do soon, that the rudimentary neurological capacity for what was later to become "culture" in the hominid line was always more potent in hominoids than monkeys (see Geschwind and Damasio 1984; Geschwind 1985, p. 272). The fact that present-day chimpanzees and gorillas have linguistic abilities or "quasi-linguistic abilities" (Savage-Rumbaugh, McDonald, Sevcik, Hopkins, and Rubert 1986; Gardner, Gardner, and Cantfort 1989) indicates that the neurological foundation for language (and hence culture) was laid under selection pressures that probably had little to do originally with language functions. This hypothesis has been recently buttressed by a ground-breaking experiment where a bonobo chimpanzee (*Pan paniscus*) was shown capable of acquiring a large repertoire of symbols to communicate without being explicitly trained to do so, and is seemingly capable of comprehending human speech sounds at the ability level of a two year old human child (see Savage-Rumbaugh, Murphy, Sevcik, Brakke, Williams, and Rumbaugh 1993).[2]

This unique asymmetry shared by hominoids (i.e., apes and humans) is probably related to expansion of the association areas (*inferior parietal lobe* in humans) located along the Sylvian fissure (Galaburda 1984; Campbell 1985, p. 341). These association areas appear to increase cortical control over the limbic system and to integrate intra- and cross-modal associations of the basic senses—vision, haptic (touch, feel), auditory (hearing), and olfactory (smell)—under the dominant visual system. Monkeys can also make intra- (i.e., vision-vision, auditory-auditory, etc.) and cross- (vision-touch, auditory- vision) modal associations, but not with the speed or ease of apes (Andersen, Asanuma, Essick, and Siegel 1990, p. 66; Horel 1988). Thus, the expansion of the neocortex and the development of the association zones that produced an asymmetry of the left and right hemispheres were probably, in part, the result of selection for adaptation to the extremes of the arboreal niche, where greater thought, memory, and integration of sensory information would increase fitness for hominoids feeling and grasping their way around the undersides of branches and the extremes of tree foliage. Only much later in the evolution of hominids (i.e., near to or on the line to humans) would these neurological changes have significance for the evolution of language and culture (see later discussion).

Behavioral and Organizational Differences. Neurological changes are reflected in the behavior of apes and monkeys. Apes reveal considerably more capacity than monkeys for deliberate and reflective action, and they appear to have more ability to use memories to guide current behavior (Passingham 1982; Jarvis and Ettlinger 1977). But especially important are behavioral changes associated with the varying organizational patterns of apes and monkeys. Monkeys form relatively tight-knit group structures, often organized along matrilines (several generations of related females) and male dominance (Jolly 1985, p. 124ff; Napier and Napier 1985, p. 76; Sade 1972; Rhine and Maryanski 1993). These matrilines and the nature of the group are sustained by females staying in the group at puberty, and by males leaving and becoming lone males or by joining an all male group or attaching themselves to another heterosexual group where multiple males are ranked in a dominance hierarchy (Maryanski 1992). In contrast, apes reveal very loose, local group structures, where most adult ties are weak or nonexistent and where intergroup mobility is high, although there appears to be a larger community structure (among chimpanzees and possibly gorillas and orangutans) within which mobility across groups occurs (Maryanski 1987, 1992). This loose and fluid structure is maintained by behaviors that are the exact opposite of those evident among monkeys. That is, unlike monkeys, both male and female apes transfer out of the local groups at puberty except among chimpanzees where only females leave at puberty (Tuttle 1986, pp. 249-256; Rodman and Mitani 1987; Harcourt 1978; Stewart and Harcourt 1987; Pusey and Packer 1987; Nishida and Hiraiwa-Hasegawa 1987). The selection pressures generating these differences in group structures and the behaviors sustaining them (for details see Maryanski and Turner 1992) were probably produced by the varying arboreal niches of apes and monkeys. Before their separation about 20 million years ago in the Miocene, apes and monkeys were not greatly differentiated in locomotion patterns (Fleagle 1988, pp. 363-373) and were probably very similar in their overall organizational arrangements (although this can never be known for sure); but, as apes were pushed to the arboreal extremes, selection seemingly worked to *decrease* the degree of group structure and the behaviors sustaining this structure. An arboreal fringe where selection once favored the emergence of the specialized anatomy found in all living apes and humans probably could not support larger, stable groups held together by matrilines. A marginal niche by definition implies a dearth of space and food, and so selection pressures must have been intense to decrease ties and bonds while increasing individuality, transfer, and mobility (Maryanski 1987, 1992).

To be more precise, especially since this conclusion is central to our arguments for alternatives to sociobiology, all four extant genera of apes evidence no ties or weak ties among adult females, including mothers and their adult daughters (Maryanski and Turner 1992). This pattern precludes the continuity of social structure across generations, as is the case with most monkey species, called "female-bonded" societies, where social structures are built along intergenerational matrilines (Jolly 1985, pp. 124ff). In all four ape genera, young females transfer out of their natal group at puberty, thus breaking the relatively strong bonds between a mother and her offspring. In three of the four ape genera, adult males do not have strong ties because, like females in all ape species, adolescent males transfer out of their natal group (with the chimpanzee as the lone exception), nor do fathers have ties with their offspring (because paternity cannot be known in a promiscuous mating pattern, with the monogamous gibbon being the exception here). These patterns of tie formation in existing apes, then, would indicate that apes are not oriented to maintaining cohesive group structures and, in fact, are somewhat individualistic and mobile (see Maryanski [1992] for a network analysis detailing this conclusion). It is likely, therefore, that most ape species in the late Miocene developed similar weak tie patterns. Otherwise it is unlikely that modern apes would reveal them, especially since such network ties are an anomaly among Old World anthropoids.

Thus, the behavioral and organizational tendencies of hominoids, along with their distinctive anatomical and (as we will examine later) neurological features, were the outcome of natural selection pressures as they worked on organisms that seemingly could not successfully compete with monkeys in the arboreal niche. As a result, they developed distinctive features that allowed them to adapt in those areas where monkeys did not go; and it is these features—altered arms, wrists, fingers, shoulders; larger, more fissured, and complex neocortex with expanded capacities for thought, reflection and integration of sensory information; and loose and fluid organizational structures revealing considerable transfer, mobility, and individuality—that would be carried onto the African savanna and be subjected to the selection pressures of this habitat. If there is a basic biological core to humans, it resides in these anatomical, neurological, and organizational features as they had to be accommodated to an open grassland niche. Even with the picture only partly drawn, it looks much different than that portrayed in various scenarios in sociobiology and behavioral ecology.

Hominoids on the African Savanna

The African savanna is a vastly different habitat than the arboreal rain-forest niches in which hominoids had originally evolved. With a cooling trend and subsequent decline in the number of forests during the Miocene, some species of apes were forced to become increasingly terrestrial and, thereby, to adapt to niches on the African savanna (see Foley [1984] on the problems of hominid adaptation). Such adaptation was constrained, however, by the anatomical, neurological, and organizational features that apes had acquired in adapting to their various niches in the arboreal habitat. What, then, did hominoids bring to the savanna? On the basis of inferences from the fossil and archaeological records and living apes, the following are reasonable conclusions about the anatomical, neurological, and organizational features that apes brought to the savanna:

1. A generalized anatomical structure with several special abilities:

   - hand and finger dexterity;
   - excellent stereoscopic and color vision;
   - capacity to rotate the arm; and
   - ability to easily assume an upright stance and become temporarily bipedal.

2. A relatively large, hemispheric mammalian brain, with a number of distinctive features:

   - elaboration and fissuration of the neocortex over the older limbic cortex;
   - asymmetry of the hemispheres of the neocortex in those regions responsible for integrating sensory modalities; and
   - cortical control and integration of other sense modalities under the dominant visual modality.

3. A set of behavioral tendencies (female transfer out of groups at puberty; male transfer, at least for some ape species at puberty; weak or no ties among adult females; weak or few ties among adult males, at least for most species; weak or moderate but transitory ties between adult males and females with infants) producing an organizational pattern with very special characteristics:

- high individuality and few enduring or strong social bonds;
- high rates of mobility and transfer from group to group within a larger regional population; and
- little group continuity over time.

It is this legacy that the selection pressures of the savanna could work on; and it is in the molding by natural selection of these ape characteristics that the biological basis of human organization is to be found.

At an anatomical level, natural selection worked to produce bipedalism, the first distinct hominid trait (see White and Suwa 1987; Latimer and Lovejoy 1990) that would allow a line of terrestrial apes to take advantage of their dominant sense modality, color stereoscopic vision, in order to see predators and food sources across the savanna grasses. Along with these changes, the dexterous prehensile hands and fingers, as well as the flexible arm and shoulder joints, would change in ways facilitating greater abilities at carrying food while walking upright; and, eventually, these changes would encourage increased abilities at using crude tools and weapons for food extraction and defense in the predator-ridden savanna (see Maglio and Cooke 1978). There were also some mutually reinforcing effects of this process: Bipedalism encourages use of hands and arms which, in turn, cycles back and makes bipedalism more adaptive.

At the neurological level, it is difficult to know how much change was occurring. The endocasts available for early hominids (i.e., species near or on the line to humans) indicate a large, fissured neocortex, but these fossilized remains cannot tell us much about the organization of the neocortex (see Falk 1983; Tobias 1987). But if we can assume that early hominids had at least a neuroanatomy similar to that of present-day apes, then we can draw some inferences about how selection processes operated. Probably the earliest selection pressure was toward increasing cortical control of the senses, especially the auditory. While the auditory modality in all primates is housed in the neocortex, primate vocalizations are still connected to the more primal limbic system with the result that mostly emotionally-laden responses to the environment are possible (Snowdon 1990).[3] A loud hominoid that emitted sounds only partially under voluntary control would likely be handicapped on an open savanna plain, especially since hominoids are much larger than monkeys and would likely have to forage alone or in smaller groupings, making them more vulnerable to predation. Hence, there was probably selection pressure for increased volutional control and integration of the senses under cortical control, leading to elaboration in the size and fissuration of the association zones of the neocortex along the Sylvian fissure. Such changes did not necessarily increase the size of the brain, as endocasts of early hominids do not indicate that the size of the brain significantly increased (Tobias 1987), but probably there was reorganization of the brain to increase the voluntary control of vocalizations and to better integrate the visual, tactile (i.e., haptic sense), and auditory modalities for increased cross-modal associations and, in turn, increased thought and reflection to facilitate survival in a more dangerous environment. Moreover, to the extent that more cohesive and stable groupings were being selected as a means of increasing survival, increased cortical capacities would perhaps be necessary to overcome the lack of a biologically based tendency among apes to form strong ties and bonds. In contrast to hominoids, selection could easily work on monkeys, such as those present-day baboons living on the African savanna, to increase their existing biological propensities for tight-knit and stable matrilineal troops (see Rhine, Bolandf, and Lodwick 1985). But for early hominids, who in all likelihood had lost these strong tie-forming tendencies in the arboreal niche, natural selection would have little to expand upon, thereby selecting for expanded cortical functions. Yet, since the brain size of early hominids (as best can be inferred from the sketchy record) did not increase dramatically, change in the neurology of the brain probably revolved around increasing complexity of the association areas of the neocortex—a process that would increase control over the senses still connected to the limbic system, while at the same time expanding the ability for thought and deliberation.

At the behavioral and organizational level, natural selection on the savanna would clearly favor primates organized for defense, mutual assistance, and food foraging in a hostile environment without the natural protection afforded by the trees, just as selection favored savanna-dwelling monkeys who are highly organized. But for early hominids who lacked a strong biological propensity for strong ties and bonds, selection pressures could have only a limited effect on the genic reprograming of apes to be like monkeys. Selection would, in essence, have to overcome 15 million years of selection *against* strong ties, cohesive groups, and continuity of structure. There was, in all likelihood, selection for increased tie formation and bonding at the genic level, but it is unlikely that hominids could be completely "rewired" neurologically to be monkeys. And, it is probably for this reason also that the number of hominoid species continued to decrease after the early Miocene, where the fossil record documents an abundance of apes; for, they could not compete with monkeys in the declining forest canopy, nor could they all develop biological propensities for strong bonds and cohesive group structures, even under heavy selection pressures. Instead, almost all ape species were selected out, leaving the current handful of nonhuman hominoids who survive primarily because of their size but, more significantly, because of their continued reliance on an arboreal habitat (the gibbon and orangutan are arboreal, but gorillas and chimpanzees occupy the forest and the transitional zones between the forest and parkland habitats). Thus, those savanna-dwelling hominoids that could develop minimal bonding tendencies among age and sex classes and who could overcome the transfer and mobility patterns of apes, were able to survive. Among those who did can be found the species on the human line (i.e., hominids), but it is reasonable to assume that, although early hominids probably evidenced more bonding and tie-formation tendencies than current apes, their biological nature was in all likelihood still biased toward relatively weak ties and fluid group structures.

How, then, did hominids survive? Our answer is that there was a far more efficient way for natural selection to produce stronger group ties than to undo millions of years of ape evolution and completely "rewire" hominoids at the genic level. It was much simpler for selection to work on already existing neurological structures to produce, in a word, the capacity for "culture"; and once this capacity existed, biological selection and evolution became less important than cultural evolution, or at the very least evolution among humans would now be primarily coevolution. And so, if humans are altruistic and disposed toward reciprocity and other group-formation tendencies, the basis for these dispositions is more cultural than biological. Let us pursue this line of argument in more detail.

The Evolution of Hominids

In the context of our synopsis above, we offer below a descriptive scenario of what occurred between the time true apes first appeared in the Miocene (about 20 million years ago) to the emergence of *Homo sapiens* some 100,000 years ago. It is in this time period that "human nature" was formed and, then, supplemented by cultural forces revolving around symbol-use and linguistic communication.

It is, of course, difficult to discern the organization of early hominids in the archeological record. Yet, this record reveals just enough to allow speculation about the first groupings of species on a branch of the human line. The various species of *Australopithecines* (5 million to 2 million years ago) were, in all likelihood, hunters-scavengers who possessed few tools and who, given their small brains and ape ancestry, had rather loose-knit patterns of social organization.[4] Selection pressures initially operated to make them upright and bipedal so that they could see and run from prey, find and chase food sources, and carry their food in their increasingly dexterous hands freed now from their locomotor functions. Perhaps sticks and stones were used as weapons, since present-day apes reveal the capacity to throw objects and use branches as clubs.

Once upright, selection began to favor the organizational capacities of hominids, but as we have argued above, it is unlikely that biological selection could work on any existing genetic tendencies for tight-knit group structure. These, we suggest, had long been lost in adapting to the extremes of the arboreal habitat; and so, if more close-knit and stable organization was to be achieved, selection would favor instead changes in the neuroanatomy of hominids so as to facilitate bonding through increased facility at communication.

Around two million years ago the effects of selection pressures on the hominid neuroanatomy can be seen in the emergence of the genus *Homo* and in the successive changes to *Homo habilis* (2.0 to 1.6 million years ago), *Homo erectus* (1.6 million years ago), and *Homo sapiens* (approximately 100,000 years ago). *Homo habilis* was similar in physical appearance to *Australopithecines*, with the exception of its cranial capacity which jumped from the 400 cc to the 500 cc range of modern apes and Australopithecines to roughly 650 cc to 750 cc (see White and Suwa 1987; Grine 1988, Fleagle 1988). Moreover, the endocast evidence suggests that the brain of Homo habilis is structurally different from the brain of Australopithecines, with a configuration that looks more like modern humans in regard to development of cortical areas in the left hemisphere (Falk 1983), where speech-production among humans occurs.

The large increase in the brain size and complexity of Homo erectus—727 cc to 1200 cc—offer further evidence of how selection was working to produce a cultural or "proto-cultural" basis of social organization. These changes in the brain brought auditory senses under cortical control and increased the capacity for intra- and cross-modal associations; and, in turn, these alterations in the integrative functions of the neocortex increased the capacity for symbolization. Just when these symbolizations became "speech" and language cannot be known, but it is likely that Homo erectus used some kind of crude language, perhaps purely visual (hand signals, for example), and maybe vocal (arbitrary sounds to designate objects), or some combination of the two. Of course, it may also be true that Homo habilis possessed the rudiments of language and cortical control of the sense modalities, with Homo erectus taking these to a new level (see Conroy 1990; Tobias 1987).

Such capacities for language or proto-language were seemingly the result of new ways of hunting and scavenging. There would be advantages on the savanna favoring animals that could organize and hunt larger game (fewer competitors, plus extra amounts of protein, fat, and other nutrients), but a small bipedal primate would need to be an organized tool-user to undertake such activity. Selection would thus favor a primate capable of planning, calculating, and cooperating in stalking and trapping big game. Such capacities would only be possible with expansion of the neocortex. In turn, cooperation through symbol-use would strengthen social bonds, with the result that groupings would become more stable and enduring. With group stability, there would be clear advantages for a male-female division of labor as well as bondings between males and females. Males could leave the group to hunt; females could gather food close to a home base and, at the same time, care for children (who would, no doubt, suckle for several years, as is the case among hunters and gatherers today). But just how far, at the genic level, these processes went before culture and socialization into cultural codes supplemented genic evolution is hard to determine. We argue that selection at the genic level did not go as far as some hard core sociobiologists claim with their assertions about inclusive fitness.

The harnessing and use of fire by Homo erectus reinforced these selection pressures (Fleagle 1988, p. 439; Shipman and Walker 1989). Fire could be used in hunting (to panic game and drive them to their deaths, usually off a cliff); and this use of fire required forethought, communication, and coordination. Fire could also be employed to cook foods, especially to soften meat, and it could be developed as a technique for hardening the tips of wooden tools and weapons. But perhaps most importantly, the use of fire encouraged sociality as members of Homo erectus groupings came together by the fire, keeping warm, expanding their time together beyond daylight hours, and encouraging communication and emotional bonds.

The ability of Homo erectus to radiate all over the world testifies to the increased cultural fitness of a fire-using, tool-making, game-hunting, and group-organizing population to adjust and adapt to varied habitats.[5] Such fitness was not programed genetically, as sociobiology would argue but, rather, was the result of Spencerian group selection processes.[6] While selection worked on the individual in producing the larger brain, once this capacity could be harnessed for symbolization and organization, we believe that the group became a crucial unit, or mediator, of selection processes. Those groupings that could better organize to hunt, gather and reproduce would be more likely to survive. But, since increased organization depended on expanded neurological capacities, selection at the individual level worked to create more efficient tool-use and organization by favoring larger brained, more communicative hominids who could organize themselves efficiently. Such organization was not achieved by selection for biologically-based propensities for inclusive fitness, altruism, and reciprocal altruism, but by selection for big brains that could create cultural (rather than genetic) codes for male-female bonding, child-adult attachments, reciprocity, and other forms of sociality.

What sociobiology sees as genetic we view as predominately cultural and the product of symbolic communication among big-brained hominids. Our argument is thus coevolutionary. Those groupings that could create values, norms, traditions, and other symbol systems that encouraged (a) an efficient division of labor between age and sex classes, (b) a stable set of bonds among males, females and offspring, (c) a sense of obligation to relatives and group members, and (d) an enduring attachment of both males and females to the young were more likely to survive and reproduce themselves. Once the large brain to allow symbol-use was created, most of these processes would be more cultural than genetic. Indeed, to create such genetic tendencies would require an undoing of the relatively low sociality of apes. Moreover, once group or cultural selection processes were operative, selection would favor ever larger brains that would improve the capacities for symbolization and communication, thereby decreasing selection at the genetic level for increased bonding.

In fact, contrary to the arguments of sociobiologists, the easiest and most "opportunistic" path to increased organization for a somewhat individualistic ape is to increase brain size so that culture can be used to *increase* sociality. To reprogram an ape genetically to be a highly territorial, hierarchical, and matri-focal monkey is far more difficult than to expand brain size in ways that allow for flexible patterns of social organization, especially since much of the difficult neurological work had already been done in the arboreal niche. Thus, hominid evolution did not involve the "selfish gene" ruthlessly pursuing maximization of its self-interest, but selection for brain size and complexity so that hominids could be better culture-producers and culture-users. By the time *Homo sapiens* emerged around 100,000 years ago, this process of increasing communicative capacities was well developed; and with *Homo sapiens sapiens* (modern humans), coevolution with the cultural side as dominant became the key feature of change in humans and their patterns of social organization.

Figure 1 models the selection pressures that produced hominid sociocultural organization revolving around hunting and gathering. A model like that in Figure 1 emphasizes the cycles of selection processes at both the individual and group level. One cycle revolves around selection pressures for bipedalism: high grasses and numerous predators. As noted earlier, if a small ape survived on the savanna, it needed to see predators and prey over the high grasses; and this ability would be facilitated by upright stance. Once upright, tool-use and increased dexterity of hands would have selective advantages for gathering, hunting, defense, and carrying. Tool-use also feeds into the other selection cycle initiated by savanna conditions: increased social organization. An organized primate on the savanna is better able to find prey and to fend off predators; and as we have emphasized, symbolic communication would have selective advantages in that it would give flexibility to such patterns of social organization. Thus, as the larger brains of Homo habilis and Homo erectus signal, a mutually reinforcing cycle revolving around an expanded neocortex, increased levels of communication, and escalated use of cultural codes was initiated. And once started, there was increased selection pressure for more brain capacity, communication, and organization in terms of culture (i.e., smarter, more communicative, and flexibly organized troops were more likely to survive in competition with other troops of primates and under the harsh dangers of an open savanna and, later, the diverse habitats of Asia and Europe).

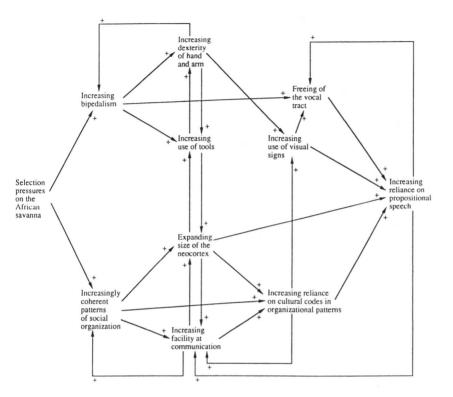

Figure 1.   Selection Pressures for Hominid Social Organization

At first a visual language may have been used, but this form of symbolic communication would be less adaptive than a spoken language (because it would be necessary to use vocalizations to get another's attention and, perhaps more significantly, it would prevent the use of tools or weapons at the same time as communication). Here again bipedalism feeds into the selective processes favoring organization by culture. It is believed that bipedalism prompted a change in vocal tract anatomy, making possible a large variety of sounds (Hill 1972; Duchin 1990) when there were sufficiently strong selection pressures for more efficient communication. Such selection for speech had to wait for growth of the neocortex to the point where it became possible to liberate the auditory sense modality from the limbic system (which is, in essence, the source of emotions) and to bring it under control of the neocortex and rational thought (see Maryanski and Turner 1992). As noted above, this may have occurred initially among other hominid species, but most certainly among those on the human line. But once this capacity for cortical control of the limbic system and the emission of emotions existed, there would be selective advantages for a speaking primate, encouraging the fine-tuning of the neocortex in ways creating the capacity for language as we know it today. The successive increases in brain size among Homo habilis, Homo erectus, and Homo sapiens, and then the fissuring (and increased complexity) in the brain of Homo sapiens sapiens, probably reflect the operation of these selection pressures.

At some point in the cycles portrayed in Figure 1, selection began to operate on the group as much as the individual level. Once the neocortex was developed to the point of organization in terms of symbolic codes, then individual and group selection combined for increased capacity to organize in terms of cultural codes, causing the expansion of the neocortex at the individual level that led to stable and flexible social groupings. By the time of *Homo sapiens sapiens*, selection was predominately "group" selection: Those populations that could use culture to organize in ways that created a set of stable bonds, a viable division of labor, and a capacity to learn and adjust organizational patterns to new or changing habitats could out-compete other hominids who were not so flexibly organized. Moreover, once cultural codes could be used to organize populations, diffusion of ideas about how best to organize became possible, enabling hominid populations to learn from each other. Up to the point of humans' current capacity for language and culturally based social organization, selection favored cultural as opposed to biological programing of group structure in hominids. Otherwise the rapid growth of the brain and its increasing complexity do not make any sense. Competition among hominids and other terrestrial primates may have been intense; and competition among culturally-organized hominids may also have existed. But the very nature of organization for hunting and gathering does not create great group selection pressures. Population densities are low, groups are dispersed, conflicts within and between groups are infrequent, and resources are easily secured even in difficult habitats. Thus, we suspect that there was little "warfare" and group selection among human hunters and gatherers, casting into doubt notions of genic selection for aggression or coercion. These too are cultural processes, initiated much later in human sociocultural evolution when humans settled down and population size as well as densities increased.

CONCLUSION

The suspicions that most sociologists have about hard core sociobiology are well founded, not because human biology is unimportant in understanding human behavior and organization but because many of the assumptions and assertions of sociobiology are unnecessary and, more significantly, inaccurate when applied to understanding the biology of human organization. There is a much simpler alternative to sociobiology; and we have attempted to paint in very broad strokes this more descriptive and historically based endeavor. The basic approach is (1) emphasize that humans are a primate, or an evolved ape; (2) consider the selection pressures that produced apes and separated them from monkeys; (3) list the behavioral and organizational characteristics of hominoids, making inferences from the organization of present-day apes; (4) explore how these were accommodated to the selection pressures of the African savanna and begin to speculate about the biological nature of early hominids; and (5) trace the evolution of hominids using the fossil and archeological records to speculate on the probable mixture of biological and cultural evolution.

Our story may not be correct, but it does rest upon the evolutionary record, as best as it can currently be extracted, rather than on often elegant but unsubstantiated models in sociobiology that reveal all of the explanatory problems of sociological functionalism and all the suspicious connotations of crude utilitarianism. What are the implications of this alternative explanation?

Probably the most radical conclusion is that humans, as a member of the superfamily, *Hominoidea*, may not be as social as sociological theory implicitly has assumed. Humans are not even social in the self-interested sense of sociobiology, with its emphasis on inclusive fitness and reciprocal altruism. But sociobiology aside, one of sociology's most fundamental assumptions is that humans are innately social, *to a very high degree*, and that humans have powerful biological needs for social bonds and group solidarity. Even the social pathologies of sociological analysis—egoism, alienation, anomie, marginality, estrangement, decentering, colonization of the life world, and so on—implicitly assume a biological basis for high sociality and solidarity.

This assumption is unsubstantiated, once we take a closer look at the biology and evolution of primates and at the obvious but very important fact that humans are an evolved ape with a biological propensity for weak-ties, loose and fluid social structures, and mobility. Indeed, what early sociologists saw as the pathologies of early urban-industrial society—loss of community, marginality, isolation, mobility, and so on—may be far more compatible with "human nature" than they assumed.

There are many further extensions of this basic conclusion about the biology of sociality. For example, we might view the apparent conflicts between collectivism and individualism, which are manifest in many different institutional arenas, as a reflection of a conflict between cultural constructions and our primate legacy. Obviously, these kinds of considerations are highly speculative, and we need not continue along these lines to make a simple point: Consideration of the historical record of primate and hominid evolution provides a fertile source of insight into the dynamics of human organization; and these insights can improve theorizing about social processes, if only by questioning implicit theoretical presumptions about "human nature." But much more is possible. Many of the dynamics of human organization, particularly some of the contradictions evident in human affairs, can be seen as influenced by the interaction effects of human culture as it was laid over our biological legacy as a hominoid who is far more individualistic, autonomous, and mobile than most sociologists have recognized or been willing to admit. Moreover, selection at the sociocultural level would, we predict, be biased by this primate legacy. Sociocultural evolution has its own internal dynamics, which have obviously generated and transmitted cultural memes and social structures violating the biological legacy of primates; and so we cannot push this point too far. But we will assert at least this much: Our primate legacy exerts a constant pressure on restrictive social structures and cultural memes, and it is an essential part of coevolutionary explanations of change toward less restrictive and constraining social structures.

ACKNOWLEDGMENTS

The authors wish to thank Peter Weingart and Gerhard Sprenger at the Center for Interdisciplinary Research (Zif) in Bielefeld, Germany for inviting us both to participate in the research project on the "Biological Foundations of Human Organization." Thanks also to Bill Durham, Peter Richerson, Rob Boyd, Signe Preuschoft, Peter Molnar, Bernt Giesen, Wulf Schiefenhövel, Boris Velichkovsky, Peter Hejl, Sandy Mitchell, Lorraine Dastow, Gerd Gigerenzer, Walter Goldschmidt, Monique Borgerhoff-Mulder, Nancy Thornhill, Sabine Maasen, John Tooby and Leda Cosmides, and all our fellow researchers for the many stimulating Zif conversations that guided the writing of this essay.

NOTES

1.   The especially free mobility of the wrists in *Hominoidea* is most likely the result of selection for arm-hanging and brachiation in the common ancestor of apes and humans; see Wolpoff (1980, p. 46) and Corruccini, Ciochon, and McHenry (1975) for a discussion of the relationship between wrist morphology and locomotor behavior.

2.   We should add that the second author of this paper just returned from a visit with Kanzi and concluded from conversations with him that, without question, this pygmy chimpanzee can quickly process and respond to human speech sounds, even spontaneous and quickly spoken utterances.

3.   The neural connections that underlie primate vocal calls are located in several regions of the brain, allowing for only rudimentary semantic signaling (see Cheney and Seyfarth 1990; Steklis 1985). Essentially the anterior ungulate gyrus (a limbic zone) has control over the production of vocal sounds (Snowdon 1990).

4.   For general references, see Foley and Lee (1989), Johanson and White (1979), Isaac (1978, 1989), and Kinzey (1987).

5.   The importance of meat in the diet of Homo erectus is unknown. But a major dietary shift toward game hunting of some kind originated with this hominid.

6. A case in point later in time are the well-known archaic *Homo sapiens*, notably the European Neanderthals. Many scholars believe that Homo sapiens neandertalensis was replaced by expanding populations of Homo sapiens sapiens. In modern times the invasion of one human population by another turns on organizational and technological superiority (see Campbell 1985).

REFERENCES

Alexander, R. 1979. *Darwinism and Human Affairs*. Seattle, WA: University of Washington Press.
Allen, G. 1969. "Hugo de Vries and the Reception of the Mutation Theory." *Journal of the History of Biology* 2:56-87.
Andersen, R.A., C. Asanuma, G. Essick, and R.M. Siegel. 1990. "Cortico-cortical Connections of Anatomically and Physiologically Defined Subdivisions Within the Interior Parietal Lobule." *Journal of Comparative Neurology* 296:65-113.
Andrews, P. 1981. "Species Diversity and Diet in Monkeys and Apes during the Miocene." Pp. 25-61 in *Aspects of Human Evolution*, edited by C.B. Stringer. London: Taylor and Francis.
Barash, D. 1982. *Sociobiology and Behavior*. New York: Elsevier.
Bell, R., and N. Bell. 1989. *Sociobiology and the Social Sciences*. Texas: Texas Tech University Press.
Boyd, R., and P. Richerson. 1976. "A Simple Dual Inheritance Model of the Conflict Between Social and Biological Evolution." *Zygon* 11:254-262.
_____. 1983. "Why is Culture Adaptive?" *Quarterly Review of Biology* 58:209-214.
_____. 1985. *Culture and the Evolutionary Process*. Chicago: University of Chicago Press.
_____. 1990. "Group Selection Among Alternative Evolutionarily Stable Strategies." *Journal of Theoretical Biology* 145:331-342.
_____. 1992. "How Microevolutionary Processes Give Rise to History." Pp. 180-207 in *History and Evolution*, edited by M. Nitecki and D. Nitecki. New York: State University of New York Press.
Campbell, B. 1974. *Human Evolution: An Introduction to Man's Adaptations*. Chicago, IL: Aldine.
_____. 1985. *Humankind Emerging*. Boston, MA: Little, Brown.
Caplan, A. 1978. *The Sociobiology Debate*. New York: Harper & Row.
Cavalli-Sforza, L.L., and M.W. Feldman. 1981. *Cultural Transmission and Evolution: A Quantitative Approach*. Princeton, NJ: Princeton University Press.
Cavalli-Sforza, L.L., M. Feldman, K. Chen and S. Dornbusch. 1982. "Theory and Observation in Cultural Transmission." *Science* 218:19-27.
Chagnon, N., and W. Irons. 1979. *Evolutionary Biology and Human Social Behavior*. North Scituate, MA: Duxbury Press.
Cheney, D., and R. Seyfarth. 1990. *How Monkeys See the World*. Chicago: University of Chicago Press.
Ciochon, R., and R. Corruccini, eds. 1983. *New Interpretations of Ape and Human Ancestry*. New York: Plenum Press.
Comte, A. (1830-1842)1896. *The Course of Positive Philosophy*. London: Bell and Sons.
Conroy, G. 1990. *Primate Evolution*. New York: W.W. Norton.
Corruccini, R., R. Ciochon, and H. McHenry. 1975. "Ostemetric Shape Relationships in the Wrist Joint of Some Anthropoids." *Folia Primatologica* 24:250-274.
Daly, M., and M. Wilson. 1978. *Sex, Evolution and Behavior*. North Scituate, MA: Duxbury Press.

————. 1988a. *Homicide*. New York: Aldine De Gruyter.

————. 1988b. "Evolutionary Social Psychology and Family Homicide." *Science* 242:519-524.

Darwin, C. (1859)1958. *On the Origin of Species*. New York: New American Library.

Dawkins, R. 1976. *The Selfish Gene*. London: Oxford University Press.

Dennert, E. 1904. *At the Deathbed of Darwinism*. Translated by E.G. O'Hara and J. Peschges. Burlington, IA: German Literary Board.

De Vries, H. 1909-1910. *The Mutation Theory*. Translated by J.B. Farmer and A.D. Darbishire. Chicago, IL: Open Court Publishing.

Dickemann, M. 1985. "Human Sociobiology: The First Decade." *New Scientist* 108:38-42.

Duchin, L. 1990. "The Evolution of Articulate Speech: Comparative Anatomy of the Oral Cavity in Pan and Homo." *Journal of Human Evolution* 19:687-697.

Durham, W. 1991. *Coevolution: Genes, Culture and Human Diversity*. Stanford, CA: Stanford University Press.

————. 1992. "Applications of Evolutionary Culture Theory." *Annual Review of Anthropology* 21:331-355.

Dyson-Hudson, R., and M.A. Little. 1983. *Rethinking Human Adaptation: Cultural and Biological Models*. Boulder, CO: Westview.

Falk, D. 1983. "Cerebral Cortices of East African Early Hominids." *Science* 222:1072-1074.

Fisher, R. 1930. *The Genetical Theory of Natural Selection*. Oxford: The Clarendon Press.

Fleagle, J. 1988. *Primate Adaptations and Evolution*. New York: Academic Press.

Foley, R. 1984. *Hominid Evolution and Community Ecology*. London: Academic Press.

Foley, R.A., and P.C. Lee. 1989. "Finite Social Space, Evolutionary Pathways, and Reconstructing Hominid Behavior." *Science* 243:901-906.

Freeman, D. 1979. *Human Sociobiology: A Holistic Approach*. New York: Free Press.

Galaburda, A. 1984. "Anatomical Asymmetries." In Cerebral Dominance, edited by N. Geschwind and A. Galaburda. Cambridge, MA: Harvard University Press.

Gardner, R., B. Gardner, and T. Cantfort. 1989. *Teaching Sign Language to Chimpanzees*. Albany: State University of New York Press.

Geschwind, N. 1985. "Implications for Evolution, Genetics and Clinical Syndromes." In *Cerebral Lateralization in Non-Human Species*, edited by Stanley Glick. New York: Academic Press.

Geschwind, N., and A. Damasio. 1984. "The Neural Basis of Language." *Annual Review of Neuroscience* 7:127-47.

Gray, P. 1985. *Primate Sociobiology*. New Haven, CT: Hraf Press.

Grine, F. 1988. *Evolutionary History of the "Robust" Australopithecines*. New York: Aldine de Gruyter.

Hamilton, W.D. 1963. "The Evolution of Altruistic Behavior." *American Naturalist* 97:354-356.

————. 1964. "The Genetical Theory of Social Behavior I and II." *Journal of Theoretical Biology* 7:1-52.

Harcourt, A. 1978. "Strategies of Emigration and Transfer by Primates, with Particular Reference to Gorillas." *Tierpsychologie* 48:401-420.

Heilbroner, P., and R. Holloway. 1989. "Anatomical Brain Asymmetry in Monkeys: Frontal, Temporoparietal and Limbic Cortex in Macaca." *American Journal of Physical Anthropology* 80:203-211.

Hill, J. 1972. "On the Evolutionary Foundations of Language." *American Anthropologist* 74:308-315.

Horel, J. 1988. "Limbic Neocortical Interrelations." In *Neurosciences*, Vol. 4, edited by H. Steklis and J. Erwin. New York: Alan Liss.

Hunt, K. 1991. "Positional Behavior in the Hominoidea." *International Journal of Primatology* 12:95-118.

Isaac, G. 1978. "The Archaeological Evidence for the Activities of Early African Hominids." In *Early Hominids of Africa*, edited by C. Jolly. London: Duckworth.

————. 1989. *The Archaeology of Human Origins*. New York: Cambridge University Press.

Jarvis, M.J., and G. Ettlinger. 1977. "Cross-Modal Equivalence in Non-Human Primates." In *Behavioral Primatology*, Vol. 1, edited by A.M. Schriver. Hillsdale, NJ: Erlbaum.

Johanson, D.C., and T.D. White. 1979. "A Systematic Assessment of Early African Hominids." *Science* 203:321-330.

Jolly, A. 1985. *The Evolution of Primate Behavior*. New York: Macmillan.

Kinzey, W. 1987. *The Evolution of Human Behavior: Primate Models*. Albany: State University of New York Press.

Krebs, J.R., and W.B. Davies. 1987. *An Introduction to Behavioural Ecology*. Oxford: Blackwell Scientific Publications.

Latimer, B., and C.O. Lovejoy. 1990. "Metatarso Phalangeal Joints of Australopithecus." *American Journal of Physical Anthropology* 83:13-23.

Lopreato, J. 1984. *Human Nature and Biocultural Evolution*. Boston, MA: Allen and Unwin.

Lumsden, C., and A. Gushurst. 1985. "Gene-Culture Coevolution: Humankind in the Making." Pp. 3-28 in *Sociobiology and Epistemology*, edited by J.H. Fetzer. Dordrecht: D. Reidel.

Lumsden, C., and E. Wilson. 1981. *Genes, Mind, and Culture*. Cambridge, MA: Harvard University Press.

————. 1982. "Precis of Genes, Mind, and Culture." *Behavioral and Brain Sciences* 5:1-37.

————. 1983. *Promethean Fire: Reflections on the Origin of Mind*. Cambridge, MA: Harvard University Press.

Maglio, V., and H.B.S. Cooke. 1978. *Evolution of African Mammals*. Cambridge, MA: Harvard University Press.

Maryanski, A. 1987. "African Ape Social Structure: Is There Strength in Weak Ties?" *Social Networks* 9:191-215.

————. 1992. "The Last Ancestor: An Ecological Network Model on the Origins of Human Sociality." *Advances in Human Ecology* 1:1-32.

Maryanski, A., and J. Turner. 1992. *The Social Cage: Human Nature and the Evolution of Society*. Stanford, CA: Stanford University Press.

Maynard-Smith, J. 1974. "The Theory of Games and the Evolution of Animal Conflicts." *Journal of Theoretical Biology* 47:209-221.

————. 1978. "Optimization Theory in Evolution." *Annual Review of Ecological Systems* 9:31-56.

Mendel, G. (1866)1948. *Experiments in Plant Hybridization*. Cambridge, MA: Harvard University Press.

Napier, J.R., and P.H. Napier. 1985. *The Natural History of the Primates*. Cambridge, MA: MIT Press.

Nishida, T., and M. Hiraiwa-Hasegawa. 1987. "Chimpanzees and Bonabas: Cooperative Relationships among Males." Pp. 165-180 in *Primate Societies*, edited by B. Smuts, D. Cheney, R. Seyfarth, R. Wrangham, and T. Struhsaker. Chicago: University of Chicago Press.

Passingham, R.E. 1982. *The Human Primate*. Oxford, England: Freeman.

Pulliam, H.R., and C. Dunford. 1980. *Programmed to Learn: An Essay on the Evolution of Culture*. New York: Columbia University Press.

Pusey, A., and C. Packer. 1987. "Dispersal and Philopatry." Pp. 250-266 in *Primate Societies*, edited by B. Smuts, D. Cheney, R. Seyfarth, R. Wrangham, and T. Struhsaker. Chicago: University of Chicago Press.

Rhine, R.J., P. Boland, and L. Lodwick. 1985. "Progressions of Adult Male Chocma Baboons (Papio ursinus) in the Moremi Wild Life Reserve." *International Journal of Primatology* 6:116-122.

Rhine, R., and A. Maryanski. 1993. "A Twenty-One Year History of a Dominant Stumptail Matriline." In *Evolutionary Biology and Behavior of Macaques*, edited by J.E. Fa and D.G. Lindburg. Cambridge: Cambridge University Press, in press.

Rodman, P., and J. Cant. 1984. *Adaptations for Foraging in Nonhuman Primates*. New York: Columbia University Press.

Rodman, P., and J. Mitani. 1987. "Orangutans. Sexual Dimorphism in a Solitary Species." Pp. 146-154 in *Primate Societies*, edited by B. Smuts, D. Cheney, R. Seyfarth, R. Wrangham, and T. Struhsaker. Chicago: University of Chicago Press.

Sade, D. 1972. "Sociometrics of Macaca Mulatta: Linkages and Cliques in Grooming Matrices." *Folia Primatologila* 18:196-223.

Savage-Rumbaugh, S., K. McDonald, R. Sevcik, W. Hopkins, and E. Rubert. 1986. "Spontaneous Symbol Acquisition and Communicative Use by Pygmy Chimpanzees (Pan paniscus)." *Journal of Experimental Psychology* 15:211-235.

Savage-Rumbaugh, S., J. Murphy, R. Sevcik, K. Brakke, S. Williams, and D. Rumbaugh. 1993. "Language Comprehension in Ape and Child." *Monographs of the Society for Research in Child Development* 58:1-169.

Shipman, P., and A. Walker. 1989. "The Costs of Becoming a Predator." *Journal of Human Evolution* 18:373-392.

Snowdon, C. 1990. "Language Capacities of Non-Human Animals." *Yearbook of Physical Anthropology* 33:215-243.

Steklis, H. 1985. "Primate Communication, Comparative Neurology, and the Origin of Language Re-examined." *Journal of Human Evolution* 14:157-173.

Steklis, H., and J. Erwin. 1988. *Neurosciences*, Vol. 4. New York: Alan Liss.

Stewart, K., and A. Harcourt. 1987. "Gorillas: Variation in Female Relationships." Pp. 155-164 in *Primate Societies*, edited by B. Smuts, D. Cheney, R. Seyfarth, R. Wrangham, and T. Struhsaker. Chicago: University of Chicago Press.

Tattersall, I., E. Delson, and J. Van Couvering. 1988. *Encyclopedia of Human Evolution*. New York: Garland Publishing.

Temerin, J., and J. Cant. 1983. "The Evolutionary Divergence of Old World Monkeys and Apes." *The American Naturalist* 122:335-351.

Tobias, P. 1987. "The Brain of Homo habilis: A New Level of Organization in Cerebral Evolution." *Journal of Human Evolution* 16:741-761.

Trivers, R. 1971. "The Evolution of Reciprocal Altruism." *Quarterly Review of Biology* 46 (4):35-57.

Turner, J., and A. Maryanski. 1979. *Functionalism*. Menlo Park, CA: Benjamin/Cummings.

Tuttle, R. 1986. *Apes of the World: Their Social Behavior, Communication, Mortality, and Ecology*. Park Ridge, NJ: Noyes.

van den Berghe, P. 1981. *The Ethnic Phenomenon*. New York: Elsevier.

————. 1986. "Skin Color Preference, Sexual Dimorphism and Sexual Selection: A Case of Gene Cultural Co-Evolution." *Ethnic and Racial Studies* 9(1):87-113.

————. 1990. *Human Family Systems: An Evolutionary View*. Prospect Heights, IL: Waveland Press.

van den Berghe, P., and D. Barash. 1977. "Inclusive Fitness and Human Family Structure." *American Anthropologist* 79:809-823.

White, T., and G. Suwa. 1987. "Hominid Footprints at Laetoli: Facts and Interpretations." *American Journal of Physical Anthropology* 72:485-514.

Williams, G. 1966. *Adaptation and Natural Selection: A Critique of Some Current Evolutionary Thought*. Princeton, NJ: Princeton University Press.

Wilson, E.O. 1975. *Sociobiology: The New Synthesis.* Cambridge, MA: Harvard University Press.

————. 1978. *On Human Nature.* Cambridge, MA: Harvard University Press.

Wolpoff, M. 1980. *Paleo-Anthropology.* New York: Alfred Knopf.

Wynne-Edwards, V.C. 1962. *Animal Dispersion in Relation to Social Behavior.* New York: Hafner.

————. 1986. *Evolution Through Group Selection.* Oxford: Blackwell.

COMPONENTS OF
SOCIOECOLOGICAL ORGANIZATION:
TOOLS, RESOURCES, ENERGY, AND POWER

Marvin E. Olsen

ABSTRACT

Socioecological organization is conceptualized as one of two fundamental realms of social organization, together with sociocultural organization. Four critical components of this realm are tool using, resource transfers, energy flows, and power exertion. Two recent complementary works by Lee Freese and Richard Adams that provide numerous insights into these four components are sketched and partially integrated. Freese's work focuses on resource transfers, which are the most basic activities within socioecological organization and are "action sustaining" for social life. Adams' work presents an "energetic" perspective that views all human life in terms of energy forms and flows, which can be transformed into power exertion. The principal point of theoretical convergence between these two works is that resource transfers are energy flows that make posssible the exercise of power. A set of theoretical principles is proposed in regard to each of the four components of socioecological organization.

Advances in Human Ecology, Volume 2, pages 35-67.
Copyright © 1993 by JAI Press Inc.
All rights of reproduction in any form reserved.
ISBN: 1-55938-558-8

INTRODUCTION

Background

Social ecology presently stands at a critical juncture. For nearly fifty years—since Amos Hawley's 1944 path-breaking paper on "Ecology and Human Ecology"—ecologically oriented sociologists have been attempting to apply ecological concepts and principles to human social organization. Major landmarks in this intellectual quest have been Hawley's (1950) classic book *Human Ecology*; Duncan and Schnore's (1959) "POET" scheme; Duncan's (1964) overview of ecological processes; Hawley's (1968) theoretical paper; Boulding's (1978) analysis of "ecodynamics"; Micklin and Choldin's (1984) collection of papers; and, most recently, Hawley's (1986) culminating theory book. These and many other writings have greatly expanded sociological awareness of, and knowledge about, the importance of ecology in human social life. However, they have not been particularly successful in integrating an ecological perspective into "mainstream" sociological thinking.

Most sociologists continue to view ecology as exterior to the major concerns of the discipline rather than as an integral part of the process of social organization. The challenge confronting ecologically oriented sociologists, therefore, is to demonstrate that ecological processes are a fundamental component of all social organization. In 1988, two social scientists—social psychologist Lee Freese and social anthropologist Richard Adams—attempted to perform this theoretical integration. Although they wrote without knowledge of each other's work, their ideas are highly complementary as well as creative, and deserve widespread attention among sociologists. (This was Freese's first writing on ecological theory. Adams had written two previous books [1975, 1982] that developed his perspective, but his 1988 book is more theoretically comprehensive. Unless otherwise noted, all references to Adams are to his 1988 book.)

Purposes

Because socioecological organization is one of the two basic realms—together with sociocultural organization—of the overall process of human social organization, a fundamental thesis of this paper is that *social ecology is an integral part of sociology*, not merely its "biological foundation" or a peripheral perspective. The paper discusses four basic components of all socioecological organization: *tool utilization, resource transfers, energy flows, and power flows*. Although these components are all highly interrelated, they can be separated for analysis, provided we always reintegrate them in our overall perspective. The discussion of each component includes a review of the relevance of those ideas for socioecological theory and some proposed principles pertaining to that topic.

More specifically, my purposes here are to: (1) extract the principal ideas of Freese and Adams concerning the four basic components of socioecological organization; (2) integrate those ideas wherever possible; (3) incorporate my own ecological thinking into this perspective; and thus (4) sketch a framework for understanding socioecological organization. This framework does not constitute an explanatory theory of socioecological organization, but merely attempts to clarify social ecological concepts that must be incorporated into any social ecological theory. In a companion paper titled "A Sociological Perspective on Social Evolution" (Olsen 1993), I examine Freese's and Adams' conceptions of the dynamics through which socioecological organization develops over time.

Three points should be made absolutely clear at the outset. First, this is a highly speculative paper that will require much refinement and elaboration in the future. Second, rather than presenting complete summaries of the works by Freese and Adams, I extract ideas from their writings that I find most intriguing and useful and sometimes modify them slightly to fit my argument. In doing this, I hope I have not misrepresented any of their thinking. Third, I make no effort to review all of the literature in numerous disciplines that lies behind this perspective, since Freese and Adams both give extensive reviews of that literature.

Terminology

Let me begin by specifying the key concepts used in the paper. *Ecology* is the branch of science, derived from biology, that examines the ways in which living organisms participate in the natural environment (both biotic and abiotic). It views all organisms as parts of ecological systems ("ecosystems"). *Human ecology*—which is the most commonly used term in the social sciences—is the branch of ecology that applies ecological perspectives, concepts, and principles to human beings, asking how they function as organisms within ecosystems. It thus examines human life from a multidisciplinary perspective, incorporating physical, biological, psychological, and social phenomena. *Sociological human ecology* (or more simply, *social ecology*) is the portion of human ecology that focuses on interrelationships between the natural environment and the process of social organization. It is thus the specific concern of sociologists.

Although the term "ecological system" is widely used in the literature, I prefer to speak of *ecological organization*. A system is always a constructed model used to analyze some real phenomenon. Systems do not exist in reality, only in the minds of analysts. Organization, in contrast, does exist in ecological and social reality. System models can be extremely useful tools in helping us understand the dynamics of real organization and formulating theoretical ideas about it, but ultimately we must be able to explain the real world. System terminology should therefore be used only in reference to analytical models, not real organization.

There are two forms of ecological organization. I use the abbreviated term *bioecological organization* to refer to biological-physical-chemical ecological processes and structures (thus including both biotic and abiotic conditions). I use the term *socioecological organization* to refer to social ecological processes and structures that occur within the overall totality of social organization. An alternative term for socioecological organization is the *functional realm* of social organization, which implies that all actions within this realm contribute to the dynamic functioning of social life. Social ecology attempts to explain this functional realm.

Socioecological organization is one of the two basic realms—or sides— of the total process of social organization. The other, parallel realm is *sociocultural organization*, which consists of interpersonal and interorganizational relationships that are infused with shared cultural meanings. An alternative term for this aspect of social life is the *relational realm* of social organization. This distinction between socioecological and sociocultural organization does not imply a dual nature of human social life. Rather, these realms constitute two sides of the same coin of social organization, and hence are totally interwoven and cannot exist apart from one another. The functional and relational sides of social organization can be separately examined, however, to provide a duality of analytical perspectives in sociology, just as a coin can be viewed as either "heads" or "tails." This paper focuses on the functional realm, since ecological processes are an integral part of socioecological organization but not of sociocultural organization.

Finally, both Freese and Adams frequently use the terms *dynamics* and *process*. Both terms depict social life as continually changing and imply that reality is active rather than static. The terms "dynamics" and "process" have somewhat different denotations, however. Dynamics implies that energy is the ultimate reality, while process implies that change is directional toward some end. Since both denotations are relevant to the thesis of this paper, I use the terms interchangeably with the understanding that both refer to the combined concept of *dynamic processes*.

Throughout this paper, I use my terms for all concepts except in direct quotations from others. Whenever my term differs from one used by Freese or Adams, his equivalent term is given in brackets.

TOOL UTILIZATION

Human Sociality

To provide a basis for examining the contributions of Freese and Adams to socioecological theory, I begin with a recent study of the origins of human sociality by Alexandra Maryanski (1992). Her study reviewed the existing literature on the social patterns of the great apes, coded those observations into a multidimensional model, and used the conclusions of that analysis to speculate about the genetic basis of human sociality. These speculations rest on the widely accepted belief that apes and humans share a common ancestor, and the fact that they are our closest living nonhuman relatives.

The conclusions drawn by Maryanski about the social behavior of apes were that:

> [A]pes loom as an anomaly in an order renowned for its high sociability. In orangutans, mostly lone individuals are reported; in gibbons, heterosexual pairs who share domestic activities prevail; in gorillas, lone males are common, while group members mostly keep to themselves; and in chimpanzees, adult males are gregarious, but are more frequently alone, while adult females are semi-solitary. Overall, apes are self-contained and highly individualistic (p. 224).

Maryanski's subsequent speculations about the genetic basis of human sociality were as follows:

> One of the great assumptions of sociology and anthropology is that high sociality is part of human nature, leading humans to seek out high levels of group involvement and embeddedness.... But humans are hominoids and, therefore, assumptions about their inherent gregariousness are questionable. At the very least, the data presented suggest that we should inquire into how strong humans' genetic social predisposition is. That natural selection pressures for greater sociality have enhanced human network ties relative to other hominoids cannot be denied. Yet... humans and the African apes recently shared a common ancestor.... Is it possible that what appears to be intense group-bonding tendencies may, in fact, be largely culturally generated and socially transmitted needs that are not rooted in humans' genetic structure (p. 24)?
>   At a biological level, humans may be far more solitary and individualistic than the collectivist-communal biases of sociology and anthropology would admit (pp. 25-26).

The main point made by Maryanski is that, genetically, humans may be quite individualistic rather than communal. Sociality is a social rather than a genetically based capacity, so that most human social organization is a learned and culturally transmitted phenomenon—a "thick veneer laid over quite individualistic creatures" (personal communication). She assumes that there has been natural selection among humans toward greater sociality, but at the social rather than the biological level. She attributes this largely to our capacity for linguistic communication, which has enabled humans to adapt more successfully to new ecological conditions, but does not attempt to explain the evolutionary process through which protohumans used their communicative ability to create social organization. Additional factors are needed to explain the existence and development of human social organization.

Proposed Tool-using Perspective

If Maryanski's thesis that human beings are genetically rather solitary creatures is valid, what has led them to cooperate in joint activities and create social organization? The usual sociological explanation of the basis for all forms of social organization—when not derived from the assumption that humans are genetically sociable—is that people create shared goals whose attainment requires cooperation and coordination, which leads to some form of social ordering. Whatever the nature of those shared goals, they are created by the human ability to imagine desired conditions that do not presently exist. Those ideas are then communicated among people who commit themselves to cooperating in joint endeavors to attain their shared goals. From this perspective, the process of social organization originates in the relational realm of sociocultural organization, while the functional realm of socioecological organization constitutes merely the means used by people to achieve their sociocultural goals. In short, this is an "ends-means" schema. Although neither the desired goals nor the collective means used to attain them may be rational (i.e., efficient, effective, or beneficial), this collective goal-attainment perspective is nevertheless quite rationalistic in nature. Without denying the obvious fact that humans do frequently employ collective ends-means schemes, we may ask whether this rationalistic ends-means theoretical perspective is adequate to explain the development of human social organization?

From an ecological perspective, the fundamental challenge facing all human beings is to survive in the natural environment. To do that, they must obtain necessary resources from the environment and transform them into useful goods and services. Since procurement and movement of resources are therefore the fundamental activities within organized human social life, resource utilization—not interpersonal communication and relationships— must constitute the fundamental basis of all social organization. Therefore, the explanation of the creation and development of human social organization must lie within the functional realm of socioecological organization, not in the relational realm of sociocultural organization. The human capabilities for symbolic communication and interpersonal relating unquestionably facilitate the process of acquiring and using resources, but interpersonal communication and relationships are only ancillary enhancements of the process of resource acquisition and utilization that underlies all human social organization. Within social organization, people surrender some of their autonomy to attain individual and collective functional benefits that are unattainable through individual action.

To obtain and use most of the resources they require, human beings must expand their limited physical capabilities in various ways. They do this by creating and using *tools* of all kinds. Broadly defined, a tool is any physical, procedural, or symbolic technique used to obtain, convey, transform, or consume resources within the functional realm of socioecological organization. This conception of tools is much broader than merely "hardware." When knowledge about tools is shared among at least some of the members of a society or other social unit, it constitutes *technology*. Following Rosa (n.d.), technology can be defined as "specialized knowledge about a procedure or set of procedures for accomplishing some task which is differentially distributed and thus provides one basis for functional interdependence." From this perspective, I argue that *the human ability to make and use tools and to accumulate differentially distributed technological knowledge about those procedures underlies all socioecological organization.* Since the apes— especially gorillas and chimpanzees—demonstrate some ability to use very simple tools, there is undoubtedly a genetic basis for this activity, although humans have obviously carried tool making and using far beyond anything done by apes.

From a dynamic perspective, the development and use of tools and the accumulation of technological knowledge can be viewed as an ongoing process that has shaped the development of human societies throughout history. Social evolution therefore originates within socioecological organization, not in sociocultural organization. Only as tools and technology are developed that enable people to adapt more successfully to their environment by increasing the efficiency and effectiveness of their resource acquisition and utilization can socioecological organization expand. Also, only as the functional realm develops in this manner can the relational realm of sociocultural organization also exhibit more complex processes and forms. Tools and technology— broadly defined—thus make possible and shape the entire "thick veneer" of social organization that transforms human beings from highly individualistic to highly sociable creatures. Without those tool-making and tool-using capabilities and our ability to communicate symbolically about useful technologies, we might likely still be only an intelligent species of apes with relatively minimal social organization.

This thesis does not overlook or reject the obvious fact that sociocultural change can produce socioecological development. That dynamic clearly occurs in both unilateral and reciprocal ways. The crucial point of the thesis, however, is that from the broad perspective of societal evolution, socioecological development is basic to sociocultural evolution, since available functional resources both enable and constrain the evolution of sociocultural organization.

Social ecological theory has long identified technology as one of the three basic "ecological factors" together with environment and population—all of which affect social organization. From the perspective proposed here, however, tools and technologies are absolutely indispensable facilitators of all functional activities in human socioecological organization. Therefore, as people create new tools and technologies of all kinds, those innovations will have direct ramifications throughout socioecological organization and indirect impacts on many aspects of sociocultural organization. If those new tools and technologies prove to be more efficient and/or effective than those that had previously been used, their effects on social organization are likely to be extensive. Tools and technology are therefore not just one factor in the human "ecological complex," but rather the crucial factor that has separated us from our prehuman ancestory and made possible human social organization.

Summary Principles

The argument made in this section can be summarized as follows:

1. Tools, broadly defined, constitute the techniques necessary to carry out all resource acquisition and utilization. Tools are therefore an integral and indispensable component of socioecological organization, as is technological knowledge about tools that becomes differently distributed among various sets of people.

2. To the extent that tools/technology require cooperation and coordination for their effective use, people become functionally interdependent within networks of socioecological organization. Tools/technology lead people to create social organization, rather than organization leading people to create tools/technology.

3. Evolutionary development of human socioecological organization has depended on the utilization of increasingly efficient and effective tools and technology. As those techniques provide increasingly abundant and useful resources, functional processes and structures within societies tend to expand and develop.

4. Activities within the relational realm of sociocultural organization are always dependent on, and therefore reflect, existing patterns of resource availability and utilization and socioecological organization. Consequently, development within the functional realm of a society makes possible and constrains the creation of more extensive and complex sociocultural organization.

5. Thus, all human social organization is ultimately an outgrowth of our ability to make and use tools and to communicate knowledge about those techniques. Tools and technology make possible functional activities within the realm of socioecological organization, which in a broad sense gives rise

to relational activities within the realm of sociocultural organization, although sociocultural change also affects socioecological organization in countless ways.

6. From an ecological perspective, the traditional sociological argument that human social organization results from collective goal-attainment efforts within the sociocultural realm (using an ends-means schema) is inadequate to account for the creation and development of social organization because that perspective ignores the indispensability of resources for human life. Social relationships and sociocultural organization cannot occur without the functional activities that provide necessary resources within socioecological organization. In turn, sociocultural organization provides both the forms and meanings of all socioecological activities.

RESOURCE TRANSFERS

Socioecological Organization

If we accept the argument presented in the preceding section that the "thick veneer" of human social organization is an outgrowth of the use of tools and technology that makes possible resource acquisition and utilization, it is imperative that we understand the role of resources in socioecological organization. Lee Freese's (1988) concept of resource transfers provides a crucial insight into that process.

Underlying Freese's perspective is the assumption that socioecological organization [social systems] is bioecological organization [ecological systems]—although of a less inclusive sort (p. 54). Socioecological organization is not a separate set of ecological processes; rather, "social systems are ecosystems of a different order in an interacting hierarchy of continuous ecological processes" (p. 116). "This level is constituted out of the ecosystem interactions when additional ingredients—the social actors and their resources—are added" (p. 116). These two forms of ecological organization constitute a two-level hierarchy because socioecological organization is always dependent on bioecological organization for necessary resources, but not the other way around. Socioecological organization cannot exist without bioecological organization, but "ecosystems can do quite nicely without human social systems" (p. 116).

Freese's key insight is that all resource acquisition and utilization within ecological organization—both biological and social—is a dynamic process that always involves the movement of resources between living forms. Therefore, *the fundamental activity within all bioecological and all socioecological organization is a resource transfer.* "Ecosystems do not exist without living organisms, and they do not exist without resources to sustain them, so we may conceive any ecological interaction as consisting of some sort of resource transfer" (p. 75). Freese defines a resource quite broadly as "any quantity that is changed by the activity of organisms," which includes "anything that may be used for sustenance, physical or otherwise, including social bonds and other nonmaterial qualities human beings take as sustenance" (p. 75). Thus *resources are energy forms that are utilized by living organisms.* Consequently, all resource transfers are energy flows, but not all energy constitutes resources for life.

We can therefore conceptualize a *socioecological resource* as anything (tangible or intangible) that is used by humans (individually or collectively) for any functional purpose (sustenance or any other objective) and is altered in some way by that usage. Resources are relevant for socioecological organization to the extent that they are transferred and then used by their recipients.

A resource transfer is a one-way activity, not a reciprocal interaction or exchange, although in reality such transfers are often reciprocated either directly (through two-actor exchange interaction) or indirectly (through sequential chains of exchange interaction). A social exchange is thus a special case of two or more resource transfers that are linked in some way. Resources may also be transferred in bundles, but Freese maintains that such activities must be viewed analytically as a compound set of separate transfers (p. 111). A resource transfer can occur almost instantaneously or can transpire across some span of time (p. 75); it can be either intentional or unintentional; the actors involved may or may not be aware of it; and those actors can be either individuals or collectivities (p. 111). Finally, "It is intuitively obvious that when the transfer of one kind of resource is connected to the transfer of a different kind, the resources, their transfers, and whatever the resources are transferred between, are interdependent" (p. 80).

Resource transfers are fundamental for socioecological organization because they make possible and sustain all of the more complex processes and structures in human life. They constitute the "substance" of social life. As expressed by Freese (using the term "social system" to refer to socioecological organization) (p. 103):

> The transfer of tangible and intangible resources has to be the fundamental interaction process of social systems because otherwise interaction and, therefore, system organization could not be sustained. So it may be said that social systems are organized and structured for resource transfers.... Resources are what people depend on each other for, and social systems endure only to the extent that they provide them. Therefore, any social system is a sustenance organization. Its basic stuff is resources, and the cogent moments of its interaction processes are resource transfers.

Although Freese does not explicitly discuss tools and technology, it is obvious that they are a crucial aspect of all resource transfers. Resource transfers never occur spontaneously or simply because actors desire them. To carry out a resource transfer, the sender must employ some kind of tool or technique to move the resource to the recipient. The more appropriate those tools are to the resources and situations involved, the more efficient and effective the resource transfer process is likely to become. As technological knowledge about appropriate tool making and using is communicated among actors and embedded within the culture of a society, its networks of socioecological organization tend to become increasingly extensive and complex. In short, tools and technology are indispensable for all human resource transfers and hence all socioecological organization.

To emphasize the relevance of tools and technological knowledge for all resource transfers, I suggest the following definitions: (1) a tool is any physical, procedural, or symbolic technique used by an actor to conduct a resource transfer; and (2) technology is differentially shared cultural knowledge about using tools and transferring resources. With this understanding, the tool-using thesis proposed in the previous section asserts that *the utilization of tools and technology makes possible all resource transfers between humans.* Sending and receiving a resource of any kind in any manner requires the use of some type of tool by the actors involved. As these techniques are repeated through time, they tend to become established parts of the ongoing process of resource transfers. As knowledge about these techniques is progressively refined, elaborated, and communicated among resource interactants, collective technology develops and is incorporated into socioecological organization.

In Freese's perspective, the elemental unit of all socioecological organization is not a single actor, but two actors [interactants] who transfer one resource (p. 105). He calls this entity a "resource group," but I propose the alternative term of *resource dyad* to avoid confusing this unit with interpersonal groups involving sociocultural characteristics such as identification and commitment, and to indicate that this unit is always limited to two actors. A resource dyad [group] is defined by "the transfer of a single resource from one interactant to another. For every different resource transferred, a different active resource group is said to exist, even if the interactants are the same" (p. 111).

Taking the resource dyad [group] as the smallest unit of all ecological organization, Freese constructs a structural model that he applies to both bioecological and socioecological organization. Without going into the details of this model, three of its features should be noted: (1) It is a system model, in which the parts are interlinked in various ways to constitute the whole system. (2) In contrast to most system modeling that begins with the whole system and follows a "decompositional" procedure to determine its successively smaller parts, Freese follows a "compositional" procedure that begins with the smallest irreducible unit—the resource dyad [group]—and builds upward by specifying the ways in which smaller units are linked into successively larger units that eventually constitute the total system. (3) The model forms a hierarchy of increasingly inclusive levels of units, in which dynamic processes move upward as well as downward. Freese therefore presumes that principles of "hierarchy theory" can be applied to the model, pointing out that: "...rates of interaction differ between the levels, decreasing as microscopic interactions compose into macroscopic effects" (p. 80).

Sociocultural Organization

For Freese, the realm of sociocultural organization is rather microsociological in nature, consisting of actors' roles, statuses, and norms and the "interpersonal groups" created by actors. This realm performs many vital functions for social life, although it does not constitute the entire process of social organization. The activities that occur within this realm "provide meaning, cognitive significance, definition and order for participants and observers of interpersonal interaction....They permit participants and observers to make sense of the flow of social interaction" (p. 99).

These interpersonal activities within sociocultural organization always rest on resource transfers and the structure of socioecological organization that results from them, according to Freese. "Actors' order-defining interaction is pointless if in some manner it does not organize, structure, and facilitate resource transfers. If it does not, interaction cannot long continue because there is nothing to sustain the interactants. Interpersonal interaction is sustained by resources" (p. 102). Sociocultural organization is thus operationally dependent on socioecological organization for its existence:

> Roles, statuses, and norms become defined, specialized, and developed, and social relations emerge, stabilize, or change, according to how they enhance resource transfers. They degenerate when they do not. When they endure, they embody the actors' accumulated experience at enhancing, expanding, or controlling resource flows of every kind actors find to be sustaining (p. 106).

Consequently, Freese views all aspects of sociocultural organization as "operational properties" rather than structural units of social organization.

In sum, socioecological and sociocultural organization constitute two distinct realms of human social organization, but the former is more fundamental and critical than the latter, in Freese's view:

> Resources alone have the capacity to sustain interpersonal groups as viable social entities. So any structure of social relations, which is *order defining*, has to be connected to some structure of resource tansfers, which is *action-sustaining*. That suggests two distinct interaction processes are behaving simultaneously and two different kinds of social entities are constituted: interpersonal groups and social systems (p. 105, emphasis added).

Proposed Perspective

As noted above, Freese places sociocultural organization [interpersonal groups] above socioecological organization [social systems] in his hierarchical model. Speaking of bioecological, socioecological, and sociocultural "systems," he says that "the last depends on the second and the second on the first, and the dependence is asymmetrical" (p. 116). This hierarchical arrangement may possibly have either of two undesirable analytical consequences. On the one hand, it can lead us to view all sociocultural organization as having only minor significance in comparison with the fundamental base of socioecological organization. Conversely, it can imply that sociocultural organization is "superior" to socioecological organization because it is at a higher level of existence. Unfortunately, both of these potential invidious comparisons are likely to distort our efforts to generate unified sociological theory.

Freese is correct, I think, in arguing that socioecological organization is ecologically more basic than sociocultural organization, in the sense that all natural resources move from bioecological organization into socioecological organization, and never directly into sociocultural organization. In that functional sense, the relational realm is always totally dependent on the functional realm. Sociocultural organization cannot exist without the resource transfers that occur within socioecological organization. That asymmetry is balanced, however, by the fact that the relational realm defines which biotic and abiotic phenomena are treated by humans as useful resources and which ones are not, as well as how functional processes are to be carried out in social life. In these ways, sociocultural organization always influences socioecological processes and structures.

To reflect the fact that socioecological and sociocultural organization influence and shape one another in a continuous reciprocal manner and to avoid implying that either realm is more important than the other in human social life, I propose that we conceive of *socioecological and sociocultural organization as parallel and highly interwoven analytical realms within the total process of social organization.* Each realm contains its own unique dynamic processes and resulting structures and can therefore be described and analyzed separately. The distinct dynamics of the two realms are nicely summarized by Freese as "action-sustaining" in the functional realm and "order-defining" in the relational realm. At the same time, because of their total interdependence, neither realm can exist apart from the other and they are both absolutely indispensable for social organization. As suggested previously, they are two distinct sides of the same coin of social organization. Without socioecological organization, all sociocultural phenomena would be hollow, resourceless shells. Without sociocultural organization, all socioecological phenomena would lose their order and meaning for humans and revert to bioecological organization.

Structurally, therefore, these two realms of social organization should be depicted at the same hierarchical level, above bioecological organization.

If we conceive of socioecological and sociocultural organization as parallel analytical realms of human social life, we should be able to identify numerous parallel concepts and processes within these two realms. As just mentioned, for example, the primary purpose of the functional realm is "action-sustaining" while in the relational realm it is "order-defining." The most basic concept in the functional realm is "functional resource," while in the relational realm it is "interpersonal action." The fundamental interaction activity in the functional realm is "resource transferring," which is paralleled in the relational realm by "personal relating." The facilitating mechanisms in the functional realm are "operational tools," while in relational realm they are "social skills." The elemental unit in the functional realm is a "resource dyad," and in the relational realm it is a "social bond." All of these parallel concepts are displayed and defined in Table 1. Additional parallel concepts can be identified within the emergent levels of social ordering/structure and shared culture. Space limitations preclude more extensive discussions of all these parallel concepts, but they are considerably elaborated in my book *Dynamics of Social Organization: Processes and Theories* (forthcoming).

Dynamic processes also display numerous parallels between the two realms of socioecological and sociocultural organization. A few of the most important of these processes are diagrammed in Figure 1, which was initially suggested by Eugene Rosa (personal communication).

Functional Ordering

Functional transfers occur through social interaction, but those activities usually give rise to broader patterns or networks of functional ordering within socioecological organization. Those emergent patterns and networks give regularity and predictability to ongoing resource transfer processes, and thus contribute to their perpetuation through time. However, all such ordering, from simple dyads to entire societies, also involves functional dependencies among the involved actors. Any resource transfer leaves both actors potentially dependent, and to the extent that transfers become woven into functional networks, the actors are likely to experience increasing interdependence.

In a resource dyad, actor A, who provides the resource, is left with a smaller amount of resources than before the transfer and is therefore functionally weaker. This means that A is more vulnerable to being affected by the actions of other actors with greater resources. Moreover, if A seeks to acquire another resource to replace the transferred one, A could become dependent on one or more of those other actors with greater resources. Meanwhile, actor B, who receives the resource, has a larger supply of resources to use and is therefore

Table 1. Parallel Characteristics of the Socioecological and Sociocultural Realms of the Total Process of Social Organization

Characteristic	Socioecological Realm	Sociocultural Realm
Description	Functional realm of social organization	Relational realm of social organization
Primary purpose	Action-sustaining = provides the substance of social organization	Order-defining = provides the form and meaning of social organization
Basic concept	Functional resource = anything that is used and thus changed by an actor	Interpersonal action = a meaningful act that one actor directs toward another actor
Fundamental interaction activity	Resource transferring = movement of a single resource from one actor to another actor	Personal relating = meaningful action by one actor that affects another actor
Facilitating mechanism	Operational tools = techniques used to transfer resources	Social skills = techniques used to relate to others
Elemental unit	Resource dyad = two actors and the transfer of a resource between them that is used by the recipient	Social bond = two actors and a meaningful linkage between them that endures for some period of time

less vulnerable to others, but has established a potential dependency on A for further supplies of that resource. This situation can be called *single dependency* and is diagrammed in Figure 2.

Since being functionally dependent leaves an actor vulnerable to being influenced or controlled by others who can supply needed resources, actors normally seek to reduce or eliminate their functional dependence on others. One way in which B can offset its dependence is to transfer some other resource to A. This establishes a situation of *mutual dependency* between these two actors, which is diagrammed in Figure 3.

A mutual dependency arrangement can be quite reliable and predictable for both actors, since each one is receiving needed resources while avoiding one-sided dependency on the other. Both of them also avoid seriously depleting their supplies of resources, since each one is receiving as well as sending resources. However, this kind of self-contained mutual dependency is usually quite difficult to sustain for long, since both actors will invariably need other resources that their partner cannot supply and hence will find it necessary to establish other functional linkages with one or more additional actors.

A second way in which both actors in a resource dyad can respond to their functional dependency is to establish additional resource linkages with other actors. In a situation of single dependency, actor A must inevitably do this to replenish the resources that are being transferred to B. If A receives resources from X, however, A's potential dependence on (and vulnerability to) others

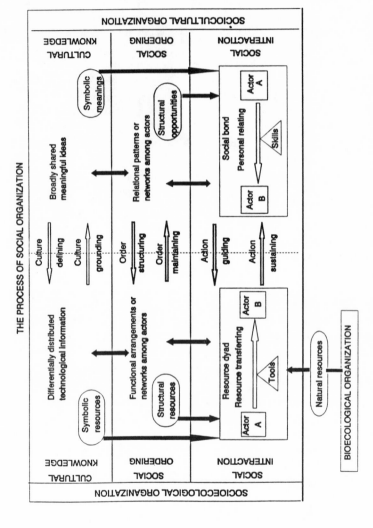

Figure 1. Processes Within the Socioecological and Sociocultural Realms of Social Organization

Perspective: Although the realms of socioecological and sociocultural organization are depicted side by side in this figure, they should be thought of as folded along the dotted line to form two back-to-back sides of social organization. Consequently, Actor A in the socioecological realm is also Actor A in the sociocultural realm, and so on throughout the diagram.

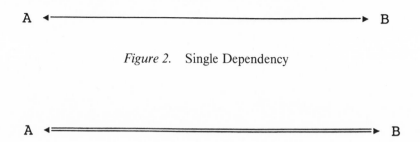

Figure 2. Single Dependency

Figure 3. Mutual Dependency

becomes actual. B, meanwhile, uses the resources received from A to take actions of some kind, which affect other actors such as Y. Since all actions involve resource transfers, B is in effect moving resources to Y (which may or may not be the same resources received from A). Actor B thus becomes increasingly dependent on A for necessary resources (regardless of whether B is consuming A's resources or passing them on to Y), without any assurance that A will continue to supply them. B is thus highly vulnerable to being influenced or controlled by A as long as the action toward Y continues. This is a situation of *serial dependency* among a chain of actors, which is shown in Figure 4.

This kind of serial dependency can extend over long chains of actors, so that no single actor has contact (or is even aware of) other actors who are located very far away on the chain in either direction. Any given actor in such a functional chain can, however, be moderately certain of (and thus able to predict) the transfers in which it will be involved as long as the overall process keeps operating. If the movement of resources is broken at any point in the chain, however, all the participants may sooner or later be adversely affected. A considerable amount of potential uncertainty is therefore always present.

It is often possible for a chain of resource transfers to become a closed loop. This is a situation of *loop dependency* among a set of actors, which is shown in Figure 5. A closed dependency loop gives considerably more certainty to a series of resource transfers and to each resource dyad within that loop, as long as the loop does not become so large that none of the participants is aware of its totality. Since every actor in the loop is functionally dependent on other participants, their levels of vulnerability are likely to be relatively similar. Also, since keeping resources flowing around the loop serves the interests of all the actors, they can all be relatively certain that it will continue. However, as with serial dependency, a breakdown of a single resource transfer anywhere in the loop may create problems for other participants, so some functional uncertainty always remains.

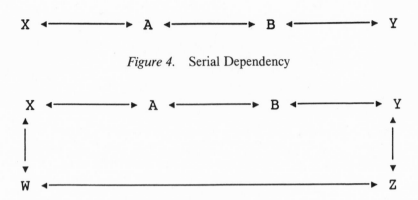

Figure 4. Serial Dependency

Figure 5. Loop Dependency

All of these examples of different forms of resource transfers represent possible functional networks that might occur among sets of actors. Moreover, both the serial and loop networks can be made much more complex by including two-way transfers within any of the resource dyads, or by linking any of the actors to more than one other actor (such as linking A to Z in the above loop). No matter how simple or complex any particular functional network is, however, all such patterns are characterized by functional dependencies. These dependencies leave the actors vulnerable to influence or control by others and uncertain about future transfers.

The key to minimizing functional vulnerability and uncertainty is to transform one-way dependencies into *shared interdependencies* among most or all of the actors within a functional network. This involves creating mutual dependencies among as many dyads in the network as possible. When all of the actors in a functional network are more-or-less interdependent on one another, no single actor is likely to become excessively vulnerable and each one can be relatively certain that the process of resource transfers will be perpetuated. Functional reliability can never be absolute, since there is always the possibility that one or more actors will fail to function adequately, or that external forces will disrupt the network. But *regularity and reliability in functional networks can be increased to the extent that all the participating actors are functionally interdependent.* A condition of complete interdependence within a network of four actors is diagrammed in Figure 6.

The essential point here is that resource transfers rarely occur in isolation within single resource dyads. Throughout all dimensions of social life, resource dyads are usually embedded within larger functional networks. Consequently, most resource transfers are interdependent parts of more encompassing patterns of socioecological ordering.

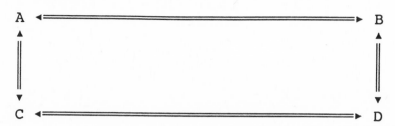

Figure 6. Complete Interdependency

ENERGY FLOWS

Dissipative Structures

Although socioecological theory could be formulated entirely in terms of tool utilization, resource transfers, and functional networks, all of these ideas are relatively descriptive rather than analytical in nature. Richard Adams' (1988) conceptions of energy flows and forms provide a more basic "energetic" perspective with which to analyze all socioecological organization. His work rests on the fundamental proposition that all existence—including human social life—ultimately consists of energy forms and flows: "[A]ll things with which we can be concerned as operative parts of the universe are energy forms and their relationships" (p .17). This energetic perspective on social organization has been proposed by numerous other theorists (see Rosa and Machlis 1983 for a review of that literature), but Adams (in all three of his books) develops it much more fully than any of those earlier writers.

Energy is usually defined as "the capacity to do work" (Adams 1988, p. 4). It includes physical energy, living energy (in animals and humans), and all objects (since matter is always reducible to energy). Energy can exist in either a potential or active state. In its potential state, energy consists of *energy forms*, which can be literally anything that "has the potential for releasing energy and is, therefore, theoretically capable of doing work" (p. 15). In addition to their energy potential or kinetic energy, energy forms also contain the embedded energy that has been used to create and maintain them through time. In its active state, energy consists of *energy flows*, which accomplish work by dissipating energy. As energy forms dissipate, or expend energy through work, they change both themselves and their environments (p. 4).

Given the energetic nature of all existence, it follows that all social life also consists of energy forms and flows. Whenever individuals or organizations act in any manner, they dissipate energy. Therefore, following Ilya Prigogine (1980) and several other previous writers, Adams refers to all social organizations as *dissipative structures* (p. 23). Regrettably, this term can be misinterpreted in two serious ways. First, the term "dissipation" in this context means only dispersing energy and does not imply the alternative meaning of wasting or squandering energy. The critical point is that all instances of social organization can be viewed as energy conveyors and transformers that contribute to energy flows and that convert energy into work that is intended to benefit some actors or units. Who benefits and to what extent are always problematic outcomes. Second, an organization that dissipates energy but does not necessarily dissipate itself in the process can balance its energy outputs with energy inputs. In that condition of balanced energy flows, the organization might be described as an "energy-maintaining structure."

Not all energy forms are constantly dissipating energy. At any given time, argues Adams, an energy form might—at least theoretically—exist in relative equilibrium with its environment if that environment were totally "benign" and exerted no pressures on the energy form to dissipate any energy (p. 18). In that case, the energy form would be a closed entity and could be called an *equilibrium structure* that merely retained its potential energy because it was not presently dissipating any energy through action. Adams rejects the traditional functional argument that social processes and conditions inherently seek equilibrium (or a condition of no change) as entirely groundless and asserts only that social organizations might theoretically exist in a state of relative equilibrium.

In reality, however, no living energy forms are ever totally closed to the environment and, hence, cannot be in equilibrium. As made clear by Freese, equilibrium is only a hypothetical condition in social organizations. Because they are always open to both the natural and social environments through inputs and outputs, these environments are constantly impinging upon them, causing them to act and therefore dissipate energy. Moreover, since organizations are constantly dissipating energy, they are always affecting their environments, which continuously changes their hypothetical equilibrium state, so that it can never be attained. Consequently, all instances of social organization can be described as dissipative structures that are *far from equilibrium.*

Whenever an environment of an energy form (including all social organizations) is not totally benign, it is constantly exerting pressures on that form to act and thus dissipate energy. In other words, all activity (i.e., all energy dissipation) is a consequence of pressures from surrounding environments. Therefore, *whenever environmental pressures lead a social actor to take action, the actor dissipates some of its stored potential energy and moves closer toward a state of entropy*, which is the total absence of potential energy. Thus the Second Law of Thermodynamics—the inevitable tendency of any instance of order to move toward increased randomness and eventual entropy—applies to all social activity. As expressed by Howard Odum (1971, p. 29) in regard to living entities, this means that, "In any real process useful potential energy becomes lost."

At the same time, all open entities—including all social units—also have the capability of absorbing energy from their environments through various kinds of inputs. They must do this if they are to maintain their internal ordering and continue functioning for long. Because every activity has an *energy cost*, "dissipative structures have to obtain the inputs of energy...necessary to their nature" (Adams 1988, p. 124). These energy costs of activity have three components: (1) the energy needed to replace the energy that is being dissipated in accomplishing work; (2) the energy needed to obtain and incorporate that new energy into the entity; and (3) the energy used within the entity to maintain its internal ordering and functioning. Consequently, the total energy cost of any activity can be much greater than the energy equivalent of the work accomplished. Social organizations are sometimes described as "islands of negative entropy" because they concentrate and organize energy and thus appear to reverse the Second Law of Thermodynamics. Although that process does occur within organizations, from a broader perspective which links organizational units with their environments, that appearance of reversing entropy is illusionary. The overall process of creating, operating, perpetuating, and expanding any instance of social organization within its environmental context always entails extensive energy costs to those environments. Consequently, what appears to be "negative entropy" within organizations is simply a process of concentrating energy from the environments and increasing their overall entropy. Thus, *all social organization is attained only by depleting the potential and active energy of its environments*, and the more extensive and complex that organization, the more severe the environmental energy depletion. In short, although the Second Law may not apply within specific organizational units at particular times, it always applies to the total process of socioecological organization.

Adams does not argue that living forms (including social organizations) have any inherent tendency to maximize the flow of energy through them. In fact, he specifically points out that numerous societies have degenerated or disappeared because they were not able to obtain adequate energy inputs to sustain themselves during periods when the surrounding environment was changing rapidly and thus placing strong pressures on them to adjust to new conditions. He does, however, accept "Lotka's Principle" that natural selection tends to favor living forms that make maximum use of available energy resources. As stated by Alfred Lotka (1922, p. 148), "In every instance considered natural selection will so operate as to increase the total flux through the system, so long as there is presented an unutilized residue of matter and available energy." Adams comments, "What Lotka tells us is that among living forms there is a relationship between the relative amount of energy that they use and their potential for survival" (p. 40).

Although social organizations are never in equilibrium with their environments because they are always taking in and expending energy, they can maintain consistency in relation to those environments. In his first book, Adams (1975, 128) referred to this as homeostasis, but in his recent work he rejects that concept in favor of three more specific conditions: (1) *steady state*, or "maintaining some constant balance or controlled ratio between inputs and outputs"; (2) *stability*, or "the ability, if displaced, to return to such a balance"; and (3) *resillience*, or "redefining the structure so as to 'adapt' to the changing environment" (p. 25). None of these conditions should be assumed to be inherent in societies, he warns, since they require negative feedback processes that may or may not occur. When those capabilities do occur, however, they can benefit a society or other organization.

The process of dissipating energy and doing work always affects the surrounding environments. Those consequences of energy dissipation on environments are called *perturbations* by Adams. "Once expended, the energy that yielded the perturbation is gone, but its effect may persist through consequent changes felt by other energy forms" (p. 48). Expressed differently, "Dissipating energy issues perturbations that alter the relative positions and compositions of parts of the environment" (pp. 58-59). Those perturbations may also act back on the energy-dissipating structure to place additional or new pressures on it for further activity. That is, environmental perturbations can "trigger" further changes in energy flows from the acting entity as well as from other entities. An *energy trigger* is "a perturbation resulting from energy dissipation that releases or inhibits the further dissipation of its own energy or that of other energy forms. Triggers, therefore, are the key mechanisms that relate one dissipative event to another" (p. 49). Triggers can operate directly on their own, or on other energy forms, and also indirectly on still other energy forms through chain reactions (p. 51).

The amount of energy required to "pull" in a trigger may be greater or less than the amount of energy flows it releases from its own or other energy forms. If "pulling" the trigger requires more energy than it releases through desired work outputs, there is a net reduction of energy potential, which is clearly not efficient from the perspective of the trigger puller (p. 53). However, if pulling the trigger requires less energy by an actor than the amount it releases through the actions of other actors, there is a net gain in work accomplished by the trigger puller. It is thus possible for any particular actor or unit to "get more for less"—which is "necessary for the continuity of any input/output structure" (pp. 53-54). Adams calls this condition "trigger minimization" and argues that, "Natural selection logic... presumes that for society to survive the net collective energy costs of triggers must be less than the work energy that is released by their action" (p. 54). "[T]here are distinct advantages of having low-energy triggers releasing larger amounts of energy" (p. 56). It must be kept in mind, however, that trigger minimization is always specific to particular actors and invariably involves greater energy dissipation throughout the larger environments.

When energy triggers are properly understood and utilized by actors, they can be specialized and directed at particular targets to release desired amounts of energy for intentional purposes. "Energy triggers can be controlled by judgments of people, judgments made at all different levels and niches of society" (p. 56). Therefore, *energy triggers constitute a crucial way in which the relational realm of social organization can control energy flows within the functional realm.*

While the effective use of energy triggers can therefore enable a society to increase greatly its energy flows and enable it to expand vastly the amount of work accomplished with relatively small energy inputs, "there is nothing in the trigger process itself that requires a low-trigger-yield energy ratio" (p. 56). Under at least two sets of conditions, a society may employ energy triggers that are highly inefficient in terms of their energy yield: (1) when a new trigger has been developed that promises great benefits but is actually quite ineffective; and (2) when conditions are very unstable and a society seeks additional energy releases at any cost.

A more common situation is employing energy triggers that have extensive unknown indirect effects, thereby possibly unleashing all kinds of undesired energy flows. At many other times, however, effective use of efficient energy triggers can greatly benefit humanity. In his 1982 book, Adams examined the manner in which the use of energy triggers by Great Britain between 1870 and 1914—through exportation of finance capital and trained administrators— released tremendous energy flows and promoted rapid socioeconomic development in the United States, Germany, and other nations.

Information

Information is an integral aspect of energy dynamics in that it is always a consequence of perturbations, or changes resulting from energy dissipation. "Irrespective of what a perturbation may be like, if it has any impact at all it leaves information on some receiving form" (p. 79). In other words, energy flows always convey information to their recipients and are often perceived, identified, and defined in terms of the information they carry (p. 81). Information is not energy, since it cannot flow and cannot do any work; that can only be done by the energy "vehicle" that conveys it. Whenever an energy flow impacts anything, however, it conveys information that humans can interpret and utilize. For example, the receiver (B) of an energy flow from an energy dissipator (A) also receives such information as: (1) A exists; (2) A possesses resources; (3) A is capable of transferring resources; (4) the nature and amount of resources received by B; and (5) B's ability to incorporate those resources.

Information can be critical in controlling and directing energy flows. In particular, energy-conveyed information is extremely important in two ways: (1) identifying and using energy-efficient triggers to release further energy flows; and (2) providing feedback about the consequences of energy flows. In general, therefore, the amount of information existing in a society and the extent of its energy flows are highly related.

> The overall picture...is that information grows proportionately to the growth of energy in the society.... Indeed, it is likely that in any viable social system, the rate of increase in complexity of information is a function of the rate of increase in per capita energy consumption of the society (p. 86).

Adams goes on to suggest that the development of human culture is a direct outgrowth of people sharing information derived from energy flows. "Culture is created out of our constant effort to associate, to relate...mental models with our experience with the energetic world" (pp. 89-90).

Interpretation

Adams' arguments concerning energy forms and flows are fully compatible with the analytical model of social organization developed in the previous two sections of this paper. Most importantly, *the resource transfers that are the fundamental activities within socioecological organization are energy flows*. A resource is anything that is used and changed by its recipient. That is, it enables the recipient to carry out some activity or work, which involves the dissipation of energy. Therefore, a received resource is an energy input that enables an actor to dissipate energy. In that process, the resource/energy input is changed into work/energy output.

While all resource transfers are energy flows, these concepts are not identical since *not all energy flows are resource transfers*. Energy flows are a more general process that occur throughout all existence, whereas resource transfers occur only among living entities. Thus, resource transfers are a special case of energy flows among organisms, people, and organizations. They are directly relevant to all socioecological organization, however, since all activities within that realm can be viewed as resource transfers/energy flows. When describing and analyzing socioecological organization, it may often be expedient to speak of resource transfers and resource dyads, since they are easier to identify and measure than abstract energy flows and forms. Nevertheless, our analytical principles might well be expressed in energy terms, since energy flows constitute the dynamics of all ecological—and hence socioecological—phenomena.

In addition, an energetic theoretical perspective makes explicit several phenomena that are often only implicit in discussions of resource transfers. These include: (1) the manner in which environmental pressures and changes promote energy dissipation; (2) the consequences of energy flows and their subsequent perturbations for both the initial actor and others; (3) the importance of maintaining a steady state in which energy inputs balance outflows, as well as the related capabilities of stability and resillience or adaptability; (4) the energy costs for environments that occur when energy is concentrated within organizations; and (5) the advantages gained by maximizing the flow of available energy through organizations. All of these ideas are implicit in Freese's discussion of resource transfers, but the energy perspective provides concepts and principles for analyzing them explicitly.

An energetic perspective also adds several ideas that are not present in discussions of resource transfers. The most important of these is perhaps the concept of energy triggers and the way in which they can be manipulated and used by people to increase the flow of energy through organizations. This, in turn, relates directly to the importance of tools and technology in social life. Tools, all of which are techniques used to transfer resources, function as energy triggers. That is, use of a tool involves the expenditure of some amount of energy (a relatively small amount if the tool is efficient) to release other energy flows (hopefully of a much greater magnitude) that will result in the accomplishment of desired work. Not all energy triggers are used as tools for transferring resources, since many triggers are relatively automatic consequences of energy perturbations resulting from energy dissipation. However, Adams' description of the manner in which actors can intentionally shape and target energy triggers to produce specific energy flows is clearly a discussion of the deliberate use of tools expressed in energetic terms. The information that is conveyed with energy flows provides the basis for shared technological knowledge and dynamic feedback processes. In sum, an "energetic perspective" appears to provide a highly useful conceptual basis for theorizing about all of the processes that occur within the functional realm of socioecological organization.

Proposed Principles

If this energetic perspective is to prove useful for developing socioecological theory, it must be formulated as a set of explicit principles. As a first step in that direction, the principles proposed below express the major ideas of Adams' energetic perspective, but they in no sense constitute a complete theoretical argument.

1. Energy flows—and hence the resource transfers and work activities they accomplish—constitute the essential dynamics of all socioecological organization. To distinguish energy flows within socioecological processes from those in the natural environment that are not influenced by humans, the former might be termed "socioenergy flows."

2. All functional activities and all instances and forms of socioecological organization can be conceptualized as energy transforming—and hence energy dissipating—processes or entities. Whenever energy is expended, that activity has effects or perturbations on the surrounding environments, and those perturbations in turn affect the initial processes or entities in various ways.

3. Whenever a resource is transferred from one actor to another, this is a socioenergy flow that at least temporarily reduces the potential energy of the sender and hence its ability to perform subsequent activities, while simultaneously increasing the ability of the receiver to perform activities. These resource/energy flows and the actors conducting them constitute the basic units of all socioecological organization.

4. All social organizational units must constantly take in new energy from their environments if they are to maintain themselves in a steady state and thus be capable of acting on a sustained basis. All units also dissipate energy to their environments in the form of work and/or waste products.

5. Since social organizations can never exist in a state of equilibrium with their environments, all organizations are constantly acting or dissipating energy as a consequence of environmental pressures and inputs.

6. Since the processes of obtaining and using energy always entail energy costs, the net socioenergy that is available to perform work is always somewhat less than the total energy consumed in any activity. This "net energy dissipation" is a critical factor shaping all socioecological organization.

7. The process of socioecological organization establishes specific instances of socioenergy concentration and ordering within which the Second Law of Thermodynamics does not appear to apply. That appearance is illusionary, however. Dissipative structures that are far from equilibrium can avoid moving toward entropy within themselves by taking in large amounts of energy from their environments, but this process always involves a net increase in total energy dissipation and hence entropy in those larger environments. The total process of socioecological organization therefore always obeys the Second Law.

8. The tools that are used to conduct resource transfers function as energy triggers which release further energy flows. Efficient triggers aimed at specific targets require less energy input than the energy they release from those targets, which benefits those who direct them, but this always entails corresponding energy costs to others.

9. As tools/triggers are used to release energy flows, this process can convey information to the recipients about energetic processes. When this information functions as feedback and is embedded in shared culture, it becomes technological knowledge that actors can use to create and control future energy flows.

10. To the extent that organizational units are able to achieve the capabilities of steady state (balance or excess of inputs over outputs), stability

(ability to regain a steady state after a displacement), and resillience (ability to adapt to changing environmental conditions), they will be successful in surviving and functioning effectively for extended periods of time.

11. Organizations that can maintain high rates of energy flows through themselves have a functional advantage over organizations that cannot, in terms of either survival or operational effectiveness.

12. Energy flows within social organization can be intentionally directed and controlled by people to achieve desired objectives. The more efficiently that is done—that is, the lower the nonproductive energy costs and wastes in those flows—the more effectively those organizations will function to attain their goals.

POWER FLOWS

Social Power

This final fundamental component of socioecological organization has only recently been emphasized by social ecologists, since power exertion has usually been thought of as occurring entirely within the relational realm of sociocultural organization. Although a great deal of power exertion—especially the exercise of authority—does take place in interpersonal and interorganizational relationships, social power flows also affect the functional realm of socioecological organization. The exercise of social power therefore constitutes a critical linkage between the functional and relational sides of social organization.

In his 1975 book, Adams made a clear analytical distinction between energy and social power: energy is the capacity to do work, while *social power is the ability to affect social life*. From a general energetic perspective, power can be viewed as a form of energy, but the analytical distinction between energy and power is nevertheless quite important for the social sciences. Energy flows originate outside of human social organization, in the physical world and in bioecological organization, and enter socioecological organization through resource transfers. Social power flows, in contrast, originate within human social organization, as people acquire the ability to control energy flows and use them to affect the actions of others. Thus *social power flows are derived from directed energy flows*. Moreover, although control over energy flows gives social actors the ability to exercise social power, the actual amounts and uses of power within social life are influenced by cultural meanings and values. "In dealing with social power . . . we are concerned . . . with the control that one actor, or party, or operating unit exercises over some set of energy forms or flows and, most specifically, over some set of energy forms or flows that constitute part of the meaning environment of another actor (1975, p. 13).

Elaboration

Adams' basic contention that power exertion in social life is derived from energy flows is unequivocal. However, he does not deal explicitly with the nature of the linkage between energy and power. To explore that linkage, we first reexamine the distinction between socioecological and sociocultural organization, following which we shall return to Adams' concept of energy triggers.

In the fundamental sense that energy flows that generate social power originate within the physical and biological realms of existence and enter human social life via the functional realm of socioecological organization, all social power is an outgrowth of energy flows/resource transfers. At that initial stage of power creation, however, it consists merely of available resources that provide a potential for power exertion. To convert that potential into overt power actions, actors must do three things: (1) assign meanings and values to those resources; (2) commit at least some of them to a particular social situation; and (3) transform the committed resources into courses of action that affect other actors. All three of these activities involve social interactions within the relational realm of sociocultural organization. Consequently, the process of power exertion always involves both realms of social organization. The functional realm provides the necessary resources, while the relational realm gives meaning and direction to power activities.

This situation is further complicated by the fact that social power can take several different forms. Some of those forms are more likely to be exercised within the functional realm, while others tend to occur more extensively within the relational realm—although no form of power exists exclusively within either realm. For instance, consider the exercise of force, which is the application of pressures (benefits, punishments, or arguments) to actors to affect their thoughts and/or actions. To apply these pressures, whatever their nature, the power wielder must transfer some resources to the power recipient—or at least threaten to do so. Consequently, the use of force tends to occur primarily within the functional realm, although if the action ceases after a threat or bluff (a relational interaction), there may not be any actual resource transfers. The dynamics of exercising authority, in contrast, occur primarily (although not exclusively) within the relational realm. The grant of legitimacy from the power recipient to the power wielder that must occur before authority can be exercised is a relational activity, although it is often affected by resource distributions and uses within the functional realm. The directive or command given by the exerciser of legitimate authority is entirely a relational act of symbolic communication. That message may, however, produce activities within either the functional or relational realms, or both.

In sum, to understand the dynamic process through which energy flows are converted into power flows in social life, we must take account of the distinctive features of both the functional and relational realms and determine the ways in which each form of power exertion is involved in both socioecological and sociocultural organization.

Adams' principal contribution to understanding the linkage between energy and power flows lies in his concept of energy triggers. An energy trigger is any expenditure of energy that unleashes additional energy flows in the environment. Triggers can be intentionally controlled by actors and aimed at specific targets to produce desired activities. They are efficient to the extent that their energy costs are less than the amount of energy they subsequently release from their targets. They are effective to the extent that they produce whatever outcomes are desired by those who use them. *The intentional use of energy triggers for specific purposes is thus an exertion of social power.* Meanings and purposes from the relational realm determine an objective to be sought and identify the energy trigger which is most relevant to that objective. That trigger is then activated by dissipating some (hopefully small) amount of energy that is directed at a specified target. If the trigger is appropriate and effective, it will then have the desired consequence of releasing much larger energy flows from the target which both alter it and have still further effects on its social environments. If this process proceeds as intended, the actors who use the energy trigger will influence or control some portion(s) of social organization. They will thus exert social power.

There is one further and very important aspect of this process of creating social power flows with energy triggers. Social actors will obviously differ greatly in their ability to utilize, control, and direct energy triggers. The greater that ability, the more social power an actor or set of actors will be able to exert. Consequently, those actors who are in a position—primarily as a result of their location in the social structure of a society or other organization—to employ effective energy triggers will be able to exert the greatest amount of social power. They thus become the power elites in that social setting. The greater the amount of power they are able to exercise through control of energy triggers, the greater the amount of power inequality—and hence social stratification—within that society.

This energetic conception of social power modifies the usual sociological explanation of how power is exerted. Traditional Marxian theory, for example, assumes that the class of people who own or control the major means of economic production in a society will automatically be able to exercise dominant power throughout that society because of their access to large amounts of critical resources. That theorizing is partially valid, in that possession of some resources is a necessary requirement for using any energy trigger. Even if a trigger requires only a very small "squeeze" to be effective, an actor must possess at least some energy resources which can be dissipated in carrying out that action. Such theorizing is incomplete in two ways, however.

First, if an energy trigger is relatively efficient, it may require only a rather small expenditure of energy to produce major consequences in social life. Therefore, actors need not possess large amounts of resources to exert considerable social power if they are able to transform their limited resources into effective energy triggers. In an industrial society, actors other than those who own the means of production may be able to exercise considerable social power if they have access to even small amounts of resources that can be used to pull efficient and effective energy triggers.

Second, even if an actor possess large amounts of resources, this does not guarantee that it will be able to wield any significant amount of social power. If an actor does not have access to an appropriate energy trigger (such as an elderly person with a large bank account but no organizational position), or if it does not know how to use its resources to pull energy triggers (such as a business owner with little knowledge of how the economy operates), that actor will not be likely to be able to use its resources to activate efficient and effective energy triggers. Consequently, that actor will not be able to exert any significant amount of social power despite its extensive resources.

In sum, even small amounts of resources can be used to exert considerable amounts of social power, but only to the extent that they can be used to activate efficient and effective energy triggers.

Proposed Principles

The proposed theoretical principles given below are intended merely to illustrate the kind of systematic theory construction that is needed to incorporate this perspective on energy-based social power exertion into sociological theory. They do not constitute any kind of complete theoretical argument.

1. Power exertion is a critical dynamic in social organization, such that all social processes and forms are affected by power flows as well as by energy flows. The ability to exercise social power is derived ultimately from socioenergy flows within the functional realm of socioecological organization that provide the resources necessary for all social activity. At the same time, all power exertion is defined and directed by the relational realm, so that power flows are always shaped by sociocultural organization.

2. Because the functional and relational realms are so thoroughly interwoven in all social organization, energy and social power flows are highly interlinked in all situations. Consequently, energy use always affects power exertion and power exertion always affects energy use.

3. The greater the socioenergy flows within a society and the greater the ability of actors to direct those flows in intended ways with effective and efficient energy triggers, the greater the potential for exercising social power

in that society. However, social power exertion is also influenced by many other social and cultural factors.

4. Those parts and members of society that enact key roles in resource transfers/socioenergy flows within socioecological processes—especially those that determine and direct the use of energy triggers—will tend to exercise the greatest amount of social power in both the functional and relational realms of a society. The ability of actors to exercise particular forms of power such as force or authority will depend on their access to the resources necessary to exert each form of power and their skill in transforming those resources into power actions such as imposing social pressures or issuing authoritative commands.

5. Although socioenergy flows/resource transfers occur in all human activities, they are particularly crucial in the economy of a society or other type of organization. The bulk of all energy/resources utilized by any social unit initially enters it through its economic sector, where energy/resources are transformed into goods and services and distributed to all other sectors. The economy of an organization therefore functions as its primary "energy/ resource gateway." In general, the greater the energy/resources flowing into an organization through its economy and being transformed into useful goods and services, the greater the flow of both wealth and power through the entire organization. Substantial increases in the amount of energy/resources flowing through an economy generally result from the substitution of inanimate energy sources for living (animal and human) energy sources.

6. The nature and efficiency of economic processes in a society or other organization directly affect the amount of surplus wealth (i.e., above the subsistence level) that is produced and can be used for nonsustenance activities. Even more critical is the amount of surplus wealth per capita; hence population size is a critical factor in this process. The total amount of surplus wealth per capita in a society directly influences the amount of social power (of all types) that can potentially be exercised in that society, which in turn affects the extensiveness and complexity of its of social organization. Consequently, those members and parts of a society that control its economic processes are especially capable of exercising social power throughout many sectors of that society.

CONCLUSION

The underlying thesis of this paper is that social ecology is an integral part of the general process of human social organization. A derivative thesis is that there is presently an urgent need for greater understanding of socioecological organization and its linkage with sociocultural organization. Four fundamental components of the theory of socioecological organization are tool utilization, resource transfers, energy flows, and power flows, which have been the concerns of this paper.

I shall not attempt to summarize all of the points made about those four components, since that is done at the end of each of the sections in which they are discussed. I simply want to stress again that all of my proposals in those sections are highly tentative and need extensive exploration and elaboration. The challenge now confronting all of us who are concerned to synthesize social ecology and sociology into a unified discipline is to integrate these four components of tools, resources, energy, and power into a single comprehensive explanation of socioecological organization.

ACKNOWLEDGMENTS

The author is indebted to Lee Freese and Eugene Rosa for their many helpful comments that considerably improved this paper.

REFERENCES

Adams, R.N. 1975. *Energy and Structure: A Theory of Social Power.* Austin, TX: University of Texas Press.
———. 1982. *Paradoxical Harvest: Energy and Exploration in British History: 1870-1914.* Cambridge: Cambridge University Press.
———. 1988. *The Eighth Day: Social Evolution as the Self-Organization of Energy.* Austin, TX: University of Texas Press.
Boulding, K.E. 1978. *Ecodynamics: A New Theory of Societal Evolution.* Beverly Hills, CA: Sage.
Duncan, O.D. 1964. "Social Organization and the Ecosystem." In *Handbook of Modern Sociology,* edited by R.E.L. Faris. Chicago: Rand-McNally.
Duncan, O.D., and L.F. Schnore. 1959. "Cultural, Behavioral, and Ecological Perspectives in the Study of Social Organization." *American Journal of Sociology* 65(September): 132-146.
Freese, L. 1988. "Evolution and Sociogenesis. Part I: Ecological Origins. Part II: Social Continuities." Pp. 53-118 in *Advances in Group Processes,* Vol. 5, edited by E.J. Lawler and B. Markovsky. Greenwich, CT: JAI Press.
Hawley, A.H. 1944. "Ecology and Human Ecology." *Social Forces* 22: 398-405.
———. 1950. *Human Ecology: A Theory of Community Structure.* New York: Ronald Press.
———. 1968. "Human Ecology." Pp. 328-337 in *The International Encyclopedia of the Social Sciences,* edited by D.L. Sills. New York: Crowell-Collier and Macmillan.
———. 1986. *Human Ecology: A Theoretical Essay.* Chicago: The University of Chicago Press.
Lotka, A.J. 1922. "Contributions to the Energetics of Evolution." *Proceedings of the National Academy of Sciences* 8: 147-151.
Maryanski, A. 1992. "The Last Ancestor: An Ecological Network Model on the Origins of Human Sociality." Pp. 1-32 in *Advances in Human Ecology,* Vol. 1, edited by L. Freese. Greenwich, CT: JAI Press.
Micklin, M., and H.M. Choldin, eds. 1984. *Sociological Human Ecology: Contemporary Issues and Applications.* Boulder, CO: Westview Press.
Odum, H. 1971. *Environment, Power, and Society.* New York: Wiley Interscience.

Olsen, M.E. 1993. "A Sociological Perspective on Social Evolution." Pp. 69-92 in *Advances in Human Ecology*, Vol. 2, edited by L. Freese. Greenwich, CT: JAI Press.

————. Forthcoming. *Dynamics of Social Organization: Processes and Theories.*

Prigogine, I. 1980. *From Being To Becoming: Time and Complexity in the Physical Sciences.* San Francisco, CA: W. H. Freeman.

Rosa, E.A. n.d. "What Is This Thing Called Technology?: Toward an Operational Definition." Unpublished paper, Department of Sociology, Washington State University.

Rosa, E.A., and G.E. Machlis. 1983. "Energetic Theories of Society: An Evaluation Review." *Sociological Inquiry* 53: 152-78.

A SOCIOECOLOGICAL
PERSPECTIVE ON
SOCIAL EVOLUTION

Marvin E. Olsen

ABSTRACT

This paper continues the perspective on socioecological organization developed in "Components of Socioecological Theory," but here focusing on the processs of social evolution. It examines the recent writings of Lee Freese and Richard Adams, looks for convergences between their theses, and then proposes several directions for further theoretical thinking about social evolution. Freese's "sociogenesis" perspective emphasizes the manner in which societies augment their environment through resource transfers and hence alter the conditions that shape their subsequent evolution. Adam's "self-organization" perspective emphasizes the manner in which energy dissipation by societies creates perturbations in their environments that trigger further energy flows in an evolutionary process. The major points of convergence between those perspectives are that the process of social evolution originates within socioecological organization and is self-generating.

Advances in Human Ecology, Volume 2, pages 69-92.
Copyright © 1993 by JAI Press Inc.
All rights of reproduction in any form reserved.
ISBN: 1-55938-558-8

INTRODUCTION

Recapitulation

In a companion paper titled "Components of Socioecological Theory: Tools, Resource, Energy, and Power" (Olsen 1993), I made two overall arguments. First, social ecology is an integral part of the general process of human social organization. Social organization can be viewed as containing two parallel and highly interwoven analytical realms: the functional realm of socioecological organization and the relational realm of sociocultural organization. Ecological concepts and processes are directly relevant to socioecological organization and indirectly relevant to some aspects of sociocultural organization. Second, four fundamental components of any socioecological organization which must be incorporated into all attempts to explain that process, are tool utilization, resource transfers, energy flows, and power exertion. Recent writings by Lee Freese (1988) and Richard Adams (1988) were extensively reviewed to identify their contributions to our understanding of these four components of socioecological organization.

Purposes

This paper continues the examination of those writings by Freese and Adams to ascertain their contributions to developing a socioecological perspective on the process of social evolution. This process is not a basic component of socioecological organization, as are tools, resources, energy, and power, but rather a consequence of the development of socioecological organization through time. It is fair to say, I think, that the principal concern of both Freese and Adams in those writings was to present a socioecological perspective on the process of social evolution.

Most traditional sociological explanations of social evolution focus primarily on the realm of sociocultural organization, asking how alterations in social-structural patterns and shared cultural ideas have shaped the emergence of modern industrial societies. Marxian theory, for example, focuses on dialectical conflict between social classes as they struggle to gain control over the major means of economic production in a society. Weberian theory emphasizes the importance of shifts in cultural worldviews, or sets of shared beliefs and values, in promoting industrialization. Functional theory views social evolution as progressive structural differentiation, in which critical social activities are moved out of households into functionally specialized social institutions. Finally, contemporary world-systems theory views the entire world as an interrelated arena of national domination and conflict in which a few powerful societies largely control the developmental fate of numerous more dependent societies.

None of these sociocultural perspectives gives any serious attention to the realm of socioecological organization and the manner in which ecological dynamics affect social evolution. Moreover, none of the classical writings on socioecological theory (Duncan 1964; Duncan and Schnore 1959; Hawley 1950, 1968, 1986) develops theoretical explanations of the process of social evolution. Although they all imply that human social organization has evolved over time, they do not attempt to explain this process in any systematic manner.

The two works by Freese and Adams that are the basis of this paper both address that challenge of formulating a socioecological perspective on the process of social evolution. Neither of them presumes to present a complete theory of evolutionary change in human social organization. But both of them insist that *socioecological conditions and dynamics underlie the entire process of social evolution.* Also, each of their works presents numerous insightful ideas concerning the role of socioecological organization within social evolution. Although Freese's and Adams' perspectives appear on the surface to be quite substantively different, there are in fact numerous points of convergence between them.

My purposes in this paper are to: (1) extract the principal theoretical ideas concerning social evolution in those works by Freese and Adams; (2) identify several points of convergence between these two perspectives on evolution; and (3) suggest some additional directions for further development of a socioecological perspective on social evolution.

This paper, like its companion, is highly speculative and will require much refinement and elaboration; it extracts from Freese and Adams the ideas that I think are most relevant rather than summarizing their entire arguments; and it makes no attempt to review all the underlying literature reviewed in their works. Despite these limitations, I hope that this paper will stimulate other social theorists to think more deeply about the relevance of socioecological processes for understanding social evolution.

The paper contains four parts. The first presents Freese's "sociogenesis" perspective on social evolution; the second covers Adams' "self-organization" perspective; the third discusses a number of points of convergence between their respective theses; and the fourth part sketches some proposed directions for further development of a socioecological perspective on social evolution.

Terminology

For readers of this paper who are not familiar with the companion piece, let me begin by mentioning the key concepts presented there. They include the differences between the fields of *ecology, human ecology,* and *social ecology;* the ideas of *ecological organization and bioecological organization*; and the fundamental distinction betwen the two realms or sides of human social organization—which I term the functional realm of *socioecological organization* and the relational realm of *sociocultural organization*—neither of which exists apart from the other. The remaining critical term in this present paper, which is not discussed in the companion paper, is *social evolution*, which refers to the historical process in which societies and many other forms of human social organization become increasingly large, complex, and formalized. This concept does not imply any kind of value judgement that modern industrial societies and their component social institutions are more desirable or beneficial than earlier forms of social organization, but merely significantly different.

Throughout this paper, I use my terms for all concepts except in direct quotations from others. Whenever my term differs from one used by Freese or Adams, his equivalent term is given in brackets.

FREESE'S SOCIOGENESIS PERSPECTIVE

Introduction

The principal thrust of the first part of Freese's paper is to propose an ecological evolutionary theory to complement natural selection theory. Natural selection applies only to individual species of organisms, and says nothing about the habitats in which they exist. Yet it presumes that those habitats change, without specifying why. It cannot account for evolutionary change in either bioecological or socioecological organization. Thus natural selection theory, which applies only to long-term species changes, must be supplemented by an ecological evolutionary theory that explains short-term changes in both biophysical and human ecological conditions.

Freese introduces his proposed theoretical perspective—which he calls *sociogenesis*—in this manner (in which his term "social systems" refers to socioecological organization, not sociocultural organization):

> The theory of natural selection, when extended to explain human social behavior, is incomplete because the natural selection of organisms and of cultural traits proceeds from the mandate to adapt to habitats. Biophysical ecosystems and human social systems, which provide habitats, are driven by a different imperative. There, evolution unfolds from the very continuation of interaction itself....This evolutionary process is said to begin in biophysical ecosystems and continue into human social systems because social systems presume ecosystem interactions but not the other way around (p. 54).

In Freese's perspective, the fundamental activity within all ecological organization [ecosystems]—both biological and social—is a resource transfer, in which a resource is moved from one organism or organization to another and subsequently used and thus altered by the recipient. Every resource transfer also affects both its sender—who then has fewer resources and hence less ability to act—and its receiver—who then has more resources and hence greater ability to act. Thus, all activity within all ecological organization continuously alters both the actors and the resources involved. Consequently, every activity affects the habitat within which all subsequent ecological activity will occur. He writes that:

> Continued interactions have autocatalytic effects in which resources are added, subtracted, and rearranged in the system. As these effects accumulate in series, they irreversibly change the conditions for further interactions and for structures of resources, causing them to be replaced. Thus, the system itself is modified by descent according to its own internal momentum (p. 54).

Evolutionary Dynamics

Evolutionary change occurs in habitats, Freese argues, because many actions by organisms—especially macroscopic actions—alter their environments in ways that are cumulative and irreversible. While some short-term, microscopic effects of actions can be reversed, even those effects are frequently cumulative, so that in the long run they are also often irreversible. Thus, the accumulated microscopic effects of actions and interactions by organisms tend to have cascading effects that become irreversible over time, contributing their small share to an irreversible macroscopic outcome. As a result of this process, the entire ecological organization in which organisms exist gradually changes and evolves. In Freese's words:

> By the mere process of living, organisms change the very conditions upon which they depend for subsistence. Their resource supply is changed by the effects of their own interactions. The individual effects may be small but the compound effects are large. Eventually they change the ecosystem. As new effects are added over sufficient series they eventually become interactive, and there emerges a different resource regimen. In other words, augmentative interactions are cumulative. As the resources of an ecosystem are developed, exploited, depleted, and otherwise transformed because of it own organic activity, eventually the system becomes something it was not. As it does, the probabilities that it can return to what it was decline. That's because some of the changes it will have endured will be irreversible (p. 71).

Whereas the process of natural selection is driven by the mandate of *adaptation to the environment*, the process of ecological evolution is driven by the mandate of *augmentation of the environment*. This latter mandate derives from the autocatalyic (i.e., self-generating) effect of ecological interactions on available resources:

> The continual addition to a system of its own interactions affects the development and depletion of resources in sequences that connect and reverberate through subsystems. Augmentation refers to the appearance of resource interactions new to some subsystem.

This should happen to some degree because ecosystems (and human social systems) are not...closed or in perfect equilibrium (p. 68).

As any of the parts of an ecological organization augment their resource interactions, those new conditions normally affect other parts in a cumulative and often irreversible manner, which through time change the entire organization. Freese views this process as evolutionary if it results in greater structural and functional differentiation—and thus complexity—within the organization, and calls it degeneration if reduces internal differentiation and complexity.

In autocatalytic systems of living organisms, unless they are degenerating, augmentation is a prime evolutionary force. As augmentative interactions appear in subsystems, resource configurations change. This changes the system, causing it to evolve into something it was not. The process by which this happens I shall call *serial differentiation* (p. 68).

Freese defines serial differentiation as "the evolutionary change that results from the autocatalytic, cumulative, and irreversible effects of interactions on system resources" (p. 72). In other words, this process is internally driven by the ongoing dynamics of ecological activity. It does not imply an irreversible destiny for any given ecological organization, but it does imply that no ecological organization can ever retreat to prior conditions because

the past state of the system becomes part of the initial conditions of the subsequent state of the system.... Such a system can gradually disintegrate or gradually evolve. If it evolves, it does so by the serial differentiation of augmentative interactions forced by induction. Differentiation itself is microscopic but it converts to macroscopic diversity, complexity, and organization in which system structures are continually redesigned by the effects of their own interactions (p. 83).

Evolution of Social Organization

The process of serial differentiation occurs in socioecological as well as bioecological organization. Over time, this process also produces evolutionary change in sociocultural organization. "Human society is not self-sustaining. If...ecosystems evolve, social systems have to continue the evolutionary process according to the same principles, however different and amplified may be the details of manifestation" (p. 116). Those principles state that:

[A]utocatalytic, cumulative, and irreversible effects on resources are properties of the interaction series of all social systems and interpersonal groups to the extent that they endure (p. 109)....

The integrity and viability of any social system or interpersonal group depend upon a continual flow of suitable resources to sustain interaction. The flow itself insures that something will be added to the interactions—the effects of the flow. These change the conditions for further interaction by changing the resource structures on which interaction depends. The structures change because resources are augmented or depleted. Thus the system itself changes, in an orderly way, and so does anything connected to it (p. 110).

These orderly changes in human social organization can be evolutionary, but they are not necessarily linear or developmental in nature. That is, they are guided by previously existing conditions and by resource availability and augmentation, not by any grand design or ultimate goals. As described by Freese:

[T]he lawful process of social change defined by autocatalytic, cumulative, and irreversible effects of resource interactions is a process of evolutionary change. It is endogenetic evolution, that is, internally generated change in a system from a deep and gradually replaceable core, in which system structures are modified by descent from their earlier forms. It is properly called evolution, not development, because there are no past forms for each unit to recapitulate, no program of information to shape morphology and function, no universal epigenetic unfolding, and no progressive functional equilibria or perfect end states that can be defined from initial conditions. The process is, nevertheless, universal....So being, any social entity incorporates its own interaction history into its evolution. Its destiny unfolds according to the resources it begins with and how it augments or depletes them during its own interaction series (p. 110).

It is important to note that Freese makes all evolutionary change in sociocultural organization [interpersonal groups] a consequence of serial differentiation in socioecological organization [social systems]. He does not allow for any independent sources of sociocultural evolution, and in fact argues that sociocultural organization tends to remain static unless pushed to change by alterations in socioecological conditions. As he states:

[T]here is no driving force to cause change in the structure and process of interpersonal groups except changing resource conditions. Interpersonal interactions arranged in a system of social relations, if they produce satisfactory resource transfers always, should not change because interactants have no incentive to change them. That they do change as a matter of course is because of the augmentation and depletion of resources that continued interaction brings....This implies interpersonal groups must change in consequence of the [socioecological] systemic interactions they themselves, or others connected to them through the system, have caused or failed to cause. To explain social change, therefore, one has to describe the changing structures of social system resource transfers that interpersonal groups have access to, are subject to, and are causes of (p. 109).

Social evolution can also occur in a negative direction toward decreasing complexity, which might be called "devolution." This can begin to transpire whenever organisms use resources at a faster rate than the bioecosystem can replenish them, leading to cumulative resource depletion (pp. 84, 115). Under those conditions, resource transfers within some resource dyads often result in the degeneration of other related functional linkages, the overall outcome of which can be ceasation of the process of resource augmentation (p. 73). When this occurs within human socioecological organization, it can have two major consequences: (1) diminishment or destruction of its bioecological foundation; and (2) decreased functional differentiation and structural complexity.

Freese has constructed a logical and integrated perspective on human social evolution which rests on the processes of resource augmentation and structural and functional differentiation within socioecological organization. While this perspective is highly suggestive, it can be expanded in other directions. Adams' theory of "self-organization" provides several ideas for that expansion.

ADAMS' SELF-ORGANIZATION PERSPECTIVE

Overview

Adams' thesis of *self-organization* is part of his broader energetic conception of social organization, in which energy forms and flows constitute the basic dynamics of all social life. Whenever an entity acts, it dissipates energy to the environment, thus creating *perturbations* in existing energy flows. Those perturbations alter the environment and all entities within it, including the initially acting entity. He introduces the idea of self-organization as follows:

> The central argument is that the inherent nature of energy is to dissipate and in so doing to emit perturbations. This dissipation itself creates structures, and the pertubations affect both these and other structures in the environment. It is this last process, taking place as continuing interaction, that constitutes "self-organization" (p. x).

This argument rests on the assumption that action always creates change. "A common weakness in classical sociology has been to regard social forces as having an inherent formal continuity; the present approach makes a contrary assumption; namely, that if things act, they change" (p. 143). More specifically, action always creates perturbations in the environment, which alter both the environment and the acting unit. "Perturbations...are the primary actors in self-organization" (p. 64).

Evolutionary Dynamics

Environmental perturbations resulting from energy dissipation affect acting units to the extent that those units must take in energy to sustain their activities. All acting entities are therefore vulnerable to, and must cope with, external disruptions coming from perturbations caused by their own actions and those of other units. These disruptions create internal *fluctuations*, or "irregularities, internal sources of error, 'noise,' and mild dysfunctions" (p. 65). By activating energy triggers to release additional internal energy flows directed at specific targets for specific purposes, the unit may be able to cope with those fluctuations successfully. The unit then evidences stability and resilliency. "The internal triggers that control and neutralize irregularities usually require little energy even though they may be critical for the structure's stability" (p. 65).

These coping activities, using targeted energy triggers, are carried out by whatever parts of the unit are affected by fluctuations. Adams does not assume that whole units have a morphostatic tendency. The affected parts act to protect themselves, but their actions dissipate energy and therefore affect other parts.

[A] structure's internal environment provides the self-triggering dynamics whereby some dissipating parts perturb the mutual conjoining of others into new energy forms. ... In energetic terms, self-organization is composed of a series of parts, each seeking its own condition of equilibrium within the immediate environmental realities. While the self-organization of an energy form must be seen as a gestalt, it can only be understood through understanding how its component parts maintain an assemblage that regenerates stability for the whole (p. 61).

This self-organizing activity can have two kinds of consequences for the unit as a whole. Although Adams does not use the systemic terms *morphostasis* and *morphogenesis*, they aptly describe those possible outcomes. Instead of morphostasis, Adams speaks of *autopoiesis*, which he defines as "the dynamic processes of a unity to maintain and reproduce itself" (p. 63). He prefers this term because it is not the entire unit which is maintaining its structure, but only some parts of it. "[W]e are not modeling an entire system but only the self-reproducing processes that operate independently of, and without concern for, other possible factors" (p. 63). Morphostasis [autopoiesis] is most likely to occur in a unit, Adams suggests, under two kinds of conditions: (1) when it seeks, or is forced by its environment, to rigidly define its boundaries; or (2) when external energy flows are limited. In either case, the unit will attempt to conserve the amount of energy it is dissipating while carrying out its activities. In other words, it will attempt to make its energy input and output flows as efficient as possible and thus preserve itself under "tight" conditions.

[W]hen a social aggregate rigidly defines its boundaries and rigidly seeks, or is forced, to include and exclude energy forms in conformance with that definition, then the energetic tendency will be to reduce dissipation of the social process to a minimum rate, to seek the most efficient use of the energy that is available.... Similarly, when the amount of energy available to a social assemblage is limited, the dissipation of that energy will lead to a more rigid definition of the boundaries of the assemblage, to its evolving increasingly closed self-organization. Thus limiting energy flow is self-organizing" (p. 149).

Morphogenesis, in contrast, is most likely to occur in a unit under the opposite kinds of conditions: (1) when it is seeking to open its boundaries; or (2) when external energy flows are abundant. In both those situations, the unit will attempt to take in as much energy from its environment as possible so as to be able to dissipate greater amounts of energy in expanding its structure and its activities. It will thus attempt to make its energy input and output flows as effective as possible and consequently expand itself under "beneficial" conditions.

> [W]hen a social aggregate is expanding—increasing its dissipation—then its boundaries are weakened and energy forms are incorporated as part of the enlarging dissipative process. Conquest introduces new sources of wealth, sources of labor, and natural resources. Economic growth involves an increase in energy dissipation, and this can only take place by ignoring existing boundaries and bringing in accessible energy forms. Boundaries change with the incorporation of new forms. If the boundaries of a previously conservative, steady state society are broken by a flood of new energy forms, the boundaries will expand in a manner that seems to maximize energy flux (p. 150).

Adams summarizes these two opposing tendencies with the following principles:

> The distinctiveness and stability of the boundaries of a dissipative process vary directly with the tendency of that process to seek a minimum dissipation rate [and] inversely with its tendency to maximize energy flux (p. 149).

Finally, a unit may degenerate or be radically altered if its parts are not capable of coping with energy disruptions and fluctuations.

> Excessive pertubations...whether internally generated or externally derived, may damage or destroy these [coping] mechanisms. Without them, the structure may be unable to control its own fluctuations and become extremely unstable, even to the point of tearing itself apart. Even without such extreme results, it becomes vulnerable to more decisive consequences from subsequent perturbations. Under these circumstances, new structures—both larger through combination or smaller through fragmentation—may well emerge (p. 65).

Which of these self-organizing directions any particular society or other unit takes at any particular time is never entirely determined by impersonal ecological or structural forces. Rather, they are ultimately controlled by intentional human purposes. Because energy flows convey information that can be used by actors as feedback and as guides for energy triggers, social actors can always—if they wish—determine the direction of their self-organizing, although not necessarily all of its details. "The salient characteristic of human groupings is that they can self-define as worthy of perpetuation, of continuity, or survival; and they can define themselves out of existence" (p. 125).

> [T]he capacity for symbolism provide[s] human beings with highly efficient and complex 'trigger' mechanisms for the release of energy flows.... By releasing these other flows, human activity—i.e., human energy—becomes involved in a larger 'self-organization' (p. 195).

Trends in Social Organization

As human societies have engaged in "self-organization" and become increasingly complex during the past 10,000 years, four broad trends have been evident throughout this evolutionary process. First, the amount of energy used per capita has steadily increased. "[T]here is no question but that an increase of energy consumption is the most fundamental characteristic of long-range, general human evolution" (p. 194).

Second, growth in economic productivity has been closely associated with the substitution of increasing amounts and diverse forms of nonhuman energy for human effort. "[T]he major increase in productivity derives from vast increases in nonhuman energy. By standing on the back of these 'energy slaves,' individual human beings can appear to be more productive" (p. 239). "Man, in his immense anthropocentricism, has tended to congratulate himself and see this only as a per capita decrease in the human energy input; until recently, he tended to overlook the cosmic significance of the massive amounts of nonhuman energy required for this advance" (1975, p. 121).

Third, increasing energy flows have steadily expanded the role of information within societies, in terms of both the manner in which it is conveyed and its usefulness in directing human activities. "The increasing dependence on nonhuman energy... brings in its train an increase in information transfers between nonhuman components of a system. It also increases the potential amount of self-organization" (p. 85). Information expansion, in turn, stimulates the growth of shared culture that is closely interwoven with energy flows. "[W]hat distinguishes human social evolution from that of all other species is that human beings couple these human and nonhuman processes as single constructions" (p. 90).

Fourth, social evolution has also involved a steady movement toward centralized power structures through which a small proportion of the population of a society can control the activities of the rest of the people. Adams refers to this as controlling the flow of human energy.

> In a broad evolutionary perspective, "development" may be seen as a high-energy version of what was first manifest thousands of years ago as efforts to domesticate other living things. The controls people gained over plants and animals to enhance their survival were replicated in the emergence of civilization as emergent hierarchies of centralized power over the larger society, i.e., domesticated people, in order to assure their own survival (p. 240).

This last trend underlies Adams's discussion of the process of power centralization in modern societies.

Power Centralization

Although the ability to exert social power results from control over energy flows, Adams made a clear analytical distinction in his 1975 book between energy and social power. Energy is the capacity to do work, while social power is the ability to affect social life. The actual amounts and uses of power within social life are therefore determined by cultural meanings and values. As humanity's ability to control socioecological processes has increased, so has its capability of exercising social power, with resulting evolution in the complexity of social organization. This linkage between energy use, power exertion, and social evolution has been, in Adams' view, almost inevitable.

> Each increment of growth in this sphere of energy forms and processes meant a new basis of power; and each increment in the exercise of power meant that the social organization had, in a sense, to expand to contain the new influence. However, this expansion has been occurring at a continuing and increasing energy cost (1975, p. 152).

In his 1988 book, Adams elaborates this perspective with the idea that a *power hierarchy* exists within every society. His argument is that as the ability to exert social power has increased in societies as a result of expanding energy flows, power flows have tended to become increasingly centralized within hierarchical social structures. "[T]here is a relationship between the energy a society can bring into play and the size and stability of the social hierarchy that will control it" (p. 112). At the top of the power hierarchy within modern societies is a *regulatory sector* that exercises dominant power throughout the entire society. This sector consists of all governmental and other collective decision-making bodies. (For convenience, Adams refers to all other parts of a society as its "working sector," although it obviously contains many distinct arenas of activity.) This development of a controlling hierarchy of social power "marks the emergence of a complex society, one which differentiates itself in terms of relative control and power" (p. 72).

Adams mentions two causes of this development of power hierarchies and regulatory sectors in complex societies. One is the functional argument that increasing specialization and interdependence among the various parts of a society require centralized regulation if the society is to function adequately. Societies that establish power hierarchies therefore have a selective advantage over those that do not.

> The emergence of hierarchy was immensely important, since it established mutually amplifying...coevolutionary systems within human society itself, i.e., the regulatory and working sectors of society. This directionality reflects the selective preference experienced by hierarchical societies over those which failed or preferred not to opt for hierarchical growth (p. 241).

The second reason is the desire by some people to dominate and control social activities, which leads them to establish a power hierarchy (with themselves at the top if at all possible). Adams is quite realistic about the human drive to exercise power.

> Although development [of power hierarchies] is adverse for some people, it benefits others. Among the beneficiaries are, of course, the members of the society's regulatory sector. Even as some of the poor grow poorer, development also enriches some of the rich and strengthens some of the powerful. Development at the motivational level persists, therefore, because it benefits the very sector of the population that has the strategic capacity to decide whether it should be pursued (p. 239).

The creation and perpetuation of a power hierarchy with a dominant regulatory sector in a society is not a simple undertaking, however. Adams discusses four kinds of difficulties that are commonly encountered by actors attempting to develop and operate a regulatory sector. The first is that the regulatory elites must devise procedures for extracting extensive amounts of resources from the rest of the society and transforming those resources into power exertion, which may be strongly resisted. "The capacity to self-organize at the top must form against the pull of the divergent interests of each of the component members" (p. 183).

Second, other parts of the society can also self-organize and thus increase their ability to counter the power of the regulatory sector, which means that it must strengthen its own power-wielding ability if it is to remain in control. "The fact that self-organization at all levels and in all components can threaten the specialized regulators will lead the latter to strengthen themselves" (p. 72).

Third, the process of societal regulation can require large expenditures of energy in complex societies, which creates additional functional problems for the regulatory sector, which limits its ability to perform its tasks. Growing societal complexity

> requires the regulatory sector to become more active, to control more energy to handle its own tasks. Thus increasing amounts of energy are brought into the process of regulation. In turn, the regulative activities themselves are subject to fluctuating stresses and must be submitted to yet further control. ... The argument proposed here is that the very increase of energy flow in regulatory activity itself makes effective regulation problematic (pp. 137-138).

Fourth, since the existence and functions of the regulatory sector depend on the ability of the rest of the society to perform its various tasks in a satisfactory manner, the regulatory sector must constantly seek to convince the other members of the society that it is serving their general interests and not merely controlling them.

In general...the regulatory sector has the most immediate stake in the integrity of the self-organization of the whole. Its members could not survive apart from the work provided by the substantive work sector. The rationale is phrased, however, in terms of the benefits to, as well as the security of, the society as a whole. Only if both sectors of the society—the workers as well as the regulators—remain convinced of this will both willingly work together (p. 190).

Despite all these difficulties, complex societies do establish power hierarchies dominated by a regulatory sector that tends to become increasingly powerful and to control numerous activities throughout the entire society. If the members of the regulatory sector can overcome the above problems, if they are adequately aware of the coordination and regulation needs of the total society, if they are committed to dealing with those matters rather than just expanding their own power and wealth, and if they are skillful at their regulatory activities, then these elites within the regulatory sector can effectively direct the course of social evolution followed by their society.

The principal way in which regulatory elites direct societal activities and development is by manipulating efficient and effective energy triggers designed for specific purposes and aimed at carefully selected targets. To the extent that elites can control this energy triggering process—in terms of both making decisions about using triggers and then activating those triggers as intended—they can exert influence and control throughout the society by expending small amounts of energy to unleash large energy/resource flows.

To explore this generalization, Adams conducted a study of energy flows and regulatory activities in 71 contemporary societies. He examined the size of the regulatory sector as a proportion of the total population of each society, in conjunction with its per capita commercial energy consumption. He found a very marked relationship between those two variables, although not a linear one. Societies using only moderate amounts of energy (generally those that are not highly industrialized) show only small expansions in the size of their regulatory sector as energy consumption increases. However, beyond a critical turning point (essentially full industrialization), each slight increase in commercial energy use is associated with a large expansion in the regulatory sector of societies. Adams summarizes his conclusions from the study in the following manner:

This pattern suggests that a nation-state must consume a certain amount of nonhuman energy before it can significantly expand its [regulatory] sector. ... Another way of expressing this relationship is that a given level of energy consumption requires a certain level of societal complexity, presumably within some finite range. This complexity will have to be reflected in a self-organization that has a specialized [regulatory] sector that is adequate to the task. Similarly, it will not support [a regulatory] sector that exceeds some limit. In short, energy is deterministically related to complexity, and complexity requires adequate self-organization. What is impressive here is the total lack of exceptions (p. 228).

CONVERGENCES BETWEEN THE THESES

Both Freese and Adams have proposed perspectives on the process of social evolution that are grounded in socioecological processes. They use different terminology: Freese speaks of an autocatalytic process of resource transfers resulting in ecological augmentation and serial differentiation, while Adams talks about energy dissipation causing perturbations that result in self-organization which leads to increasingly centralized power exertion. Nevertheless, both of them use a common socioecological frame of reference and a self-organizing system model to describe the process of social evolution. Moreover, since all resource transfers are energy flows (although not all energy flows are resource transfers), both writers are dealing with essentially the same process. We can, therefore, identify several points of convergence between their respective arguments.

1. The most fundamental point made by both perspectives is that the *process of social evolution originates within the realm of socioecological organization*. Both writers insist that social organization can evolve only to the extent that changes occur within the functional realm. They both reject the traditional sociological argument that social evolution originates in the relational realm of sociocultural organization.

2. Also of critical importance is the fact that both perspectives view *the process of social evolution as self-generating*, as emphasized by the terms "sociogenesis" and "self-organization." Internal functional dynamics inevitably change the processes and structures of socioecological organization through time. In human social life, to exist is to act, and to act is to change. While external forces and conditions constantly impinge upon the functional activities of societies and thus influence evolutionary processes, social evolution is shaped largely by internal dynamics.

3. The most basic activity in the evolutionary process is resource transfers/energy flows, since this constitutes the essence of socioecological organization. All resource transfers/energy flows affect the actors that initiate them in two ways: (1) directly, by depleting the amount of potential resources/energy available to those initiating actors; and (2) indirectly, by altering the natural and social environments, which sooner or later affects the initiating actors. All transfers/flows also affect the receiving actors, since they provide those receivers with useful resources/energy. Finally, other actors that are functionally connected with the receivers in any way are eventually impacted to some extent by the ramifications or perturbations of those transfers/flows. Thus, *all functional activities and all patterns of socioecological organization are continuously being affected and altered by resource transfers/energy flows*.

4. All these changes constitute a self-organizing process that is cumulative and irreversible, since changes build on themselves through time. And the

further that process moves from its initial starting point, the more cumulative and irreversible it becomes. Under most circumstances, a society cannot retreat to an earlier form because the set of socioecological conditions that produced that form no longer exist. Resources have been augmented and energy flows have increased in magnitude and often taken new forms. As a general principle, therefore, *the socioecological organization which exists at any point in time is built on the organization that has existed in the past, is to some extent unique, and constitutes the foundation for all socioecological organization that will occur in the future.*

5.   The two perspectives do emphasize different aspects of the evolutionary process. Freese stresses structural conditions, arguing that through serial differentiation, socioecological organization becomes increasingly complex. Adams, meanwhile, focuses on the functional processes of morphostasis and morphogenesis and the conditions under which they occur. However, *structural and processional descriptions of social evolution are merely two ways of viewing the same process,* so that the two perspectives are totally complementary in this respect.

6.   While Adams allows for equilibrium as a possible temporary condition of socioecological organization in which evolution is not occurring, Freese's position on this matter is more realistic. He argues that *equilibrium is only a hypothetical condition that never actually occurs in reality* since societies and all other open units are continuously affecting their environments. This means that (a) their hypothetical equilibrium state is always changing, which (b) constantly forces the unit to take action (and thus dissipate energy) to cope with new conditions, which (c) always keeps it out of equilibrium and therefore evolving.

7.   The attention that Adams gives to *the transmission of information that always accompanies energy flows,* as well as its consequences for feedback, energy triggers, and cultural accumulation greatly enhances our understanding of the evolutionary process. The idea of information transmission in conjunction with resource transfers/energy flows is fully compatible with Freese's perspective, although he does not explicitly deal with information.

8.   While many aspects of both perspectives are derived from existing theory concerning system dynamics, each one adds a new and potentially critical idea to the ability of system dynamics to explain social evolution. Freese's contribution is the idea that *the process of serial differentiation (which interacts with natural selection) is made possible by activities that augment the amounts and forms of resources available to a unit from its environments and are used by it as it acts and evolves.* Adams' contribution is the idea that *energy triggers can be intentionally used in a targeted manner to release additional energy flows that can enable a unit to cope with disruptions and increase its functional capabilities.* These two ideas are clearly compatible, since energy triggers (which

often function as tools) provide the mechanisms or procedures that make possible resource augmentation.

9. For Freese, social evolution is normally cumulative and irreversible, but he does not specify the direction or forms of this process beyond increasing structural complexity. Social evolution, in his view, is essentially a stochastic process that is influenced by the resources that are available to a society and the step-by-step process of using and augmenting them. Adams goes beyond Freese in this matter, suggesting *four broad directional trends in social evolution:* increasing energy use; a shift from human to nonhuman energy forms; expanded use of information; and power centralization. All of those trends are fully compatible with Freese's more general focus on complexity, however, and give it additional specification.

10. The two perspectives disagree in one critical respect. Freese very explicitly allows no independent source of change originating within sociocultural organization. Its evolution is entirely an outgrowth of changes in socioecological organization, although as those changes become manifest in the relational realm of society, they may take a variety of forms. Adams, in contrast, gives the relational realm a proactive rather than a totally reactive role in social evolution. While the structure and functioning of sociocultural organization in a society are highly influenced by its patterns of socioecological organization, *the relational realm can direct and shape both the flows of energy and the exercise of social power throughout that society.* The principal means through which that occurs is the intentional use of targeted energy triggers by the regulatory sector of society.

DIRECTIONS FOR FURTHER THEORETICAL DEVELOPMENT

In this final section, I propose several directions that might be pursued in the future as we seek to develop a unified socioecological theoretical perspective on the process of social evolution.

Evolutionary Directions

Both Freese and Adams conceive of social evolution as self-generating, cumulative, and normally irreversible, but neither of them says very much about the directions in which this process proceeds through time. Freese discusses only the broad idea of differentiated structures, while Adams speaks about increased organization. Nevertheless, most conceptions of social evolution, especially on the societal level, stress the point that as societies evolve they change in identifiable directions. Two such directions are implicit in the writings by Freese and Adams but require additional specification: structural complexity and functional adaptability.

Structural Complexity

Any theory of social evolution, if it is to be compatible with biological evolution, must take account of increasing structural complexity, which is a factual certainty. Freese's idea of serial differentiation emphasizes the fact that socioecological organization also tends to become increasingly complex as it evolves. Structural complexity usually involves three features: (1) an increase in the number of component parts within a society or other social entity; (2) creation of functional dependencies and interdependencies among the component parts, although all of the potentially possible bonds between the various parts rarely occur; and (3) emergence of a relatively stable structure of functional linkages among the parts that is identifiable and that endures through some period of time. To understand social evolution within socioecological organization, we need to specify principles that explain the development of each of these three features of structural complexity.

Freese's structural model of socioecological organization contains four levels of increasing complexity, with resource dyads [groups] forming unions, which in combination compose associations, which form assemblies that are the principal subunits of total ecological systems (p. 80). This is a static rather than evolutionary model, however, and does not specify any dynamic principles concerning the processes through which socioecological organization develops any of the above three forms of increasing structural complexity. Critical variables within any such explanatory principles for the development of structural complexity might be likely to include: (a) the extent of resource transfers/energy flows that are occurring; (b) factors that influence the extent to which such transfers/flows become differentiated; (c) the kinds of subsequent activities that those transfers/flows generate; and (d) the actions taken by actors to stabilize and perpetuate their functional linkages with other actors.

Functional Adaptability

Adams' treatment of social evolution implies that as societies and other organizational entities develop, they tend to improve their ability to cope with their natural and social environments. This idea of functional adaptability usually contains three features: (1) increasing ability to obtain necessary resources/energy flows from the natural and social environments; (2) improving efficiency in transferring and utilizing resources/energy within social life; and (3) greater effectiveness in controlling resources/energy and applying them to the attainment of desired objectives.

Adams argues that all three aspects of functional adaptability do tend to occur, although certainly none of them is inevitable. He does not, however, propose any theoretical principles concerning the dynamics of any of those processes. He merely adopts Lotka's Principle, which asserts that "in every instance considered natural selection will so operate as to increase the total flux through the system, so long as there is presented an unutilized residue of matter and available energy" (Lotka 1922, p. 148). In other words, there is an observed relationship between the amount of energy used by an entity and its potential for survival. This is an empirical generalization, not a theoretical principle, and it pertains only to survival, not necessarily evolution. Critical variables within any such explanatory principles of the development of functional adaptation might be likely to include: (a) the role of tools/ technology in obtaining and transferring resources/energy; (b) the use of energy triggers to generate further resource transfers/energy flows; (c) factors that affect the usefulness of those transfers/flows to their recipients; and (d) how those transfers/flows alter surrounding environments.

The Process of Devolution

Both Freese and Adams discuss the possibility that social evolution can occur in a negative as well as a positive direction, creating disorganization and possible elimination of any specific instance of socioecological ordering. Freese suggests that this occurs when resources are used at a faster rate than they are replenished, while Adams describes it as increasing entropy resulting from energy dissipation. These ideas should provide useful insights into many instances of devolutionary change within socioecological organization.

They are directly relevant, for example, to William Catton's (1980) analysis of ecological carrying capacity, overshoot, and crash. For each species within an ecological organization [ecosystem], there is an ecological carrying capacity, which is the maximum population size that can be sustained on a permanent basis at a given standard of living. That carrying capacity can be raised in either of two ways: (1) improving the tools or procedures used to obtain necessary resources; or (2) reducing the standard of living of part or all of the population. There is an absolute limit to the carrying capacity of any environment for any species, however, which is set by the total amount of resources that exist in it. When the population of a species exceeds the carrying capacity of its environment, it is in a condition of overshoot.

A condition of overshoot may persist for some period of time, depending on the ability of the population to use coping techniques such as taking resources away from other species, obtaining them from outside that environment, or drawing down finite resource supplies. Eventually, however, a species that is overshooting the carrying capacity of its environment will experience a population crash as a result of starvation, disease, declining fertility, predation by other species, destruction by external invaders, or (in the case of humans) warfare. Normally, this crash is not just a population decline back down to the environment's carrying capacity, but a severe depletion of a large proportion (or sometimes all) of that population.

A second example of social devolution would be the ecological process of environmental destruction, in which a species depletes and despoils its environment to the point that the carrying capacity is reduced to near-zero or zero for that species (or even all species). When this occurs, the offending species is likely to be largely or entirely eliminated within that ecosystem. In many situations, some other species with different resource requirements may enter into, or expand within, that ecosystem, resulting in ecological succession. However, if the environmental destruction has been severe—such as pollution of all fresh water or soil—it may be impossible for any species to survive in that ecosystem. These two examples indicate the kinds of devolutionary processes that should be taken into account by any attempt to explain socioecological evolution.

Power Centralization

Adams' thesis that as humans increase their control over energy flows they expand their capacity to exercise social power is clearly fundamental to a socioecological perspective on social evolution. Since social power is the ability to affect social activities, the greater our ability to exert power, the more elaborate and extensive the social organization we can create. Quite clearly, therefore, socioecological theory must be integrated with sociological theories of power creation, power structures, and power use if we are to understand how resource/energy dynamics are transformed into power dynamics. Since social power exertion is always shaped and directed by the relational realm of sociocultural organization, such theoretical integration will undoubtedly increase our understanding of the ways in which the functional and relational realms of social organization affect one another.

Equally important is Adams' contention that as societies evolve, they tend to develop increasingly centralized power structures. If this tendency is in fact inherent in social evolution, it will have numerous consequences for social stratification and political systems. Adams gives both functional and relational reasons for this trend. In the functional realm, certain "key functionary" roles become critical in maintaining and operating socioecological activities, and as that realm becomes increasingly complex, it requires ever-greater coordination and regulation if it is to operate effectively. Modern societies therefore create a regulatory sector consisting of public (governmental) functionaries who are given the legitimate right to exercise authority in many sectors of the society, as well as private (corporate and other organizational) functionaries who exercise power in the economy and other functional activities. In the relational realm, a small proportion of the population attempts—for many different personal and collective reasons—to maximize its ability to exert power and often also gain wealth. It thus becomes an elite socioeconomic class that may be able to exercise disproportionate amounts of all forms of social power.

Carrying this line of reasoning further, it might be argued that as power becomes centralized in a society, a small "controlling elite class" tends to develop, consisting of extremely powerful persons who act within both the functional and relational realms. Their exercise of power is likely to extend across many different sectors of the society. In addition to this top controlling class, there will also be numerous sets of "subelites" whose activities are directed or guided by the controlling elites, although these less-powerful actors tend to operate only within specialized sectors of the society. The actors located toward the center of this power structure—the controlling elites, the various subelites, the entire regulatory sector, and the upper socioeconomic class—will exercises extensive influence and control in modern societies.

The purposes for which those actors exert power (and the manner in which they do that) are likely to be determined largely by their own interests. However, their actions may be constrained to some extent by other factors such as: (a) cultural ideologies of social responsibility; (b) personal desires to serve and improve society; (c) the necessity of keeping the society operating in a relatively stable and effective manner so as to keep resources flowing to them and to ensure that most people are satisfied with the existing power arrangements; (d) established political participation practices and norms such as public elections; (e) their own ability to exercise power in an effective manner; and (f) organized opposition from other parts of the society.

If these possibilities do occur in societies as they acquire the ability to exercise increasing amounts of social power and as they develop increasingly centralized power structures, we must express these tendencies as principles of social evolution. In particular, those principles should specify the conditions under which the actions of actors at the center of a societal power structure may or may not benefit the larger society and thus facilitate its development [sociogenesis or self-organization]. They must also specify the interacting factors that affect the consequences of power centralization for societal development, such as: (a) how the controlling elites use their power; (b) the limitations on their activities from all of the above sources; (c) scientific and technological discoveries that affect resource transfers and energy flows; (d) existing conditions in the natural environment; and (e) activities of other societies within the world system.

Promotion of Social Cohesion

A fundamental dimension of social evolution is the degree of social cohesion or unity within a society or other organization. As argued by Emile Durkheim (1933), societies tend to expand and/or increase their solidarity as they evolve.

Durkheim's thesis was that "organic solidarity"—which is now usually called "functional cohesion"—tends to become increasingly important in modern societies as they experience increasing division of labor among individuals and organizational units. Functionally specialized actors inevitably become highly interdependent on one another as they loose functional self-sufficiency. They must therefore engage in reciprocal functional transactions that tie them together into a functionally unified entity. This thesis is obviously directly relevant to a socioecological perspective on social evolution. Many questions concerning this process of functional cohesion remain unanswered, however. For example: Under what kinds of conditions are relatively self-sufficient actors willing to become functionally specialized and thus surrender their functional autonomy? How can complex networks of interdependent functional transactions be coordinated and regulated so that the society or other organization becomes unified rather than chaotic? What conditions create the mutual trust among functionally specialized actors that is necessary for a smoothly operating and effective society?

In partial answer to those questions, Durkheim argued that increasing functional cohesion never replaces or eliminates the need for "mechanical solidarity"—which is now usually called "normative cohesion." In this more traditional process, shared values and norms bind a society together as those cultural ideas become institutionalized in organizations and internalized in individuals. Functional cohesion supplements normative cohesion in modern societies, thus adding a second basis for societal solidarity, but never replaces it. Indeed, functional cohesion can occur only to the extent that it rests on a sound foundation of normative cohesion that creates trust and cooperation among the members of a society.

The point here is that the process of functional cohesion could easily be incorporated within a socioecological perspective on social evolution. The process of normative cohesion, meanwhile, describes another way in which the relational realm of sociocultural organization is interwoven with the functional realm of socioecological organization. And the interdependence of these two cohesion processes suggests some important ways in which the overall dynamics of social organizational evolution can be understood as a single integrated process.

CONCLUSION

The idea of directional change pervades the sciences today. The universe is constantly expanding; stars go through "life-cycles"; the earth's biosphere increases in diversity; organisms evolve from simple to complex forms. Similarly, sociology, since its inception in the middle of the nineteenth century by Condorcet and Comte, has been thoroughly infused with conceptions of social evolution. The theoretical ideas proposed by sociologists and other social scientists to explain this process have generally been rather crude, however, and have consistently avoided grounding the process in the dynamics of bioecological evolution. This is not surprising, since biological thinking about evolution has focused almost exclusively on the evolution of specific organisms and has not developed a comprehensive theory of ecological evolution that social scientists could use. Moreover, that organismistic focus in biology has given rise to highly ideological theories of social evolution occurring through natural selection and "survival of the fittest." Consequently, social scientists have given virtually no attention to constructing an ecologically based theory of social evolution.

That theoretical vacuum in the social sciences has finally been addressed in recent writings by Lee Freese and Richard Adams. Although neither of them has thus far taken explicit account of the work of the other, their ideas are highly complementary. This paper has attempted to identify several points of convergence between their writings and some implications for further theoretical development, in an effort to sketch the outlines of an integrated and more comprehensive perspective on social evolution. The essential thesis of this perspective is that *the process of social evolution originates within socioecological organization, not sociocultural organization, as energy flows provide resource transfers that are transformed by people into power exertion.* As a consequence of this process, human social organization has become increasingly functionally adaptive and structurally complex. A corollary thesis, which constitutes the heart of both Freese's and Adams' thinking, is that *the evolutionary process is self-organizing*, based on fundamental principles of energy dissipation and serial differentiation that in the long run tend to be both irreversible and cumulative. Continuing evolution of social organization is never inevitable, however, since the manner in which humans conduct and direct their activities can just as likely result in social devolution as in social evolution.

With this perspective provided by Freese and Adams, two major challenges face social scientists seeking to develop a more complete and detailed understanding of social evolution. First, we must specify how general evolutionary principles apply to various dynamics and forms within human socioecological organization. Second, we must explore the many ways in which developing socioecological organization influences and shapes socioecultural organization in an evolutionary manner.

Beyond those theoretical challenges lies the pragmatic and ethical question of whether human beings can learn to direct the process of social evolution toward ecologically sustainable and socially just forms of social organization.

REFERENCES

Adams, R.N. 1975. *Energy and Structure: A Theory of Social Power.* Austin, TX: University of Texas Press.

————. 1988. *The Eighth Day: Social Evolution as the Self-Organization of Energy.* Austin, TX: University of Texas Press.

Catton, W.R., Jr. 1980. *Overshoot: The Ecological Basis of Revolutionary Change.* Urbana, IL: University of Illinois Press.

Duncan, O.D. 1964. "Social Organization and the Ecosystem." In *Handbook of Modern Sociology,* edited by R.E. L. Faris. Chicago: Rand-McNally.

Duncan, O.D., and L.F. Schnore. 1959. "Cultural, Behavioral, and Ecological Perspectives in the Study of Social Organization." *American Journal of Sociology* 65(September): 132-146.

Durkheim, E. 1933. *The Division of Labor in Society.* Translated by G. Simpson. Glencoe, IL: The Free Press.

Freese, L. 1988. "Evolution and Sociogenesis. Part I: Ecological Origins. Part II: Social Continuities." Pp. 53-118 in *Advances in Group Processes,* Vol. 5, edited by E.J. Lawler and B. Markovsky. Greenwich, CT: JAI Press.

Hawley, A.H. 1950. *Human Ecology: A Theory of Community Structure.* New York: Ronald Press.

————. 1968. "Human Ecology." Pp. 328-337 in *The International Encyclopedia of the Social Sciences,* edited by D.L. Sills. New York: Crowell-Collier and Macmillan.

————. 1986. *Human Ecology: A Theoretical Essay.* Chicago: The University of Chicago Press.

Lotka, A.J. 1922. "Contributions to the Energetics of Evolution." *Proceedings of the National Academy of Sciences* 8: 147-151.

Olsen, M.E. 1993. "Components of Socioecological Organization: Tools, Resources, Energy, and Power." Pp. 35-67 in *Advances in Human Ecology,* Vol. 2, edited by L. Freese. Greenwich, CT: JAI Press.

SOCIOLOGY, HUMAN ECOLOGY, AND ECOLOGY

Curtis E. Beus

ABSTRACT

Sociology has long eschewed the inclusion of environmental or other "nonsocial" variables in sociological analyses. Even the 70-year-old subdiscipline of sociological human ecology has focused almost exclusively on explaining human social organization with only minimal attention given to societal-environmental interactions. This history is reviewed. With the advent of the modern environmental movement, a new sociological subdiscipline, environmental sociology, was created by those sociologists interested in the ecosystemic role played by humans. However, environmental sociology has not yet lived up to its original intent to develop a "core" of knowledge about the interrelationships of social systems and ecosystems—what is refered to as the "new human ecology." The development of a new human ecology for sociologists and other human ecologists is discussed, and the paper concludes by suggesting how the new human ecology might help to develop innovative, interdisciplinary approaches to address the complex and difficult problems now facing humans worldwide.

Advances in Human Ecology, Volume 2, pages 93-132.
Copyright © 1993 by JAI Press Inc.
All rights of reproduction in any form reserved.
ISBN: 1-55938-558-8

I believe that the real problems confronting man in the contemporary world can best be illuminated—insofar as social science can illuminate them—by stating them and attacking them as ecological problems.

—Duncan (1961, p. 140)

INTRODUCTION

Despite what would seem on the surface to be growing interest, concern, and action surrounding many environmental and social issues, human societies in the 1990s face even more "real problems" than they did three decades ago when the eminent sociologist Otis Dudley Duncan issued the above challenge (Odum 1989; Schnaiberg forthcoming). Problems such as ozone depletion, global warming, desertification and deforestation on a massive scale, species extinction, acid precipitation, energy shortages, and the use of nuclear power, were either unheard of or scarcely taken seriously 30 years ago. Furthermore, long-recognized problems such as population growth, hunger, poverty, soil erosion, and air and water pollution have continued to increase in severity over the past 30 years.

Given the seriousness of these problems, have sociologists accepted Duncan's challenge and begun to frame their investigations in ecological terms? For the most part, no. Shortly after the first Earth Day in 1970, G. Edward Stephan observed, "Anyone concerned about the present ecological crisis would be hard pressed to find much literature on the subject contributed by sociologists" (1970, p. 218). The situation in the 1990s remains much the same. Most sociologists continue to exclude ecological insights, concepts, and variables from their analyses, and therefore have little to say about many of the problems listed above, or about how these problems shape societal conditions. This paper outlines why contemporary sociology—including its subdiscipline of sociological human ecology—is largely irrelevant to many of these problems; reviews recent efforts by some sociologists to make sociology more ecological; and discusses possibilities for the future of the ecological approach in sociology.

THE CHICAGO SCHOOL OF HUMAN ECOLOGY

Like European sociology, American sociology—which did not really come into its own until after the turn of the century—for the most part followed Durkheim's admonition that "a social fact can be explained only by another social fact" (1950, p. 145). Although many early American sociologists such as Franklin Giddings, Lester Ward, W.I. Thomas, and Charles Horton Cooley differed from their European counterparts by taking a more individualistic, social-psychological approach to sociology, they were similar to the Europeans in their avoidance of any "subsocial" explanations of sociological phenomena. This changed, however, with Robert E. Park's addition to the sociology faculty at the University of Chicago. His considerable influence, and the preeminence of Chicago's Sociology Department during the period, ultimately placed human ecology in the mainstream of American sociological thought in the 1920s and 1930s.

The Ascendence of Classical Sociological Human Ecology

During the first two decades of this century, American sociology struggled to establish itself as a legitimate field of study. Only a handful of universities had departments of sociology and, moreover, most faculty in these departments were not trained in sociology. As a result, a good deal of confusion existed as to what should be covered by the new discipline. A comprehensive text, *Introduction to the Science of Sociology*, produced by Robert L. Park and Ernest W. Burgess in 1921, proved to be a watershed for American sociology. R.E.L. Faris, in fact, called it "one of the most influential works ever written in sociology" (1970, p. 37). This book served to crystallize sociological thought in the United States, inegrating concepts such as symbiosis, succession, invasion, and competition (often explained by presenting extended excerpts from the writings of plant and animal ecologists such as Frederic E. Clements, Eugenius Warming, and William M. Wheeler) into its treatment of more orthodox sociological subjects such as conflict, social control, and collective behavior. This text served to legitimate human ecology and introduce it into mainstream sociology, and soon after its publication, a host of studies under the general heading of human ecology began to flow out of the Chicago school.

Park, Burgess, and Roderick D. McKenzie, a student of the Chicago school, are generally recognized as the founders of sociological human ecology. In fact, Amos Hawley (1950), the most widely known contemporary sociological human ecologist, attributes the first use of the term human ecology to Robert Park and his colleagues in 1921. Robert McIntosh (1985) disagrees, however, and suggests that the term was familiar to bioecologists by 1914. Regardless of who first coined the term, there can be little doubt that it was the Chicago sociologists who first used human ecology as a conceptual framework upon which to build a considerable intellectual school of thought.

The work of Park, Burgess, McKenzie, and their students is commonly referred to as the classical school of sociological human ecology. One of the central tenets of classical sociological human ecology is the division of human social organization into two levels, the biotic and the cultural. "There is a symbiotic society based on competition and a cultural society based on communication and consensus" (Park 1936a, p. 13). Park conceived the biotic level to be analogous to Darwin's notion of the "web of life" and regarded it as essentially subsocial and, therefore, the appropriate level of study for human ecology. The cultural level, with its emphasis on values, norms, communication, and individual agency, was viewed as outside the purview of human ecology.

At the biotic or community level, society was believed to be organized not by individuals' conscious acts, but by competition in the struggle for existence. Competition was seen as the driving force behind the division of labor and the allocation of space. Park (1936a) described how competition in human communities resulted in "competitive cooperation" which ultimately led to relatively stable "symbiotic relationships" and "communal equilibrium." "Under the pressure of competition, each individual and group were said to carve out both residential and functional niches in which they could best survive and prosper" (Berry and Kasarda 1977, p. 4). As a result, people would segregate into residential areas or occupational groups described as "natural areas," natural because they were seen as the result of inexorable forces beyond the control of individuals. Change, Park explained, is initiated when external "intrusive factors" impinge on the social system. However, when these disruptive factors are introduced, "Competition operates . . . to bring about and restore the communal equilibrium" (Park 1936a, p. 7).

Another central idea of classical sociological human ecology that is closely related to the idea of natural areas is Burgess' theory of the radial extension of concentric zones in cities. From the city center outward, Burgess identified five zones: the central business district, the zone in transition, the zone of workingmen's homes, the residential zone, and the commuters' zone. Burgess suggested that if factors such as natural and artificial barriers or city plans did not interfere with the radial expansion of cities, then all metropolitan areas would "exhibit a perfect exemplification of these five urban zones" (1928, p. 108).

Though the above is obviously an oversimplified summary of the classical school of thought in sociological human ecology, it suffices to illustrate the essence of the Chicago school's approach. The influence of Herbert Spencer and Emile Durkheim is evident in the ideas of the classical sociological human ecologists, though seldom explicitly recognized by them. Also very influential, and readily cited by Park, McKenzie, and the other early sociological human ecologists, are the writings of Darwin, as well as the works of Frederic E. Clements and other early bioecologists. In addition to their use of ecological concepts such as competition, symbiosis, natural areas, and equilibrium described above, the early sociological human ecologists also utilized other ecological concepts such as succession, invasion, dominance, selection, evolution, and climax stage as analogs of social processes (e.g., see, Burgess 1928; McKenzie 1924, 1926; Park 1936a, 1936b, 1939).[1]

The Fall of Classical Sociological Human Ecology

Thus, during the 1920s and 1930s, sociological human ecology rapidly rose to become one of the most dominant perspectives in American sociology, especially in terms of sociological research. Faris suggests that because of the prodigious amount of research in what he terms urban ecology, the Chicago department "unintentionally and perhaps unwillingly acquired the reputation for almost exclusively concentrating on spatial distributions in its own city" (1970, p. 51). Indeed, for a period Chicago sociology was practically synonymous with human ecology, and human ecology with spatial distributions. Some, such as Humphrey and Buttel, have even suggested that "from roughly 1925 to 1945, human ecology was the major focus of the entire discipline of sociology" (1982, p. 8). As Berry and Kasarda relate, however, the rapid rise of sociological human ecology would soon be matched by an equally rapid decline: "The period of eminence of the ecological approach was relatively brief. . . . By 1950, the ecological approach as developed by Park, his colleagues, and students at the University of Chicago was virtually dead" (1977, p. 3).

Why did sociological human ecology experience this flash-in-the-pan type of beginning? A number of circumstances have been suggested which contributed to the undermining of human ecology as the dominant school of thought in American sociology. Until the mid-1930s, Chicago sociology enjoyed near hegemonic control of the entire American sociological scene. With the ownership and editorship of American sociology's official journal, the *American Journal of Sociology*, firmly ensconced in Chicago, a growing resentment within the discipline resulted in the establishment in 1936 of a competitor publication, *The American Sociological Review* (*ASR*), now the discipline's preeminent publication. Faris (1970) relates how the founding of *ASR*, together with the rapid increase in the number and quality of other departments of sociology in the United States, created more parity in the discipline, thereby limiting Chicago's influence and hence contributing to the decline of sociological human ecology as well. Berry and Kasarda (1977, p. 17) suggest that a "strong social-psychological trend" in American sociology (which, ironically, was also fostered at the University of Chicago, by sociologists such as George Herbert Mead and W. I. Thomas), together with the development of psychometric scaling techniques for use in social psychological research, also contributed to sociological human ecology's demise. In addition, Humphrey and Buttel (1982) note that human ecology— a macrosociological, functionalist perspective—was superseded by the functionalist theories of Talcott Parsons and Robert K. Merton, which attempted to incorporate human values, culture, and power within their framework. These were elements excluded from classical sociological human ecology.

Although these trends were undoubtedly related to the fall of classical sociological human ecology from its dominant position, they were not the primary cause. Classical sociological human ecology, as epitomized by the Chicago school, failed for almost precisely the same reasons the earlier organismic approach epitomized by Comte and Spencer had failed: a general vagueness and lack of theoretical grounding, and the uncritical application of biological analogies. Between 1938 and the mid-1940s, sociological human ecology was blitzed with numerous attacks (e.g., see Alihan 1938; Gettys 1940; Firey 1945; Hatt 1946; Hawley 1944; Hollingshead 1946). While all of these critiques had their effect on the field, without a doubt the most hard-hitting and influential critique of classical sociological human ecology was Milla A. Alihan's 1938 book *Social Ecology: A Critical Analysis.*

In what Theodorson (1982, p. 4) calls a "devastatingly [critical analysis of the] theoretical elements of classical human ecology," Alihan methodically demonstrated many inherent weaknesses in the approach of Park, his colleagues, and students.[2] Alihan particularly attacked the classical school's division of social organization into the biotic and cultural levels, contending that such a distinction is impossible to maintain in theory or practice. She criticized the human ecologists for overemphasizing competition as the primary causal force in social organization and for excluding cultural and human volitional factors from their analyses. Alihan found the human ecologists' position on environmental determinism to be contradictory and untenable, noting that they often recognize the existence of "such volitional factors as purpose, but even then usually tell us how hopelessly the iron laws of nature determine it" (1938, p. 248).

Probably the most common theme woven throughout Alihan's analysis is her opposition to what she viewed as the uncritical and sloppy use of biological analogies.

> The application of ecological analogy, the concomitant accretions of alien concepts from several other disciplines, and the modification of these have resulted not only in the deviation from the ecological subject matter, but also in the change of the entire character and scope of the system. . . . The pitfalls would be less hazardous if the borrowed concepts readily responded to the subject matter to which they are applied, but generally the analogy is labored and, if anything, distorts rather than describes or explains (Alihan 1938, p. 249).

Alihan noted that one reason for this distortion is the "fact that the starting point of the [human] ecologists was sociology" (1938, p. 245). Alihan argued that because the sociological human ecologists were trained as sociologists with no training in general ecology, they merely superimposed their understanding of sociological concepts onto the often ill-suited ecological terms they had borrowed.[3] Her criticisms, which were for the most part well-founded, revealed the need for sociological human ecologists to better understand and more accurately reflect the ecological meanings and implications of the terms they imported for use in sociological human ecology. Paradoxically, however, rather than stimulating improvements in human ecological theory and research in sociology, Alihan's criticisms seem to have "contributed mainly to reinforcing the predilection of sociologists to remain aloof from biology" (Catton 1992, p. 70).

What adds to the irony is the fact that this same person who so vigorously chastened the sociological human ecologists of her time also seemed to genuinely admire many elements of their work. As G. Young says, "Alihan's was a reassessment, not a total rejection. There is frequent admiration for human ecology in her book" (1983, p. 95). In the preface of her book Alihan wrote, "The ecological school is one of the most definite and influential schools in American sociology at the present time. It has to its credit not only an important series of factual studies but also a firmly established doctrine" (1938, p. xi). Alihan made it clear that her primary concern was to point out fundamental flaws and "inconsistencies revealed in the theory" (1938, p. 251), but also made it equally clear that she found many of the sociological human ecologists' empirical studies very valuable (1938, pp. 249-251). At the end of the text she expresses her hope that the disarticulation between the school's valuable empirical work and its poorly developed theoretical base might be reconciled for, as she warns, "where consonance between theory and fact is foregone there is no science" (1938, p. 252).

THE NEOORTHODOX AND SOCIOCULTURAL SCHOOLS OF SOCIOLOGICAL HUMAN ECOLOGY

By 1950, sociological human ecology "had been subjected to more than a decade of sharp criticism and was seriously undermined" (Theodorson 1982, p. 5). Despite the fact that many of the critics of this period meant to evaluate and redirect more than to condemn and destroy, sociological human ecology nevertheless lost support, followers, and credibility. Consequently, by 1950 the field had been relegated to marginal status within sociology. It is somewhat ironic that in 1950, the year that many commentators use to demarcate sociological human ecology's fall from grace, two major sociological human ecology texts appeared. James A. Quinn's (1950) *Human Ecology* proved, however, to be little more than a belated attempt to justify many of the elements of classical sociological human ecology, despite his claims to the contrary (Duncan and Schnore 1959; G. Young 1974). Conversely, *Human Ecology: A Theory of Community Structure*, by Amos Hawley (1986), had a lasting impact and provide the nexus around which a school of thought, commonly referred to as neoorthodox sociological human ecology, would develop. As suggested by the name, this approach sought to maintain certain elements of the classical school while revising others in response to the criticisms of the Chicago human ecologists.

At about this same time, the objections of some to the early sociological human ecologists' exclusion of cultural, normative and volitional factors from human ecological theory and practice led to the formation of what came to be called the sociocultural school of sociological human ecology (e.g., see, Firey 1945; Firey and Sjoberg 1982; Wilhelm 1962). According to Firey and Sjoberg, this school has a dual orientation:

> In the first place, there is a concern with the meanings which the members of a particular society have relative to various aspects of their physical environment—meanings which, of course, form a part of that people's culture. . . . In the second place, there is a concern on the part of the sociocultural ecologist with the ways in which environmentally relevant meanings get built into the structures of people's social relationships, especially in the form of norms and institutions (1982, p. 152).

Because of the emphasis they place on symbolic meanings and structures of social relationships, the sociocultural human ecologists have much in common with the social psychological perspective in contemporary sociology. Consequently, the sociocultural human ecologists tend to take a "micro" approach in their studies, focusing on individual decision making, motivations, and attitudes, while neoorthodox scholars focus more on aggregate-level, "macro" phenomena such as large groups, cities, populations, or societies (Bailey and Mulcahy 1972, p. 37). Despite these differences, Theodorson (1982) sees the sharp divisions that developed early on between the sociocultural and neoorthodox schools as having largely abated. This seems to be borne out, at least on the side of the sociocultural human ecologists, by Firey and Sjoberg (1982), who not only no longer see the two approaches as competitive but, indeed, see a synthesis between the two as imperative.

Amos Hawley, however, contends that, "Human ecology is not qualified to deal with the normative order in a social system" (1968, p. 337). While his most recent comments on the subject do not totally dismiss cultural factors from the neoorthodox approach, he objects strongly to the encroachment of "individualism" into sociological human ecology (1984, 1986). Hawley warns, "I think the price of looking upon human events from the perspective of the individual is a failure to recognize system properties" (1984, p. 9). For Hawley, human ecology is a "macrolevel approach to the study of human organization" (1986, p. 6). As such, Hawley views sociological human ecology as more sociological than much of sociology itself,[4] and therefore rejects approaches that would introduce the subjective and volitional elements of individual human behavior. While there has certainly been some convergence between the two schools of thought as Theodorson suggests, it appears that a synthesis of the two perspectives is still far off.[5]

Amos Hawley's Redirection of Sociological Human Ecology

While the sociocultural school has made significant contributions to sociological human ecology, the neoorthodox approach is clearly the more dominant of the two perspectives. This is largely due to the influence of one person. As mentioned earlier, most sociological human ecologists failed to answer the bell after the bevy of blows they sustained from critics during the 1930s and 1940s. One of these critics, Amos Hawley, published in 1944 what would become a landmark critique of sociological human ecology. In contrast to those who abandoned the field of study—both critics and advocates—Hawley's influence and involvement as both critic and advocate of sociological human ecology has continued to this day. Hawley's 1944 critique had three major points:

> [R]esponsibility for the existing chaos in human ecology, it seems to me, rests upon certain aberrant tendencies which have dominated most of the work that has been done. The more significant of these may be described as: (1) the failure to maintain a close working relationship between human ecology and general or bioecology; (2) an undue preoccupation with the concept of competition; and (3) the persistence in definitions of the subject of a misplaced emphasis on "spatial relations" (1944, p. 399).

Somewhat ironically, the person most responsible for propagating the definition of human ecology as "the study of the spatial and temporal relations of human beings" was Hawley's mentor Roderick D. McKenzie (1924, p. 288).[6] This definition, said Hawley, "permitted human ecology to be construed as merely the description of distributions of social phenomena" (1944, p. 402). The focus on spatial relations had become so pervasive, continued Hawley, that "one of the techniques employed in ecological research—mapping—has been mistaken for the discipline itself" (p. 402). Finally, Hawley summarily dismissed the centrality of spatial relations to human ecological inquiry by contending that "Spatial and temporal considerations are incidental to the investigation of ecological problems" (p. 402).

After a critical exegesis on the nature of competition and its role in human ecology, Hawley said that he did not mean to "imply that competition has no place in ecological thought," but rather that his criticism was "directed solely at the loose and extravagant use of the concept which enabled it to become accepted as the basic theoretical element in human ecology" (1944, p. 401).

Finally, with respect to his third criticism regarding sociological human ecology's relationship to bioecology, Hawley offered this admonition:

> Unless human ecology has a problem of its own, then it is nothing and may as well be forgotten. But just as urgent is the necessity that a discipline be coherent within itself and consistent with the point of view it pretends to present. There is no basis, in other words, for calling a study human ecology, if it is not ecological (1944, p. 402).

The "problem of its own" that Hawley suggested should be the focus of sociological human ecology was "the community, the form and development of which are studied with particular reference to the limiting and supporting factors of the environment" (1944, p. 403).

What has happened since Hawley attempted to redirect sociological human ecology more toward mainstream ecology nearly 50 years ago? Has the field "repented" of its "sins" of aloofness from bioecology, undue preoccupation with the principle of competition, and overemphasis on spatial relations? Indeed, has Hawley followed his own advice? Looking at his first criticism, we need to ask if sociological human ecology has "developed a closer working relationship with general or bioecology?" Hawley himself recently answered this question:

> [H]uman ecology with its sociological coloration has drifted apart from many of the current uses of the term ecology. That is contrary to what was expected in earlier days. It was then thought that human ecology was an extension to bio-ecology and that there might be a fruitful exchange of ideas (Hawley 1944). That has not occurred in any marked degree for reasons that are obscure (Hawley 1984, p. 3).

Despite Hawley's early stance indicating an urgent need for human ecologists to increase "awareness that they are logically committed to follow out in the study of man the implications of ecology" (1944, p. 399), in recent years he has changed his position considerably. He now suggests that "the mutualism between bioecology and human ecology, present from the beginning, has abated somewhat in recent years" (1986, p. 3).

Although Hawley certainly does not call for a complete divorce of human ecology from bioecology, he contends that "human ecology must draw out the implications of its assumptions and test the inferences with data from human collective life without expecting, to say nothing of demanding, close parallels with the models and conclusions of bioecology" (1986, p. 126). Hawley views this drawing away from bioecology as necessary because he says that the intrinsic limitations on human behavior are indeterminate, or, in other words, that human beings possess a nearly infinite ability to adapt to any situation. According to Hawley, this characteristic makes humankind's relationship to its environment fundamentally different from other species' environmental relationships, thus rendering comparisons and parallels between human ecology and bioecology dubious at best.

In Hawley's recent efforts to establish a more theoretical base for human ecology, he has not only established more distance between human ecology and bioecology but has also attempted to move human ecology more into mainstream sociology. In fact, in a 1984 commentary on the state of sociological human ecology Hawley says, "I think there has been a great deal of convergence between human ecology and the parent discipline. Whether that is to be regarded as fortunate or not depends on how one views the objectives of social science" (1984, p. 3). It is interesting that in 1944 Hawley appeared to view bioecology as the parent discipline of human ecology, whereas today he sees human ecology as squarely within the realm of sociology. The evolution in Hawley's thinking about how sociological human ecology should relate to bioecology is evident throughout his writings, from his 1944 critical essay, to his 1950 landmark text, to his 1968 article in the *International Encyclopedia of the Social Sciences*, to his 1986 theoretical treatise on contemporary sociological human ecology. With each subsequent publication Hawley has tended to establish more distance between bioecology and sociological human ecology.

What has Hawley done with regard to the role of competition in contemporary sociological human ecology? In the development of his theoretical propositions on community structure, Hawley rejects sociological human ecology's earlier notions of "natural" laws and outcomes, stating that "inevitability is as foreign to human ecology as human ecology is to Greek drama," and then continuing, "It becomes desirable, therefore, to exorcise the notion of competition as a generalized causal principle for complex phenomena, for that has been the conceptual peg on which the 'natural' and 'automatic' cloaks have been hung" (1986, p. 127). Hawley argues that as an explanation for social outcomes and events, competition is an obscure and insufficient concept as it fails to recognize and account for other types of relationships such as symbiotic and commensalistic interactions.

With respect to the status of spatial relations in human ecology, Hawley has also remained true to his critical stance of 1944, eschewing the classical school's static treatment of space, distance, zones, and gradients. Hawley conceives of space primarily in terms of space-time relationships, focusing on how they constrain and facilitate interdependence and other interactions within populations (1986, pp. 39-40).

The work of Amos Hawley in sociological human ecology does indeed reflect many elements of the redirection he advocated nearly 50 years ago. He has attempted to purge the field of the uncritical and "extravagant" use of competition as a causal force, and he has attempted to redefine sociological human ecology away from the narrow conception of spatial patterns by focusing on dynamic concepts such as human interdependence and social change. (Although Hawley has largely rejected major roles for spatial patterns and competition within sociological human ecology, other contemporary sociological human ecologists continue to center their work on these concepts, a subject to which we will return.) The one area of his early critique of sociological human ecology from which Hawley has retreated is the idea that human ecology and bioecology should develop a closer working relationship. Despite his biting remarks in 1944 about the unecological nature of sociological human ecology, in subsequent publications Hawley has considerably changed his position on the relationship between sociological human ecology and bioecology. He has made all of these changes in an attempt to legitimate sociological human ecology as a "macrolevel approach to the study of human organization" (1986, p. 6), and thus bring it closer to the sociological mainstream.

Human Ecology as Macrosociology

Hawley was not the first sociological human ecologist to suggest that human ecology was macrosociology. Twenty-five years before Hawley made this statement, another influential sociologist of the neoorthodox school of sociological human ecology, Leo F. Schnore (1961), suggested that "*'human ecology' might be best regarded as a type of 'macro-sociology'*" (p. 139, emphasis in original). Schnore further stated that "the central role given to organization—as dependent or independent variable—places ecology clearly within the sphere of activities in which sociologists claim distinctive competence, i.e., the analysis of social organization. If human ecology is 'marginal' to sociology, what is central" (p. 139)?

Hawley's and Schnore's equation of human ecology with a macrolevel approach to the study of human social organization begs the question: What, if any, difference is there between sociological human ecology and sociology generally? Before Schnore's declaration that human ecology was nothing more than macrosociology, Duncan and Schnore asserted that "the study of society as a system or pattern of organization constitutes the core problem [for sociology]. . . . As a result, a rather amorphous area, usually called 'social organization,' seems to provide sociology's central concern" (1959, p. 132). In a response to Duncan and Schnore's paper, Peter Rossi likewise acknowledged, "The proper study of sociology is social organization. On this perspective there is probably the greatest degree of agreement in our discipline" (1959, p. 146). Given the generally widespread agreement that sociology is essentially the study of social organization, and given Hawley's and Schnore's assertions that human ecology is primarily concerned with the same, we must ask: Why does sociology need human ecology at all? If sociological human ecology is simply another name, using different terms, for what sociologists already do, of what value is it?

Despite his earlier collaboration with Schnore in 1959, Duncan voiced this very concern in response to Schnore's comments:

> The description of human ecology as a "type of macrosociology" may be reassuring to students attracted to ecological problems but anxious to preserve their membership in good standing in the sociological fraternity. Such a description could, however—though I am sure this is not the effect Schnore was after—foster a new "myth," that human ecology is just another name for what sociologists are already doing, and are perfectly capable of doing, without benefit of ecological ideas (1961, p. 140).

Duncan was warning his fellow sociological human ecologists of what would likely befall the field should it allow itself to become indistinguishable from sociology in general.

Duncan's essay appears to be an attempt to erase any doubts as to the importance he placed on keeping sociological human ecology closely allied with bioecology, and in so doing bringing sociology to bear on real-world ecological problems. Duncan definitely did not share Hawley's and Schnore's view that human ecology—defined as the study of social organization—should move to the center of the sociological scene. Although he appears to advocate a more central role for human ecology within sociology, his view seems to be that sociology must move toward human ecology, with the emphasis on ecology. He even goes so far as to say that the resolution of ecological problems should be central to sociology, maintaining that if this is not the case, then sociology is "'peripheral' to what is going on in the world and is not worthy of cultivation by responsible scholars" (1961, p. 140).

Duncan's reading of the situation at the time appears to have been that there was little chance that sociology would shift en masse toward a more ecological version of sociological human ecology, but he recognized a real danger that sociological human ecology might blend into the sociological mainstream and thereby facilitate its own demise. For as both Duncan (1961) and Hawley (1944) pointed out, sociological human ecology must have something unique to offer; if not, then, as Hawley said, "it is nothing and may as well be forgotten" (1944, p. 402).

Duncan's POET Model

Duncan not only voiced concerns about Hawley's and others' redirection of sociological human ecology away from bioecology, but he also began to develop an approach that he hoped would help reconnect the field with mainstream ecology. Duncan's model involved four variables: population, organization, environment, and technology (P, O, E, T), the interactions of which he termed the "ecological complex" (1959). Critics of the POET model often refer to the fact that it is too abstract and simple to be used in any concrete analyses. Duncan himself recognized this, and hoped readers of his work would "credit the author with being aware of the many complications concealed by the use of arrows linking the broad and heterogeneous categories of the ecological complex" (1961, p. 148). Not wishing to make any grandiose claims as to what could be accomplished using the POET approach, Duncan explained that the model was merely a "somewhat arbitrarily simplified way of identifying clusters of relationships in a preliminary description of ecosystem processes" (1961, p. 145). Duncan's goal was to get sociological human ecologists to shift their level of thinking "from the social system to the ecosystem," and he hoped that his simple abstraction would help them to begin to see the ecological processes of which the human community is a part.

Duncan realized that his model was not a theory as such but, rather, a framework for describing the interrelationships of human ecological processes. Although it definitely had some serious shortcomings (most of which Duncan readily admitted), such as its relegation of the "environment" into a "residual category including *all* aspects of the ecosystem other than human populations, their social organizations, and their technology" (Dunlap and Catton 1979b, p. 63, emphasis in original), the approach was a significant contribution to sociological human ecology. Duncan's analysis of the Los Angeles smog problem using the POET model illustrated how Duncan believed sociological human ecology could be brought to bear on a real-world human ecological problem (1961). Few sociological human ecologists followed Duncan's lead, however, with most choosing instead to continue to ignore the human role in ecosystems and the ecological constraints on human societal phenomena, thereby further widening the gap between bioecology and sociological human ecology. Shortly after his pioneering work, Duncan himself chose to turn his professional attention to other sociological endeavors, undoubtedly frustrated by sociological human ecologists' refusal to broaden the scope of their work to encompass an ecosystemic view of human social life.

Organization for Sustenance

In 1926, Roderick D. McKenzie characterized the task of sociological human ecology as the study of "spatial and sustenance relations in which human beings are organized" (1926, p. 141). McKenzie himself never fully developed his idea of sustenance relations, and most others from that time until the present have ignored McKenzie's concept of sustenance in favor of the more readily observable concept of spatial relations with which McKenzie is most often associated.

In the late 1950s, Jack P. Gibbs and Walter T. Martin returned to McKenzie's notion of sustenance organization and suggested that this concept be utilized as a basic theoretical system for human ecology (1959). Like Duncan and his POET approach, Gibbs and Martin recognized that their concept of sustenance organization was not a complete and all-inclusive theory. Rather, they were attempting to delimit the field in an effort to make it more manageable. While warning that the connection between biology and human ecology should not be carried too far, Gibbs and Martin believed that there was nevertheless a vital link between the two insofar as "sustenance organization must meet certain indispensable biological needs" (1959, p. 34).

Gibbs and Martin insisted that spatial relations are of interest to human ecologists only as they influence organization for sustenance (1958), and they also condemned the uncritical use of biological analogies, noting that, "From

Park to Hawley borrowed concepts have dominated theory without contributing to its advancement" (1959, p. 34). Their goal was to provide a base upon which could be built a theory of how human populations organize themselves for the exploitation of natural resources in their efforts to survive and progress. As such, Gibbs and Martin conceived of human ecology—the study of sustenance organization—as closely allied with, but not coterminous with, economics. Like other neoorthodox sociological human ecologists, they excluded "values, motives, attitudes, [and] sentiments . . . from the universe of inquiry" (1959, p. 33).

Like others of both the classical and neoorthodox schools, Gibbs and Martin have been criticized for excluding cultural and ideational factors from their scheme, and their sustenance organization approach was also criticized for being too economistic and narrow. While Gibbs and Martin were correct in condemning the overemphasis on spatial distributions in sociological human ecology, they merely traded one extreme for another.[7] Although the idea of sustenance organization is represented to varying degrees in the work of some contemporary sociological human ecologists, such as Hawley (1986) and Bidwell and Kasarda (1985, 1987), Gibbs and Martins' attempt to redefine sociological human ecology as the study of sustenance organization has had only a moderate impact on the field.

SOCIOLOGICAL HUMAN ECOLOGY'S CURRENT PREDICAMENT

Human ecology has long held a tenuous position in relation to sociology. Buttel attributes this position to the "inherent duality in human existence—humans as strands in the web of life in the larger biosphere on the one hand, and humans as creators of unique and distinctly social 'environments' on the other hand" (1986, p. 338). Thirty-nine years earlier, A. B. Hollingshead indicated that this same quandary also perplexed human ecologists of the classical school: "The [human] ecologist's problem appears to be posed by the unique position man occupies in the realm of things: to wit, his place in nature as an animal and his role in societies as a possessor of culture" (1947, p. 194). For human ecologists outside sociology, this problem is indeed a little sticky (e.g., see Sargent 1974); however, for sociologists it is particularly troublesome and has undoubtedly been the source of considerable cognitive dissonance. On the one hand, most sociological human ecologists feel compelled to be "good" sociologists and explain social facts via other social facts, but on the other hand, many agree with Hawley's 1944 assertion that they have no business calling their work ecology if it is not ecological.

There are three possible resolutions to this problem with which sociological human ecology has wrestled for 70 years, only one of which is a resolution of the duality itself. The other two are merely ways to cope with the uncomfortable dilemma faced by sociological human ecologists. One possible resolution would be for sociological human ecologists to focus on humankind's biological role in ecosystems, while deemphasizing the unique aspects of human culture and society. Obviously, this avenue has not been attractive to sociologists and has not been pursued for very good reasons. A second possible resolution to the problem would be to eliminate the duality by finding some way to integrate the biological with the social aspects of human existence in a logical and compatible manner. This is obviously a tall order, especially for a limited number of scholars within a single social science. Needless to say, sociological human ecologists have not succeeded in this endeavor and, indeed, few have even attempted it (although Duncan's POET model and, to a lesser extent, Gibbs and Martins' sustenance organization approach were attempts in this direction). The third possible resolution would be to downplay or even ignore the biological nature of humans, while focusing almost exclusively on their unique cultural and social aspects. Given sociology's historical legacy of eschewing nonsocial explanations, the tendency of sociological human ecologists to view human ecology as a subdiscipline within sociology (rather than as a multidisciplinary field) and the inherent difficulty of reconciling the problem of human duality, clearly this is the path most contemporary sociological human ecologists have chosen.

Paul M. Siegel in a paper whose primary purpose is to salvage some of the ecology rejected by Amos Hawley, suggests two possible domains of study for sociological human ecology:

> On the one hand, human ecology might take as its domain the ecosystem . . . taking the point of view that man is an integrated, natural component of ecosystems and focusing on ecosystem processes, which surely include but are not coextensive with societal processes. . . . On the other hand, human ecologists claim the study of *social* organization as their domain. On this view ecosystems or biological communities may offer models of organization which can prove fruitful when employed in the study of social organization (1984, pp. 22-23, emphasis in original).

These two domains are similar to the second and third resolutions presented above. The second domain presented by Siegel, the study of social organization, is essentially the one claimed by most sociological human ecologists today. Siegel notes that this option "requires much less modification of the traditional concerns" of sociological human ecologists, as the only requirement to be met when utilizing ecological concepts is "their utility in the study of social organization." As a result, says Siegel, "One need not be concerned that ecosystem models *must* apply to social organization *because* it is ecological" (1984, p. 23, emphasis in original). In other words, sociological human ecologists have merely defined social organization as "ecological," and have therefore proceeded to use ecological terms and concepts in describing and explaining organizational phenomena with little or no concern for how their work relates to ecology in general.

Organizational Ecology

This equation of human ecology with the study of social organization has recently taken a new turn as sociologists have now developed a branch of sociological human ecology, referred to as organizational ecology, which is presently attracting considerable attention (Carroll 1984, 1988). The "population ecology of organizations" developed by Michael T. Hannan and John Freeman was the first effort in this new organizational ecology approach, and has spawned several other studies along the same lines (e.g., see, Carroll 1985, 1987; Freeman and Hannan 1983; Hannan and Freeman 1977, 1988, 1989; Lincoln 1979). Utilizing population ecology theories based on competition and selection, this approach attempts to explain increases and decreases in "populations" of organizations and "niche" diversification as related to the proliferation of organizational types or "species."

In an unflinching critique reminiscent of Alihan's assault on the classical sociological human ecologists 45 years ago, Ruth C. Young (1988) recently challenged the validity of applying ecological models to the study of populations of organizations. Among her chief criticisms of the approach, she claims that its definitions of terms are vague, difficult to follow, and even nonexistent in several instances. Consequently, she says the Hannan and Freeman articles are "difficult to read, whereas the biological ecology literature from which their model is derived is not" (p. 21). In addition, Young says, "Different concepts seem to have similar definitions and are not distinguishable from each other" (p. 21). All of this, says Young, "confounds attempts to understand the meaning of propositions and leads to grave problems of measurement" (p. 21). Finally, Young contends that the model's heavy emphasis on competition is unfounded. As a result of these and other problems, she says, "One must conclude that the concepts of biological ecology do not lend themselves readily to organizations" (p. 21). In short, Young sees in the Hannan and Freeman approach similar fundamental problems that beset sociological human ecologists of the classical school, such as the careless use of analogies and undue emphasis on the concept of competition. Despite Young's harsh comments, this approach to organizational ecology remains one of the most influential schools of thought in contemporary sociological human ecology.

Another influential contribution to the new organizational ecology approach in sociological human ecology is the work of Charles E. Bidwell and John D. Kasarda (1985, 1987). Their "ecosystem" theory of social organization equates formal organizations with ecological communities. The organization (community), which consists of various "populations," together with the organization's resources and other "environmental" factors, make up the organization's "ecosystem." Bidwell and Kasarda utilize numerous ecological concepts, such as niche, carrying capacity, symbiosis, and commensalism, in their organizational theory and apply their theoretical framework to a study of school districts in Michigan. In their two-volume human ecology treatise, all of the ecological concepts they use refer strictly to *social* phenomena and are used only as heuristic devices to describe and analyze *social* organization. In other words, Bidwell and Kasarda explain social facts with other social facts, but do so with an "ecological" model.

While not relying on the monistic causal principle of competition as does the Hannan and Freeman model, Bidwell and Kasarda's ecosystem model of organizations appears to suffer from many of the same problems as does the population ecology approach. Specifically, its vague definitions of terms, and in some instances its lack of definitions, results in many of the same inconsistencies and vagueness Young pointed out in the work of Hannan and Freeman.

For example, Bidwell and Kasarda (1985) define populations simply as subsets of an organization's membership that conduct common types of work activities, or "activity patterns." In their model, activity patterns are used analogously to species in biological communities (p. 36). On the next page, however, the authors state that "the activity pattern construct is analogous to the sociologist's or social anthropologist's social position construct" (1985, p. 37). They state emphatically, however, that the activity pattern construct does not reflect social roles, as they "make no assumption about the moral basis of the rules of activity patterns" (1985, p. 37).

Although there is a distinction in the social sciences between social positions and social roles, the two concepts are nevertheless closely related. The generally accepted relationship between the two is that, "A *social role* is the expected behaviour associated with a *social position*. A position is simply the label or the means of identifying a particular social role" (Mitchell 1979, p. 159, emphasis in original). If Bidwell and Kasarda conceive of social position as devoid of any role expectations, this would seem to reduce occupants of social positions to mere automatons that somehow perform activities of which they are unaware. Moreover, since the two concepts are so intricately interrelated, Mitchell suggests that social position and role "are only analytically separable" (1979, p. 159) Therefore, in practice it becomes nearly impossible to conceive of a social role such as a doctor (or a barber, as in the example used by Bidwell and Kasarda) without defining a doctor in terms of what a doctor does, just as it is practically impossible to conceive of a species without referring to the role it plays in an ecosystem (unless one is willing to limit the species concept to some static notion of morphology).[8]

Another logical problem with Bidwell and Kasarda's analogy between biological species and organizatonal populations is the fact that persons in organizations can and do perform different sets of activities and thus can belong to two or more "species" simultaneously. While Bidwell and Kasarda acknowledge this discrepancy between their use of the concept and the biological use, they skim over the difference as if it were unimportant.

Other inconsistencies and contradictions could be pointed out in Bidwell and Kasarda's use of the ecosystem concept as applied to social organizations, but the purpose here is not to conduct an extensive critique. Rather, I wish to echo Duncan's criticism of Kenneth Boulding's analogical use of the term "ecosystem" by stating that "ecosystem is much too valuable a conceptual scheme to be sacrificed on the altar of metaphor" for, as Duncan also pointed out, "Human ecology has already inspired a generation of critics too easily irritated by figures of speech" (1961, p. 143).

Although there are other approaches within organizational ecology (for a discussion of them, see Carroll 1984, 1988), these two perspectives are currently the most prevalent in sociological human ecology. The population ecology of organizations espoused by Hannan and Freeman and the organizational ecosystem approach of Bidwell and Kasarda, as well as the other models of organizational ecology, are examples of sociological human ecology that are ecology in name only. While the models may or may not provide insights into the structure and dynamics of social organizations (this is not the point here), these types of models use ecological concepts only metaphorically, and often poorly. In addition, none of these approaches offers any possibility for its adherents to address ecological problems which, as Duncan suggested 30 years ago, should be the focus of human ecology.

Ecological Demography

Recently, Krishnan Namboodiri (1988) suggested that "ecological demography (a partnership between demography and human ecology) promises the most systematic and comprehensive treatment of the core of sociology—the study of societies and social systems" (p. 619). Namboodiri advocates combining demography—"the scientific study of population structure and dynamics and their determinants and consequences" (p. 620)— with sociological human ecology in an effort to better analyze a host of sociological phenomena (e.g., see p. 631). Namboodiri views the primary purpose of sociology as "the systematic study of interdependence within and among social organizations" and, as such, he contends that *human ecology is not peripheral to sociology. It is sociology proper* (p. 622, emphasis in original). Namboodiri, like Schnore and Hawley before him, sees sociological human ecology as coterminous with the study of social organization and, therefore, central to sociology. He also believes that a partnership between sociological human ecology and demography is "inevitable," and suggests that if theoretical paradigms are compared for their ability to handle the "core" of sociology, "the ecology-demography twosome will be hard to beat in the contest" (p. 631).

While it is still too early to know whether Namboodiri's call for a merger between sociological human ecology and demography will occur, its still possible to evaluate his basic argument. It is not at all clear in Namboodiri's article just how this marriage between the two perspectives would take place. It is also not clear just how he conceptualizes sociological human ecology. He seems to lump the work of Hawley, Hannan and Freeman, Carroll, Duncan, and other sociological human ecologists into a generic sum, despite the fact that their approaches vary considerably.

Pulling these different perspectives in sociological human ecology together into one coherent theoretical perspective would be difficult enough (if, indeed, even possible), yet Namboodiri proposes not only to do this but also to blend them with demography into a theoretical perspective that "will before long be widely recognized as the core of sociology" (1988, p. 631). This, of course, is bold talk, and may even happen (though it is highly unlikely). But even if it were to happen, there is little evidence that this new human ecology-demography synthesis would take an ecosystemic or even a truly ecological approach to the study of human society, despite the fact that Namboodiri mentions briefly the role of biophysical factors in human ecology. His approach, like most other "ecological" approaches in sociology, seems to emphasize almost exclusively the study of social phenomena while excluding or deemphasizing *nonsocial* factors.

Unecological Sociological Human Ecology

Although the work of Park, Burgess, McKenzie, and other early sociological human ecologists was also primarily aimed at shedding light on human social organization, it nevertheless reflected more direct ties with and influence from bioecology than does contemporary sociological human ecology (Catton 1992). The two examples from the organizational ecology and the ecological demography perspectives discussed above provide evidence of the nearly complete detachment from bioecology of prominent schools of thought in contemporary sociological human ecology. Catton (1984) provided another example of this detachment when he compared two contemporary texts, a bioecology text by Eugene Odum (1975) and a sociological human ecology text by Berry and Kasarda (1977), and found a disparity of 57 to 14 in the number of ecological terms used in the two texts.[9] Contemporary sociological human ecology suffers not only from the misuse of many of the ecological concepts it does apply but also from a general disregard for many of the advances and current concepts in contemporary bioecology.

In addition to the chronic problems of overemphasis on competition in social systems and uncritical use of analogy, the aspect of classical sociological human ecology that has probably received the harshest criticism—the spatial distribution of social phenomena—also continues to be represented in the work of many contemporary sociological human ecologists. This tendency has existed throughout the neoorthodox school's attempt to revamp sociological human ecology and is reflected in Shepard's remark in 1967 that, "'Human Ecology' has become that branch of sociology dealing with urban geography" (1967, p. 891). More recently, Humphrey and Buttel said of contemporary sociological human ecology:

> Moreover, there has been a more recent trend among human ecologists to study the static and dynamic aspects of population distribution in cities without any regard to the underlying biophysical processes that affect these trends, including specific environmental constraints and opportunities that influence and are influenced by human populations. A growing amount of this literature involves technical descriptions of changing segregation patterns and other spatial aspects of population distribution. This does little, if anything, to advance our knowledge of human ecology, the environment, or metropolitan or community growth (1982, p. 47).

Much of human ecology as practiced in sociology today fits anthropologist John W. Bennett's characterization as "focusing on the geographical distribution of social components in space" (1976, p. 71). This assessment, though simplified, is not entirely unwarranted. Relatively recent research, such as that of Sly and Tayman (1980, p. 119), still utilizes Chicago school concepts such as "cores" and "rings" in an effort to reexamine the "theory of ecological expansion" in metropolitan areas. Avery Guest likewise suggests that Burgess' concentric zone approach "has a high degree of usefulness" in sociological studies of the city (1984, p. 305). For many sociologists, the terms ecological and spatial remain synonymous even today.

The aim in presenting a sketch of the development of sociological human ecology has not been to provide a complete analysis or history, but rather to illustrate how the field has consistently floundered despite a few efforts to provide it with some direction. Hawley, in his 1944 critique, stated that "after twenty years [human ecology] remains a somewhat crude and ambiguous conception. A perusal of the literature that has accumulated under the name can hardly fail to produce bewilderment" (p. 398). If the ambiguity that existed then could cause bewilderment, then the state of affairs surrounding contemporary sociological human ecology might well produce complete stupefaction in anyone foolish enough to try to make sense of it all. Not only do many of the concepts and methods of the original Chicago school still persist in varying degrees, but, as could be expected, many new ideas and positions have been added.

In addition to the changes that have taken place in sociological human ecology, many other disciplines have entered the fray with their own particular emphases and paradigms. Human ecological perspectives are now present in sociology, bioecology, anthropology, geography, economics, psychology, home economics, demography, political science, epidemiology, and philosophy, as well as in other fields and by some who reject disciplinary boundaries altogether. The result of this current state of affairs is that contemporary human ecology may well be an even "cruder and more ambiguous conception" than it was in 1944.

The diversity and complexity that pervades present-day human ecology leads one to ponder how sociological human ecology should relate to the current morass. As I have attempted to demonstrate, the response of sociological human ecologists has been to essentially cloister "their" field by distancing themselves from bioecology and human ecologists of other fields. This has been done primarily by redefining human ecology as a macrosociological approach to the study of social organization, thereby moving it more into mainstream sociology.

THE EMERGENCE OF ENVIRONMENTAL SOCIOLOGY

Sociology, and even sociological human ecology, has generally deserved the criticism it has received, both from within and without, for not including human-environment interrelationships in the study of social behavior and social organization. Stephan (1970) believes that the reason for sociology's lack of attention to ecological factors is that sociologists have seldom considered them as important to begin with. "Problems involving the acquisition of food, the elimination of waste products, the survival of a species—*de rigueur* for the general, or biological, ecologists—have been regarded as 'sub-social' by [sociological] human ecologists" (p. 218). This tendency is painfully obvious in this statement by Janson: "If *human ecology* is the study of man's interaction with his external environment, then let us define *social ecology* as the part of human ecology that deals with social and societal aspects of that environment and thus falls within the realm of sociology" (1980, p. 433, emphasis in original). While Janson's recognition that human ecology involves human-environment interactions is laudable, his witting acceptance into the "realm of sociology" of only that "part" (as if an easy separation can be made) of human ecology which deals with the "social" environment is typical of sociology's historical tendency to ipso facto relegate all else to subsocial status and, therefore, not appropriate for consideration by sociologists. Justly or not, sociology has hung its hat on Durkheim's dictum and has vigorously opposed any "nonsocial" explanations making their way into the discipline.

Exemptionalism versus Ecologism in Sociology

William R. Catton, Jr. and Riley E. Dunlap (1978a, 1980; Catton 1983) suggest that it is not merely the influence of Durkheim that has created the near xenophobia of sociologists toward "nonsocial" facts. They contend that sociology developed during an age of exuberant growth and faith in social progress and that the discipline has consequently been imbued with a worldview or paradigm that impedes recognition of the importance of ecological factors. Catton and Dunlap (1980) therefore argue that "sociology stands in need of a fundamental alteration of its disciplinary paradigm" (p. 15). They identify a Human Exemptionalism Paradigm (HEP) which they say has guided sociology since its inception, and suggest a New Ecological Paradigm (NEP) which, they say, "may better serve the field in a post-exuberant age" (p. 15).

These sociological paradigms are the counterparts of corresponding broader sociocultural paradigms present in society at large (Dunlap and van Liere 1978, 1984), and are not meant to be thought of as scientific research paradigms in the sense used by Thomas Kuhn (1962). Rather, they operate as sets of background assumptions over which theories are constructed. "It must be emphasized," state Catton and Dunlap, "that these assumptions are virtually never made explicit; yet, they clearly influence the practice of sociology" (1980, p. 24). Catton and Dunlap (1978a, 1978b, 1980) even go so far as to suggest that the HEP-NEP distinction is more central to sociological understanding than are the various competing theoretical perspectives in sociology. This, they say, is because these "ostensibly diverse and competing theoretical perspectives in sociology are alike in their shared anthropocentrism" (1978a, p. 41).

While not dismissing the importance of the HEP-NEP distinction, Buttel (1978) nevertheless argues that it ought not take precedence over traditional theoretical perspectives in sociology. This critique of Catton and Dunlap's work has led to spirited debate, and has helped to sharpen the focus of the HEP-NEP distinction in sociology as well as to find some common ground in the paradigm-theory controversy (Buttel and Humphrey forthcoming; Freudenburg 1989; Catton and Dunlap 1980). The basic underlying assumptions of both the HEP and NEP are presented in Table 1.

The work of Catton and Dunlap, together with the efforts of Alan Schnaiberg (1980) and others, resulted in the emergence during the mid-1970s of environmental sociology, a new subdiscipline within sociology (Buttel 1986, 1987; Dunlap and Catton 1979a; Freudenburg 1989). Dunlap and Catton explain, "Environmental sociology involves recognition of the fact that physical environments can influence (and in turn be influenced by) human societies and behavior.... Indeed, its acceptance of 'environmental' variables as meaningful for sociological investigation is what sets environmental sociology apart as a distinguishable field of inquiry" (1979a, p. 244).

Table 1. Major Background Assumptions of the Human Exemptionalism Paradigm (HEP) and the New Ecological Paradigm (NEP)

	Human Exemptionalism Paradigm (HEP)	*New Ecological Paradigm (NEP)*
A. Assumptions about the nature of human beings:	Humans have a cultural heritage in addition to (and distinct from) their genetic inheritance, and thus are quite unlike all other animal species.	While humans have exceptional characteristics (culture, technology, and so forth), they remain one among many species that are interdependently involved in the global ecosystem.
B. Assumptions about social causation:	Social and cultural factors (including technology) are the major determinants of human affairs.	Human affairs are influenced not only by social and cultural factors, but also by intricate linkages of cause, effect, and feedback in the web of nature; thus, purposive human actions have many unintended consequences.
C. Assumptions about the context of human society:	Social and cultural environments are the crucial context for human affairs, and the biophysical environment is largely irrelevant.	Humans live in and are dependent upon a finite biophysical environment which imposes potent physical and biological restraints on human affairs.
D. Assumptions about constraints on human society:	Culture is cumulative; thus, technological and social progress can continue indefinitely, making all social problems ultimately soluble.	Although the inventiveness of humans and the powers derived therefrom may seem for a while to extend carrying-capacity limits, ecological laws cannot be repealed.

Source: Adapted from Catton and Dunlap (1980, p. 34).

The creation of the field of environmental sociology suggests the following question: Why was environmental sociology necessary to begin with, given the fact that sociological human ecology has existed for 70 years? The answer, as might be surmised, is that sociological human ecology had become so distorted that it could not (or would not) deal with the societal-environmental issues raised with the advent of the environmental movement. The irony need hardly be stated. Human ecology, the study of humanity's interaction with its environment, missed the proverbial boat. It became necessary to create a new sociological subdiscipline to deal with society's urgent ecological problems.

While most sociologists are scarcely aware of their adherence to the HEP, some sociological human ecologists have actually operationalized the notion of human exemptionalism. Hawley, for example, states that one of the characteristics of humans in his theory of human ecology is that "the intrinsic limitation on the human being's behavioral variability is indeterminate. Expansiveness is unimpeded by any known restriction on the kind or the extent of refinement of activity in which the human individual can engage" (1986, p. 6). Hawley further suggests that this characteristic "opens wide the door to divergences of the human from other species in the implications the other postulates have for the kind of environmental relation established" (p. 125).

The indeterminate limits on human behavior proposed by Hawley are likely related to his contention that with humans, "population is not regulated by the physical and biotic environment. Although the environment may be finite, organizational determinants will come into force long before the environment itself operates as a restraint on population" (1973, p. 1200). He goes on to suggest:

> If the line of reasoning followed here is correct, at some time in the course of technological and economic development *population size becomes a neutral factor* in the amounts and kinds of uses of natural resources to be expected. The power for technical and organizational innovation implicit in the already accumulated fund of knowledge is inestimable, and it is constantly being enlarged (p. 1200, emphasis added).

It is apparent from these statements that Hawley is operating from an HEP perspective. His postulate that human behavior has indeterminate limits, therefore making humans unlike any other species, confirms his acceptance of HEP assumption A in Table 1. Hawley's statement that in the course of technological and economic development population size becomes a neutral factor in resource use suggests his adherence to HEP assumption B. His belief that organizational determinants will stop population growth long before the environment becomes a limiting factor is evidence of his acceptance of HEP assumption C. His reference to the inestimable power for technical and organizational innovation contained in the ever-enlarging "fund of knowledge" confirms his acceptance of HEP assumption D. Hawley, like many sociological human ecologists, has developed his human ecological perspective from a largely unecological worldview.

A New Human Ecology for Sociology?

With the preceding discussion in mind, the reader may have come to the conclusion that from a truly ecological point of view, sociological human ecology is a lost cause. To this I would respond both yes and no. Given the current trajectory of the prominent schools of thought in sociological human ecology, it is likely that the field will become so indistinguishable from conventional or mainstream sociology as to essentially disappear, as Duncan (1961) warned 30 years ago. The efforts of prominent sociologists such as Hawley, Schnore, and Namboodiri to legitimate human ecology by equating it with a macrosociological approach to the study of social organization have practically stripped contemporary sociological human ecology of any bioecological content. Further, although they have not been successful in their promotion of sociological human ecology as central to the study of sociology, they have succeeded in distancing the field from bioecology and even from other approaches to the study of human ecology.[10]

Environmental sociology, on the other hand, is a relatively young and vibrant branch of sociology that started with the rather lofty goal of seeking "nothing less than the reorientation of sociology toward a more holistic perspective that would conceptualize social processes within the context of the biosphere" (Buttel 1987, p. 466). Although this has not occurred, environmental sociology has nevertheless become a well-established subdiscipline as a result of its zealous beginnings. As stated previously, environmental sociology is based on the idea that physical environments can and do influence human societies and human social behavior, and vice versa (Dunlap and Catton 1979a). Buttel (1986, 1987) refers to this concept as the core of environmental sociology and even goes so far as to refer to this core as the new human ecology. He offers this characterization of the ecological stance of the new human ecology:

> Analysts working from the new human ecology have generally asserted that a "genuine" environmental sociology—indeed, a sociology that is relevant to the pressing problems of the modern world—must shed its anthropocentrism and reject the notion that humans, because of their capacity for culture, technological innovation, and so on, are exempt from the ecological laws that govern the existence of lower species (1987, p. 468).

This position stands in stark contrast to the position of sociology generally, and sociological human ecology specifically.

Ecological problems such as the recent oil spills in Prince William Sound in Alaska and the Persian Gulf, the Chernobyl nuclear disaster, the extermination of thousands of species annually, global climate change, and thousands of other acute and chronic environmental problems are not likely to go away. Indeed, if the past three decades are any indication we can expect many more environmental problems to emerge in the years to come. Environmental concern and awareness, which had been on the decline throughout the 1970s in the United States, have rebounded sharply during the 1980s and early 1990s. This is due in large part to the growing number and visibility of environmental problems, but is also a response to recent and current political leaders who have tended to deemphasize environmental programs and policies (Dunlap 1991; Dunlap and Scarce 1991). We can probably expect interest in human-environmental relationships to continue to grow for the foreseeable future, both in the general public as well as in many academic disciplines, sociology included. Beginning sociologists who want to understand the human role in ecosystem processes are probably not likely to gravitate toward sociological human ecology as it is now practiced within sociology, but rather toward environmental sociology. Whatever sociological human ecologists there may be who cannot abide watching their field melt away into mainstream sociology are also likely to gravitate toward environmental sociology.

Environmental sociology, however, is not limited to the study of the core issues which Buttel refers to as the new human ecology. It also encompasses a wide variety of sociological approaches that include environmental variables or issues of one form or another. Among the areas of study in environmental sociology are: environmental attitudes, values, and behaviors; the environmental movement; technological risk and risk assessment; political economy of the environment and environmental politics; the "built" environment; wildland recreation; resource management problems; natural hazards and disasters; social impact assessment; as well as other areas (Buttel 1987; Dunlap and Catton 1979a). Environmental sociology is not likely to completely metamorphose into a new human ecology, as the diversity of these various approaches to studying environmental issues, policies, and problems will not and probably should not be eliminated from environmental sociology. However, environmental sociology is fast approaching an age where it must begin to seriously address the core issues upon which the subdiscipline was founded.

Despite the pluralism that currently exists in environmental sociology, it nevertheless seems likely that a significant portion of environmental sociologists will become human ecologists of a new breed, as the old human ecology's prominence further wanes and dissipates into the sociological mainstream. Dietz says he favors the term new human ecology, "because of its implications *outside* sociology and because human ecology within sociology could be reinvigorated and redefined by environmental sociologists" (1988, p. 2, emphasis in original). I contend that the new human ecology, the core of environmental sociology, *will* redefine sociological human ecology, and in so doing open up a dialogue long since broken off with bioecologists and many others who are interested in studying the integral role that human social systems play in ecosystem processes.

TOWARD A THEORETICAL BASIS FOR
THE NEW HUMAN ECOLOGY

Social scientists generally, and sociologists specifically, are often viewed as unscientific by those in the natural sciences (Barkow 1989; Lenski 1988). Barkow and Lenski, both of whom are sociologists, see the lack of unambiguous, falsifiable theories as a major impediment to the advancement of scientific knowledge in sociology. Both of these authors likewise suggest that sociological theories need to develop more conceptual links and continuity with other scientific disciplines. These same criticisms apply to sociological human ecology (Hawley 1984) and environmental sociology (Buttel and Humphrey forthcoming), as neither subdiscipline has developed a theoretical framework upon which a cumulative, rigorous science can be built, or which facilitates linkages with other disciplines.

Buttel notes that the "HEP/NEP schema of Catton and Dunlap has had a curious influence on environmental sociology" (1986, p. 345). It is curious, he says, because while it has become essentially obligatory to cite the NEP conceptual basis in any work done at the center of environmental sociology, there has been little "fleshing out" of the broad domain assumptions that make up the competing paradigms into "more precise theoretical statements and testable hypotheses." Buttel (1987) points out that the only major works spawned by the HEP-NEP model are Catton's (1980) development of an historical analysis of the ecological impacts of industrial societies, and the voluminous body of work using HEP-NEP concepts in sample survey research on different publics' commitment to the "Dominant Social Paradigm" versus the "New Environmental Paradigm" (see, e.g., Cotgrove 1982; Dunlap and van Liere 1978, 1984; Milbrath 1984). Despite this work, however, Buttel (1978, 1986, 1987) has remained somewhat critical of Catton and Dunlap's HEP-NEP distinction because it is couched at a highly abstract "metatheoretical" level and thus "has not been readily usable in empirical research" (1987, p. 469). The reason for this lack of empirical work using the HEP-NEP distinction, say Humphrey and Buttel (1982, p. 15), is that, "HEP and NEP fall short of being true paradigms because their assumptions say little about the principal 'laws of motion' or social forces that shape how society is organized and how it changes over time."

Buttel and Humphrey argue that traditional sociological theoretical perspectives are the appropriate vehicles for environmental sociological analyses, provided they reflect the assumptions of the NEP (Buttel 1978, 1986,

1987; Humphrey and Buttel 1982; Buttel and Humphrey forthcoming). These authors are particularly impressed with many elements of the political economy perspective of Alan Schnaiberg. Schnaiberg's (1980) concepts of the societal-environmental dialectic and the treadmill of production are singled out as particularly insightful in explaining the inherent expansiveness of capitalistic societies and how this places ever-increasing stress on resources and the environment. Yet, Buttel criticizes many of Schnaiberg's ideas, as he did Catton and Dunlap's, for their abstractness and consequent difficulty in operationalization. For example, Buttel and Humphrey (forthcoming) note that it is not clear whether Schnaiberg's concept of the self-reinforcing treadmill of production applies only to advanced capitalist economies or whether it also applies to underdeveloped and socialist economies. Buttel also notes that Schnaiberg's work tends to be less ecologically sophisticated than that of Catton and Dunlap in that it tends to lump ecological issues into an "undifferentiated mass of problems of 'ecological disruption'" (1986, p. 349).

Buttel acknowledges that there is but a "small core of largely theoretically oriented work" in environmental sociology, most of which is framed at a highly abstract level" (1987, p. 466). Consequently, "the bulk of environmental sociological scholarship tends to consist of a 'normal-science' working out of middle-range empirical puzzles" (p. 466). Though much high quality, valuable, empirical work is currently being done under the heading of environmental sociology, much of it is disjointed as the field is currently without clear theoretical guidance. "Less focused on its theoretical and metatheoretical core (the 'new human ecology'), environmental sociology has become more diverse and fragmented, and afflicted with many of the same problems as sociology at large" (p. 484). A unified theoretical perspective is needed to generate more interest in environmental sociology and the emerging new human ecology. But more importantly, a unified theoretical perspective would be invaluable in assisting sociologists to better conceive of and explain societal-environmental reciprocal relationships, and it should allow for greater cross-fertilization with human ecologists in other fields.

Dunlap and Catton (1979b, 1983; Catton 1987) suggest that the simple POET model, or ecological complex, first introduced by Duncan in 1959 could provide the basis for an improved framework to analyze societal-environmental interactions. While those few sociological human ecologists who have employed the ecological complex have done so with an almost exclusive concern for examining social organization (O), Dunlap and Catton suggest that for environmental sociologists the emphasis must be on the environment (E) as it influences and is influenced by the "social complex" (population [P], organization [O], and technology [T] [Park 1936a]). "Just as biological ecologists can speak of an ecosystem as a biotic community and its environment, so the proposed framework for environmental sociology treats Duncan's ecological complex as comprising Park's social complex and its environment" (Dunlap and Catton 1983, p. 12). Further elaborating on the POET model, Dunlap and Catton differentiate the organization component into a cultural system, social system, and a personality system. Based on the work of Odum (1975, 1989), they also conceive of the physical environment as serving three distinguishable and often competing functions: dwelling place, source of supplies, and repository for wastes (see Catton and Dunlap 1989 for a more detailed treatment of this tripartite model of environmental functions, including a minor revision of terms).

Applying Liebig's "law of the minimum" to these three competing functions, Catton and Dunlap (1989) relate how any number of factors can act as limiting in ecological relations. Although we tend to think in terms of energy or raw materials as the limiting factors in societal growth and progress, Catton and Dunlap suggest that even if essentially unlimited supplies of energy, raw materials or food are found, other factors such as the ability of the environment to absorb waste heat and materials or to provide adequate living space may act to limit societal progress and growth.

While still not a theory as such, Dunlap and Catton's further elaboration on Duncan's POET model appears to offer potential for further development. Although the POET schema does not provide the theoretical basis for explaining social or ecological change, it nevertheless "enables one to see the complex, reciprocal relationships among population, organization, technology and environment" (Buttel and Humphrey forthcoming). Figure 1 is an attempt to expand upon Dunlap and Catton's elaboration of the POET model while also incorporating some of the more dynamic theoretical aspects of the works of Freese (1988) and Adams (1988).

Olsen's preceding two essays in this volume thoroughly review Freese's (1988) theory of how changes and disruptions in resource transfers provide the basis for evolution of both ecosystems and social systems, and Adams' (1988) theory of social evolution as the self-organization of energy. Olsen attempts a synthesis of key elements of both while also going beyond these two theories by using their ideas to break new ground on the dynamics of social power. Olsen says that "there is presently an urgent need for greater understanding of socioecological organization and its linkage with sociocultural organization" (1993a, p. 65).[11] His work is a major step toward developing that linkage as he presents an elaborate model of how socioecological and sociocultural organization are *parallel and highly interwoven analytical realms within the total process of social organization*" (1993a, p. 47, emphasis in original).

In both Freese's and Adams' theories, however, the socioecological level of organization is posited to be heavily impacted via energy and resource flows with the biophysical environment. Therefore, just as important as understanding the linkages between socioecological and sociocultural organization is the need to further understand the linkages between bioecological and socioecological organization. Freese's perspective places considerable emphasis on how disruptions in resource flows in bioecological systems directly affect human social organization. Likewise, Adams suggests that "perturbations" in the biophysical environment, caused by energy dissipation, directly feed back to alter human social organization. While the primacy of this relationship is implicit throughout Olsen's synthesis of these two theoretical works, the model he provides for the process of social organization treats bioecological organization as simply the source of natural resources and provides little insight into the resource interactions between social systems and ecosystems (Olsen 1993a, p. 50).

Freese (1988) argues that "biophysical ecosystems and human social systems are different manifestations of the same evolutionary process" (pp. 116-117). This, he says, is because "resource transfers running through ecosystems to social systems connect; and that means evolution in the one is a continuation of evolution in the other, respecting the additional resource interactions that social systems enable" (p. 117). Developing an understanding of this "continuation" between ecosystems and social systems is an area of research that has been largely neglected by both environmental sociologists and traditional sociological human ecologists. The exploration of this interface between social systems and ecosystems is not only essential for establishing core knowledge for the new human ecology in sociology, but also for establishing links with other disciplines, especially bioecology.

The natural environment in Figure 1 is presented as if comprised of the three interacting yet competing functions suggested by Catton and Dunlap (1989). When human population density was lower, and before the advent of industrial technologies, segregation of these three functions was seldom a serious problem. However, in today's highly populated, industrial world, Catton and Dunlap suggest, "Segregation of the three functions has become increasingly important while at the same time becoming increasingly difficult" (1989, p. 4). The fact that the three functions are highly interrelated and increasingly contradictory is represented by the overlap of the three circles representing these functions in Figure 1. Other species besides humans also use the natural environment to obtain resources, dispose of wastes, and as habitat or living space. This is represented by the central circle labeled Non-Human Nature in Figure 1. As human populations and their concomitant social organizations utilize the environment in any of the three capacities, not only does this have ramifications for the ability of the physical environment to continue to provide these functions for humans in the future, but it also directly affects the resource base and living space for other species as well.

Freese (following bioecologists) says that resource flows can be broken down into materials, energy, and information flows, although all three are highly interdependent and are "integral to the complex field of interactions an ecosystem contains" (1988, p. 69).[12] This roughly coincides with Adams' (1988) theory, which views materials and information as intrinsic to his concept

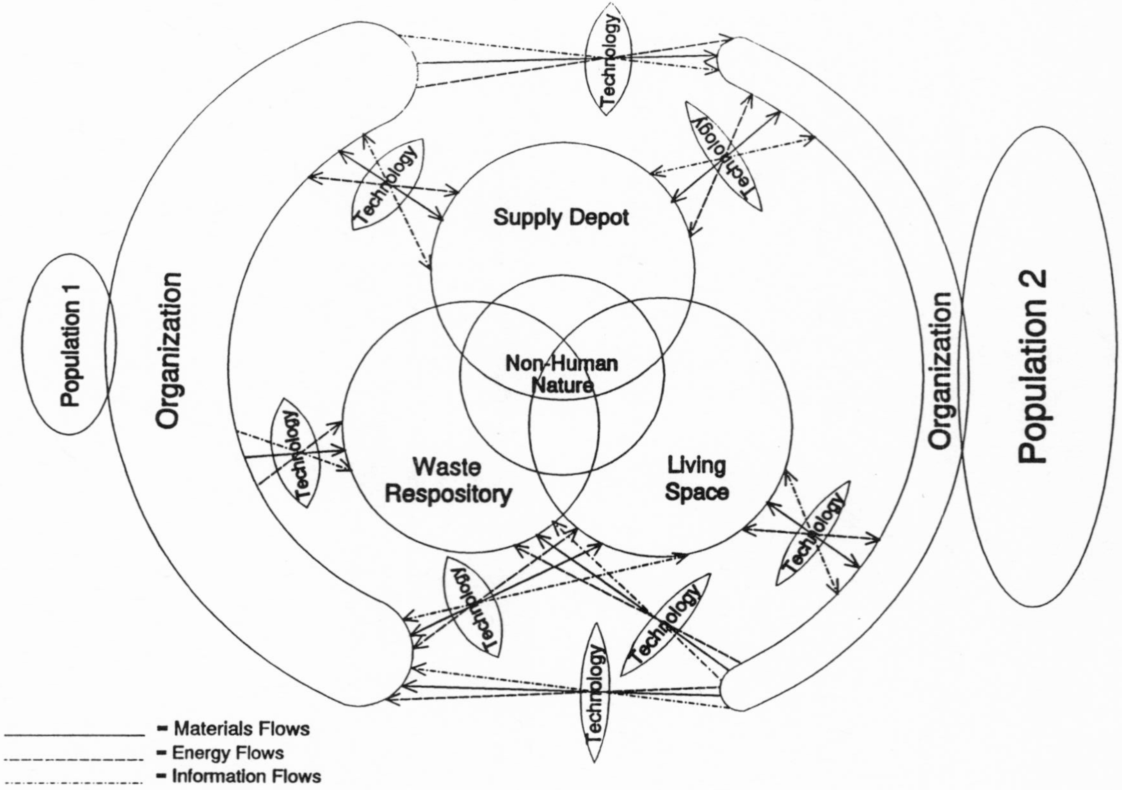

Figure 1. Revised POET Model

of energy forms. The flows of materials, energy, and information are represented in Figure 1 by three intersecting lines to reflect their complex interplay in actual resource transfers. The relationships between human social organization and environment as supply depot and living space are represented by two-headed arrows to reflect the fact that resources can flow in either direction. For example, in addition to heavily drawing nonrenewable resources from the environment, humans commonly increase the amount of renewable resources they draw by employing advanced agricultural methods, intensive forestry, or supplementing fisheries through hatcheries. In terms of living space, not only do humans invest tremendous materials, energy and information into designing and manipulating the environment as human habitat, but the environment as living space provides numerous resources in return such as the privacy, protection, and security provided by homes; entertainment and leisure from parks, museums, wilderness, and so forth; mobility from the system of roads and highways; and enhanced communication through the infrastructure of various telecommunications systems.

I would argue, however, that the flow of resources between human society and environment as waste repository is largely unidirectional. Only when waste disposal impedes the function of environment as living space (e.g., toxic waste sites that render neighborhoods or whole communities unfit to live in) or threatens the supply function of the environment (e.g., groundwater contamination, acid precipitation's effect on forests, or the impact of global warming on world agriculture), do we become aware of the effects of waste disposal. The impact of waste on human habitat and sustenance resources has therefore only been widely recognized relatively recently. Hence, concern over this aspect of the physical environment is a relatively new phenomenon compared to the other two.

Implicit in all these resource transfers are the roles of human social organization and technology. It has long been recognized that members of certain populations make much greater demands on the environment than do members of other populations in terms of resources used, wastes created, and space utilized. The two ovals in Figure 1 represent human populations of substantially different sizes. Moreover, the two populations in this model are organized very differently. The smaller population, in this instance, is organized much more elaborately than the larger one. In other words, the smaller population supports a much larger economy, a more complex polity, a more extensive educational system, and so forth. This greater degree of social organization for the smaller population translates into relatively greater per capita resource transfers between population 1 and the physical environment than is the case for population 2.

Both Adams (1988) and Olsen (1993a, 1993b) view tools and technology as "triggers" whereby organized human populations are able to use small amounts of resources to unleash much larger volumes of resources. Adams says,

"Human technology has indeed changed the surface of the earth, but it has not eliminated the self-organizing properties of the environment. It is also a trigger that has increasingly set the environment loose in a cascading exhibition of the Second Law of Thermodynamics" (1988, p. 129). Technology can increase a population's demand for energy, materials, and information, just as it can sometimes expand supplies of all three. Likewise, technology can "have extensive unknown indirect effects, thereby possibly unleashing all kinds of undesired energy flows," or, if used effectively, it can improve conditions (Olsen 1993a, p. 57).

Catton (1980, 1987) argues that in preindustrial times, technology primarily increased human carrying capacity by increasing the resources available for human consumption, whereas in modern industrial societies it often actually *decreases* carrying capacity as the technology itself consumes enormous amounts of resources (especially fossil fuels, which Catton says provide a type of phantom carrying capacity). Modern, industrial technology has so expanded human beings' ability to do work, consume resources, and create wastes, that Catton refers to modern tools and technologies as "prosthetic organs" which have transformed *Homo sapiens* into *Homo colossus*. In Figure 1, technology is represented between two arcs that resemble a lens to indicate that technology can act to either magnify resource demands (Catton 1987) or resource supplies (Hawley 1973). The important point is that technology plays a pivotal role in all resource transfers. The thicknesses of the technology "lenses" of the two hypothetical populations are also different, reflecting the fact that different societies' technologies can have very different effects on resource transfers, both in terms of increasing demand for resources and in terms of augmenting supplies and conserving non-renewable resources.

The model in Figure 1 is admittedly an oversimplification. It says nothing about how energy, materials, and information interact in resource flows, and it says nothing about the internal dynamics of social organization.[13] But used as a schematic framework, it points out that the interactions between the environment and human populations, organization, and technology (the social complex) are highly variable depending on how societies are organized and how their technology triggers operate. The model also hints at the complex ways that resource flows impact different functions of the physical environment, both for humans and other species.

The theoretical perspectives of Catton and Dunlap, Freese, Adams, and Olsen appear to be highly complementary to this revised POET model. By incorporating their theoretical principles on the dynamics of social and ecological change, this type of approach could prove useful in developing a basis for a cumulative theoretical core for those sociologists interested in societal-environmental relations. This theoretical core could prove to be the nexus around which could be built a truly new human ecology within sociology. More importantly, this theoretical approach is not built merely on natural science analogies but provides numerous points of convergence between the natural and social sciences that could foster interdisciplinary human ecological studies that include natural scientists, social scientists, and virtually anyone interested in the study of human ecology as a scientific approach to understanding and even attenuating or solving complex ecological problems in which human societies are integrally involved.

ACKNOWLEDGMENTS

Special thanks are due to William R. Catton, Jr., Riley E. Dunlap, Lee Freese, and Gerald L. Young for helpful comments on an earlier version of this manuscript. I am also indebted to the editor for making available to me his unpublished book chapter on the subject of this essay.

NOTES

1. Young (1974, p. 5) points out that early on, biologists also borrowed concepts from the social sciences, but contends that "whatever their original roots...the biologists were instrumental in giving certain concepts ecological validity and it is from the biologists that they were borrowed by early human ecologists."

2. It is noteworthy that Robert E. Park, in reviewing Alihan's (1938) book, *Social Ecology*, denies that he and his colleagues at Chicago were even attempting to construct a theory (Duncan and Schnore 1959).

3. For a good discussion of Alihan's criticism of the careless use of biological analogy, see Catton's (1992, pp. 89-90) discussion of Alihan's comments about the classical human ecologists' use of the term succession.

4. Some macrolevel sociologists tend to view the study of macrolevel structures and organization as to only legitimate subject matter for sociology, and therefore view individual or "micro-" level social phenomena as psychology (e.g., see Mayhew 1980, 1981).

5. For more information on the similarities and differences between, and possible synthesis of, the sociocultural and neoorthodox perspectives of sociological human ecology, see Bailey and Mulcahy (1972) and Firey and Sjoberg (1982).

6. Catton (1992) notes that in fairness to McKenzie, this phrase also included the words "as affected by the selective, distributive, and accommodative forces of the environment." Catton relates how sociologists of the time could have chosen to emphasize the effects of environmental forces as McKenzie suggested, but instead chose to dwell almost exclusively on his notion of spatial relations.

7. Gibbs and Martins' concept of sustenance organization was undoubtedly an improvement over the preoccupation with human spatial relations, but it only focused on the environment as a source of resources for human sustenance, and it ignored other functions of the physical environment such as living space and waste repository (Catton and Dunlap 1989).

8. In an example utilizing basketball to demonstrate the difference between what he calls systemic interaction and interpersonal interaction, Freese (1988, p. 97) confirms the impossibility of separating social position from social role: "The very idea of a basketball player is meaningless without the roles, statuses, and norms that define and characterize the play."

9. Also of interest in this text by Berry and Kasarda (1977) is its title, *Contemporary Urban Ecology*. Catton (1992) suggests that one reason for sociological human ecology's near total

disregard for bioecological factors is its urban bias, which he says is evident in work from the Chicago school of human ecology right up to the present day. Catton notes that almost all sociological human ecologists have seen the rural "hinterlands" as dependent on urban centers, while almost none have viewed cities as dependent on rural areas, which is the common view among bioecologists and even among many human ecologists in other social sciences, such as anthropology, where the urban bias is not so strong. Another manifestation of the continuing urban bias in sociological human ecology can be seen in a text edited by George Theodorson that was first published in 1961 under the title *Studies in Human Ecology*, but which was revised and republished in 1982 under the title *Urban Patterns: Studies in Human Ecology*.

10.   This is especially evident in the fact that the work of sociological human ecologists is conspicuously absent from the proceedings of the international conferences of the interdisciplinary Society for Human Ecology (Borden, Jacobs, and Young 1986, 1988; Pratt, Young, and Jacobs 1990).

11.   See Olsen (1993a, 1993b) for a discussion about, and definitions of, socioecological and sociocultural organization.

12.   Duncan (1964) likewise discussed the complex interplay of materials, energy, and information flows in ecosystems and social systems. However, his discussion was more descriptive and did not present a theory of how resource flows affect social change.

13.   Olsen's two essays in this volume, and especially his model of the process of social organization wherein he develops the relationships between sociocultural and socioecological levels of organization, coincide well with the revised POET model in Figure 1. For a different theoretical approach to developing the POET schema, see Bailey's paper in this volume.

REFERENCES

Adams, R.N. 1988. *The Eighth Day: Social Evolution as the Self-Organization of Energy*. Austin, TX: University of Texas Press.

Alihan, M. H. 1938. *Social Ecology: A Critical Analysis*. New York: Columbia University Press.

Bailey, K.D., and P. Mulcahy. 1972. "Sociocultural versus Neoclassical Ecology: A Contribution to the Problem of Scope in Sociology." *The Sociological Quarterly* 13(Winter): 37-48.

Barkow, J.H. 1989. "Broad Training for Social Scientists." *Science* 243(February 24): 992.

Bennett, J.W. 1976. *The Ecological Transition: Cultural Anthropology and Human Adaptation*. New York: Permagon Press.

Berry, B.J.L., and J.D. Kasarda. 1977. *Contemporary Urban Ecology*. New York: McMillan.

Bidwell, C.E., and J.D. Kasarda. 1985. *The Organization and its Ecosystem: A Theory of Structuring in Organizations* (Monographs in Organizational Behavior and Industrial Relations, Vol. 2). Greenwich, CT: JAI Press.

_____. 1987. *Structuring in Organizations: Ecosystem Theory Evaluated* (Monographs in Organizational Behavior and Industrial Relations, Vol. 7). Greenwich, CT: JAI Press.

Borden, R.J., J. Jacobs, and G.L. Young, eds. 1986. *Human Ecology: A Gathering of Perspectives*. Selected Papers from the First International Conference of the Society for Human Ecology, University of Maryland, April. College Park, MD: The Society for Human Ecology.

_____. 1988. *Human Ecology: Research and Applications*. Selected Papers from the Second International Conference of the Society for Human Ecology, College of the Atlantic, October. College Park, MD: The Society for Human Ecology.

Burgess, E.W. 1928. "Residential Segregation in American Cities." *Annals of the American Academy of Political and Social Science* 140(November): 105-115.

Buttel, F.H. 1978. "Environmental Sociology: A New Paradigm?" *The American Sociologist* 13(November): 252-256.

_____. 1986. "Sociology and the Environment: The Winding Road Toward Human Ecology." *International Social Science Journal* 109: 337-356.

_____. 1987. "New Directions for Environmental Sociology." *Annual Review of Sociology* 13: 465-488.

Buttel, F.H., and C.R. Humphrey. Forthcoming. "Sociological Theory and the Natural Environment." In *Handbook of Environmental Sociology*, edited by R.E. Dunlap and W. Michelson. Westport, CT: Greenwood Press.

Carroll, G.R. 1984. "Organizational Ecology." *Annual Review of Sociology* 10: 71-93.

_____. 1985. "Concentration and Specialization: Dynamics of Niche Width in Populations of Organizations." *American Journal of Sociology* 90: 1262-1283.

Carroll, G.R. 1987. *Publish and Perish: The Organizational Ecology of Newspaper Industries.* Greenwich, CT: JAI Press.

_____ (ed.). 1988. *Ecological Models of Organizations.* Cambridge, MA: Ballinger.

Catton, W.R., Jr. 1980. *Overshoot: The Ecological Basis of Revolutionary Change.* Urbana: University of Illinois Press.

_____. 1983. "Need for a New Paradigm." *Sociological Perspectives* 26(1): 3-15.

_____. 1984. "Research and Policy Issues in Sociological Human Ecology: An Agenda for the Future." Pp. 385-426 in *Sociological Human Ecology: Contemporary Issues and Applications*, edited by M. Micklin and H. M. Choldin. Boulder, CO: Westview Press.

_____. 1987. "The World's Most Polymorphic Species." *BioScience* 37(June): 413-419.

_____. 1992. "Separation versus Unification in Sociological Human Ecology." Pp. 65-99 in *Advances in Human Ecology*, Vol. 1, edited by L. Freese. Greenwich, CT: JAI Press.

Catton, W.R., Jr., and R.E. Dunlap. 1978a. "Environmental Sociology: A New Paradigm." *The American Sociologist* 13(February): 41-49.

_____. 1978b. "Paradigms, Theories, and the Primacy of HEP-NEP Distinction." *The American Sociologist* 13(November): 256-259.

_____. 1980. "A New Ecological Paradigm for Post-Exuberant Sociology." *American Behavioral Scientist* 24(1): 15-47.

_____. 1989. "Competing Functions of the Environment: Living Space, Supply Depot, and Waste Repository." Paper presented at the Conference on Environmental Constraints and Opportunities in the Social Organization of Space, University of Udine, Italy, June 7-10.

Cotgrove, S. 1982. *Catastrophe or Cornucopia: The Environment, Politics and the Future.* New York: Wiley & Sons.

Dietz, T. 1988. "Towards a Human Ecology of Industrial Societies: Some Comments on Theory and the State of Environmental Sociology." *Environment, Technology, and Society* 52(Spring): 2-4.

Duncan, O. D. 1959. "Human Ecology and Population Studies." Pp. 678-716 in *The Study of Population*, edited by P. M. Hauser and O. D. Duncan. Chicago: University of Chicago Press.

_____. 1961. "From Social System to Ecosystem." *Sociological Inquiry* 31(Spring): 140-149.

_____. 1964. "Social Organization and the Ecosystem." Pp. 36-82 in *Handbook of Modern Sociology*, edited by R.E.L. Faris. Chicago: Rand-McNally.

Duncan, O.D., and L.F. Schnore. 1959. "Cultural, Behavioral, and Ecological Perspectives in the Study of Social Organizations." *American Journal of Sociology* 65(July): 132-152.

Dunlap, R. E. 1991. "Trends in Public Opinion Toward Environmental Issues: 1965-1990." *Society and Natural Resources* 4: 285-312.

Dunlap, R.E., and W.R. Catton, Jr. 1979a. "Environmental Sociology." *Annual Review of Sociology* 5: 243-273.

_____. 1979b. "Environmental Sociology: A Framework for Analysis." Pp. 57-85 in *Progress in Resource Management and Environmental Planning*, edited by T. O'Riordan and R. C. d'Arge. Chichester, England: John Wiley & Sons.

_____. 1983. "What Environmental Sociologists Have in Common (Whether Concerned with 'Built' or 'Natural' Environments)." *Sociological Inquiry* 53: 113-135.

Dunlap, R.E., and R. Scarce. 1991. "The Polls—Poll Trends: Environmental Problems and Protection." *Public Opinion Quarterly* 55: 713-734.

Dunlap, R.E., and K.D. van Liere. 1978. "The New Environmental Paradigm: A Proposed Measuring Instrument and Preliminary Results." *Journal of Environmental Education* 9: 10-19.

_____. 1984. "Commitment to the Dominant Social Paradigm and Concern for Environmental Quality." *Social Science Quarterly* 65(December): 1013-1028.

Durkheim, E. 1950. *The Rules of the Sociological Method.* Glencoe, IL: The Free Press.

Faris, R. E. L. 1970. *Chicago Sociology: 1920-1932.* Chicago: University of Chicago Press.

Firey, W. 1945. "Sentiment and Symbolism as Ecological Variables." *American Sociological Review* 10(April): 140-148.

Firey, W., and G. Sjoberg. 1982. "Issues in Sociocultural Ecology." Pp. 150-164 in *Urban Patterns: Studies in Human Ecology,* edited by G.A. Theodorson. University Park, PA: The Pennsylvania State University Press.

Freeman, J., and M. T. Hannan. 1983. "Niche Width and the Dynamics of Organizational Populations." *American Journal of Sociology* 88: 1116-1145.

Freese, L. 1988. "Evolution and Sociogenesis. Part I: Ecological Origins. Part II: Social Continuities." Pp. 51-118 in *Advances in Group Processes,* Vol. 5, edited by E.J. Lawler and B. Markovsky. Greenwich, CT: JAI Press.

Freudenburg, W.R. 1989. "The Emergence of Environmental Sociology: Contributions of R. E. Dunlap and W. R. Catton, Jr." *Sociological Inquiry* 59(4): 439-452.

Gettys, W.E. 1940. "Human Ecology and Social Theory." *Social Forces* 18(May): 469-476.

Gibbs, J.P., and W.T. Martin. 1958. "Urbanization and Natural Resources: A Study in Organizational Ecology." *American Sociological Review* 23(3): 266-276.

_____. 1959. "Toward a Theoretical System of Human Ecology." *Pacific Sociological Review* 2(Spring): 29-36.

Guest, A. M. 1984. "The City." Pp. 277-322 in *Sociological Human Ecology: Contemporary Issues and Applications,* edited by M. Micklin and H.M. Choldin. Boulder, CO: Westview Press.

Hannan, M.T., and J. Freeman. 1977. "The Population Ecology of Organizations." *American Journal of Sociology* 82: 929-964.

_____. 1988. "The Ecology of Organizational Mortality: American Labor Unions, 1836-1985." *American Journal of Sociology* 94: 25-52.

_____. 1989. *Organizational Ecology.* Cambridge, MA: Harvard University Press.

Hatt, P. 1946. "The Concept of Natural Area." *American Sociological Review* 11(August): 423-427.

Hawley, A.H. 1944. "Ecology and Human Ecology." *Social Forces* 22(May): 398-405.

_____. 1950. *Human Ecology: A Theory of Community Structure.* New York: Ronald Press.

_____. 1968. "Human Ecology." Pp. 328-337 in *International Encyclopedia of the Social Sciences,* edited by D. L. Sills. New York: Macmillan and The Free Press.

_____. 1973. "Ecology and Population." *Science* 179(March 23): 1196-1201.

Hawley, A. H. 1984. "Sociological Human Ecology: Past, Present, and Future." Pp. 1-15 in *Sociological Human Ecology: Contemporary Issues and Applications,* edited by M. Micklin and H. M. Choldin. Boulder, CO: Westview Press.

_____. 1986. *Human Ecology: A Theoretical Essay.* Chicago: The University of Chicago Press.

Hollingshead, A.B. 1947. "A Re-Examination of Ecological Theory." *Sociology and Social Research* 31(January-February): 194-204.

Humphrey, C.R., and F.H. Buttel. 1982. *Environment, Energy, and Society*. Belmont, CA: Wadsworth.

Janson, C.-G. 1980. "Factorial Social Ecology: An Attempt at Summary and Evaluation." *Annual Review of Sociology* 6: 433-456.

Kuhn, T.S. 1962. *The Structure of Scientific Revolutions*. Chicago: University of Chicago Press.

Lenski, G. 1988. "Rethinking Macrosociological Theory." *American Sociological Review* 53: 163-171.

Lincoln, James R. 1979. "Organizational Differences in Urban Communities: A Study in Organizational Ecology." *Social Forces* 57(3): 915-930.

Mayhew, B.H. 1981a. "Structuralism versus Individualism: Part I, Shadowboxing in the Dark." *Social Forces* 59: 335-375.

_____. 1981b. "Structuralism versus Individualism: Part II, Ideological and Other Obfuscations." *Social Forces* 59: 627-648.

McIntosh, R.P. 1985. *The Background of Ecology: Concept and Theory*. New York: Cambridge University Press.

McKenzie, R.D. 1924. "The Ecological Approach to the Study of the Human Community." *American Journal of Sociology* 30(November): 287-301.

_____. 1926. "The Scope of Human Ecology." Pp. 141-154 in *Papers and Proceedings of the 20th Annual Meeting of the American Sociological Society*. Washington DC: The American Sociological Society.

Milbrath, L.W. 1984. *Environmentalists: Vanguard for a New Society*. Albany, NY: State University of New York Press.

Mitchell, G.D. 1979. *A New Dictionary of the Social Sciences*. Hawthorne, NY: Aldine.

Namboodiri, K. 1988. "Ecological Demography: Its Place in Sociology." *American Sociological Review* 53(August): 619-633.

Odum, E.P. 1975. *Ecology: The Link Between the Natural and Social Sciences*. New York: Holt, Rinehart and Winston.

_____. 1989. *Ecology, and Our Endangered Life-Support Systems*. Sunderland, MA: Sinauer Associates.

Olsen, M.E. 1993a. "Components of Socioecological Organization: Tools, Resources, Energy, and Power." Pp. 35-67 in *Advances in Human Ecology*, Vol. 2, edited by L. Freese. Greenwich, CT: JAI Press.

_____. 1993b. "A Socioecological Perspective on Social Evolution." Pp. 69-92 in *Advances in Human Ecology*, Vol. 2, edited by L. Freese. Greenwich, CT: JAI Press.

Park, R. E. 1936a. "Human Ecology." *American Journal of Sociology* 42(July): 1-15.

_____. 1936b. "Succession, an Ecological Concept." *American Sociological Review* 1(2): 171-179.

_____. 1939. *An Outline of the Principles of Sociology*. Chicago: University of Chicago Press.

Park, R.E., and E.W. Burgess. 1921. *Introduction to the Science of Sociology*. Chicago: University of Chicago Press.

Pratt, J., G.L. Young, and J. Jacobs, eds. 1990. *Human Ecology: Steps to the Future*. Proceedings of the Third International Conference of the Society for Human Ecology, October. Sonoma, CA: The Society for Human Ecology.

Quinn, J.A. 1950. *Human Ecology*. New York: Prentice-Hall.

Rossi, P. 1959. "Comment" on the article by Duncan and Schnore in the same issue. *American Journal of Sociology* 65(July): 146-149.

Sargent, F., ed. 1974. *Human Ecology*. New York: American Elsevier.

Schnaiberg, A. 1980. *The Environment: From Surplus to Scarcity*. New York: Oxford University Press.

————. Forthcoming. "The Political Economy of Environmental Problems and Policies: Consciousness, Conflict, and Control Capacity." In *Handbook of Environmental Sociology*, edited by R.E. Dunlap and W. Michelson. Westport, CT: Greenwood Press.

Schnore, L.F. 1961. "The Myth of Human Ecology." *Sociological Inquiry* 31: 128-139.

Shepard, P. 1967. "Whatever Happened to Human Ecology?" *BioScience* 17(December): 891-894.

Siegel, P.M. 1984. "Human Ecology and Ecology." Pp. 21-49 in *Sociological Human Ecology: Contemporary Issues and Applications*, edited by M. Micklin and H. M. Choldin. Boulder, CO: Westview Press.

Sly, D.F., and J. Tayman. 1980. "Metropolitan Morphology and Population Mobility: The Theory of Ecological Expansion Reexamined." *American Journal of Sociology* 86: 119-138.

Stephan, G.E. 1970. "The Concept of Community in Human Ecology." *Pacific Sociological Review* 13(Fall): 218-228.

Theodorson, G.A., ed. 1961. *Studies in Human Ecology*. Evanston, IL: Row, Peterson and Company.

————, ed. 1982. *Urban Patterns: Studies in Human Ecology*. University Park, PA: The Pennsylvania State University Press.

Wilhelm, S.M. 1962. *Urban Zoning and Land Use Theory*. New York: The Free Press.

Young, G.L. 1974. "Human Ecology as an Interdisciplinary Concept: A Critical Inquiry." *Advances in Ecological Research* 8: 1-105.

————, ed. 1983. *Origins of Human Ecology*. Stroudsburg, PA: Hutchinson Ross.

Young, R.C. 1988. "Is Population Ecology a Useful Paradigm for the Study of Organizations?" *American Journal of Sociology* 94: 1-24.

SOCIAL ENTROPY THEORY:
AN APPLICATION OF NONEQUILIBRIUM
THERMODYNAMICS IN HUMAN ECOLOGY

Kenneth D. Bailey

ABSTRACT

Sociological human ecology was once dominated by equilibrium models, which have become largely obsolete since the development of nonequilibrium thermodynamics by Prigogine and others. This paper presents a nonequilibrium approach based on social entropy theory. While drawing from nonequilibrium thermodynamics and systems theory, the newer approach can accommodate equilibrium if desired, but it is not dependent upon it. Following an assessment of classical sociological human ecology, social entropy theory is presented and its relationship to nonequilibrium thermodynamics is discussed, emphasizing the connection of social entropy to thermodynamic entropy. A macrovariable model with microscopic links is developed for social entropy theory, and the paper concludes with an assessment of its potential for sociological human ecology.

Advances in Human Ecology, Volume 2, pages 133-161.
ISBN: 1-55938-558-8

INTRODUCTION

A systems approach has been prevalent in (if not central to) sociological human ecology since its inception. One of the founders of sociological ecology, Robert E. Park, relied heavily upon the notion of interrelationships among the components of the ecological system. However, Park's ecological system, following the custom of the time, emphasized equilibrium. Park (1936) said that ordinarily, minor fluctuations in the biotic balance do not disturb the existing equilibrium. Later sociological ecologists followed Park in emphasizing equilibrium or balance, although their systems terminology emphasized the concept of ecosystem rather than the balance of nature (see Duncan 1961, 1964).

While sociological ecologists who used the equilibrium concept have never been criticized to the extent that sociological functionalists were, it nevertheless is clear that, for a number of reasons, the trend in science today is away from an emphasis on equilibrium and toward nonequilibrium thermodynamic approaches that emphasize the concept of entropy rather than equilibrium (see Dyke 1988; Dyke 1992; Weber, Depew, and Smith 1988; Brooks and Wiley 1988; Bailey 1984, 1990a). One almost fatal confusion in many sociological applications of classical equilibrium theory occurred because "true" or "stable" equilibrium in thermodynamic terms is maximum entropy in an isolated or closed system. Maximum entropy is system death rather than the fortuitous state of balance desired by sociologists. Thus, sociological equilibrium theory essentially has no thermodynamic foundation and is often poorly conceptualized and inadequately measured (see Russett 1966).

Modern systems theory, following Prigogine (1955, 1962, 1984), is generally a nonequilibrium approach. This approach looks at entropy rather than equilibrium, and has recently been applied to sociology in *Social Entropy Theory* (Bailey 1990a). The purpose of this paper is to apply nonequilibrium thermodynamic entropy theory to sociological ecology. The paper begins with a brief review of classical sociological ecology, specifically, the equilibrium approach. After a short critique of this approach, the principles of entropy theory as currently interpreted by Wicken, Dyke, Bailey and others are presented.

The basic thrust of modern nonequilibrium thermodynamics as applied to social science is to show how entropy can remain constant or even decrease in social systems in apparent violation of the Second Law of Thermodynamics. Ecological forces that contribute to the production and decrease of entropy are examined in detail. The relationship between statistical and thermodynamic entropy is also discussed, and the measurement of entropy is presented. The discussion culminates with an application of Social Entropy Theory to ecology and a discussion of the contributions it makes.

PAST APPROACHES

While sociological human ecology is still vibrant and exciting, it can easily be argued that it is theoretically mature and is consolidating rather than expanding. This is particularly true of macroecology, and perhaps less true for microecology.

Classical sociological human ecology was based largely upon plant and animal ecology, and thus had a large theoretical tradition from biology to draw upon. This biological tradition yielded a number of concepts still in use today, such as dominance, invasion, succession, niche, environment, and symbiosis.

The problem was that classical sociological ecology, as well as the approaches that followed, was rather heavily criticized, and it proved vulnerable to a portion of this criticism. A dominant theme in this criticism was the proper role of biotic as opposed to social and cultural factors. Another problem in the classical approach was an emphasis (sometimes explicit and sometimes implicit) on equilibrium. I will briefly review the classical, neoclassical, and sociocultural approaches to sociological human ecology. This discussion is drawn largely from my unpublished doctoral dissertation (Bailey 1968).

The Classical School

Classical sociological ecology was inspired by plant and animal ecology. It emphasized the principle of "competitive cooperation," that Homo sapiens was an organism in the web of life shared with other animals and with plants. The symbiotic community (a territorially organized population) utilized competition for regulating numbers and maintaining a biotic balance between competing species. Two other functions of competition, dominance and succession, were also emphasized. Thus the biotic level is the concern of human ecology, but it is distinct from the cultural level. The cultural level rests on the symbiotic community, and factors that appear on the biotic level are seen on the cultural level. The cultural level is woven from symbolic communication and consensus. Human ecology, so constituted, is an attempt to explain the maintenance and restoration of the biotic balance and social equilibrium.

This theoretical approach had several advantages. It emphasized the interrelationships between levels in the ecosystem, and it allowed for conceptualization on a macrolevel. But perhaps its strongest point was its emphasis on stability and order as an abiding phenomenon in the midst of continual flux (competition). Several brilliant studies spawned by this school remain as classics, for example, Burgess's concentric zone theory—a theory that postulated a process of adaptation resulting in a series of distinct zones illustrative of city expansion (Burgess 1925, pp. 47-62) and Hoyt's sector theory, which postulated distinct sectors extending outward from the central city business district (Weiner and Hoyt 1939, pp. 60-70). Both of these formulations are reflected in Berry's later factor models of urbanization (Berry 1964, p. 156).

But the treatment of cultural phenomena apart from ecological processes soon proved unpalatable to sociologists. This disenchantment was exacerbated by some negative research findings. Davie's study of New Haven demonstrated that the Burgess zonal hypothesis, which had been devised for Chicago, could not be considered as an empirical representation of every American city (Davie 1938). Such substantive criticisms, along with devastating theoretical attacks, of which Alihan's (1938) book is a prime example, soon sounded the death knell for classical sociological ecology.

Alihan was particularly critical of the distinction between the biotic and cultural levels of human organization. She said that this distinction depended upon a priori assumptions. Thus, it is very important to discover whether or not these assumptions are valid. Among the assumptions she listed were: (1) of a relationship between the organic level and physical structure; (2) of a connection between spatial and economic phenomena; and (3) that the division of labor has a more organic basis than customs and mores. Alihan was also critical of the concept of competition. She concluded that the classicist's theoretical statements are contradictory, and that the biotic and cultural levels are empirically equivalent. Another critic was Gettys (1940), who generally agreed with Alihan's critique of the classical position.

The Sociocultural (Voluntaristic) School

The tide of criticism that was directed at classical thought culminated in a school of sociological ecology that not only discarded the distinction between biotic and cultural levels of human organization, but also placed primary emphasis upon culture and values. This approach is well represented in Firey's (1947) work. Along with other socioculturists, Firey concluded that the theories espoused by the classical (and some neoclassical) sociological ecologists all had a common denominator, called ecological determinism, based on two premises (Firey 1947, p. 30): "(a) Physical space is a self-given phenomenon, and its qualities are wholly independent of cultural values; (b) Social systems are passive adapters to spatial distance and have no further role than one of compliance."

Firey showed, in a study of Boston, that land use is not always governed by principles of economic efficiency. Rather, the use of a particular parcel of land is often determined by the particular values attached to it. Thus, the Boston Common and Beacon Hill occupy sites that could be used profitably by business interests simply because of the value placed upon them by Boston residents.

Firey's study is perhaps best seen as a complementary approach to material determinism. Firey (1947, p. 31) contended that his study provided support for the existence of "a logical alternative to the 'intrinsic' society-space relationship." Both cultural values and economic factors were thought to be relevant to explaining variations in land use. Proponents of this school have not been too active in recent years.

The Neoclassical or Neoorthodox School

Gibbs and Martin, two proponents of the neoorthodox school, rejected values as central to their explanations. But they did this with the understanding that their choice depended upon the problem being studied. They contended that two of the four questions most relevant to human ecology are "what is human ecology to explain" and "what is the universe of inquiry?" Gibbs and Martin considered the examination of organization for sustenance to be the central problem for social ecology. Much of their work was in the tradition of Emile Durkheim, consisting of deductive theories that are concerned with relationships between such things as the division of labor in society and urbanization. Gibbs and Martin (1962, p. 677) wrote, "It will be noted that the non-material aspects of man's culture that do not pertain to technology or sustenance organization whether conceived as values, motives, attitudes, or sentiments have been excluded from the universe of inquiry." Elsewhere, they wrote (Gibbs and Martin 1959, p. 33), "The problem of human ecology, however, is to develop generalizations about sustenance organizations at a level that does not include individual motivations and attitudes."

Duncan and Schnore (1959) presented the ecological complex of population, organization, environment, and technology—given the acronym POET. Their work with the ecological complex constitutes a major part of neoclassical human ecology. The ecological complex seems the best available concept with which to construct an ecological frame of reference for two reasons. First, it constitutes a classificatory scheme that is potentially exhaustive and thus capable of handling a large number of variables on a macroscopic level. Also, three of the four components of the ecological complex (population, organization, and environment) are already defined in the general systems literature and, thus, are conducive to treatment from a systems viewpoint. This is extremely important, for without some concept such as system it is extremely difficult to take a large number of variables into account.

As I noted recently (Bailey 1990a), the efficacy of the POET model is not a matter of debate, since the ecological complex has been evaluated in a number of discussions and applications (including Duncan 1959, 1961, 1964; Schnore 1960-1961; Duncan and Schnore 1959). More recently, Micklin (1984) has analyzed POET from a theoretical standpoint, suggesting that each of the four components can be treated alternatively as independent or dependent variables, although most studies choose organization as the dependent variable of interest.

Elsewhere, Poston, Frisbie, and Micklin (1984, p. 96) lament the tendency of social ecologists to emphasize POET as an analytical entity or "heuristically useful typology" while generally neglecting the ecosystem framework on which it rests. They continue:

> Initially, this misplaced emphasis on format rather than content may have stemmed partially from Duncan's reluctance to assign prematurely *systemic* properties to the interrelationships among the four dimensions of the complex.... It is also probably fair to say that the complexity of the ecosystem concept deterred even those most convinced of its analytic potential (1984, p. 96, emphasis added).

I can quickly bring the analysis of the POET model up to the present time by briefly quoting from my recent article (Bailey 1990c, p. 387):

> Other analysts have commented on the four components. Analysts of the environment include Hawley (1968; 1981; 1986), Michelson (1970), and Berry and Kasarda (1977); population has been discussed by Berry and Kasarda (1977), Poston and White (1978) and Hawley (1986); organization has been analyzed by Berry and Kasarda (1977), Frisbie and Poston (1978), Aldrich (1979), Hawley (1986), Carroll (1987; 1988), Hannan and Freeman (1977; 1988) and Delacroix, Swaminathan, and Solt (1989); technology has been treated by Frisbie and Clarke (1979;1980). But for the most part analysts of POET relate a single variable from one component to the other three components in a recursive model, such as Sly (1972) did by relating migration (P) to organization (O), environment (E), and technology (T).

ASSESSMENT

What can sociological human ecology in the 1990s take from the past? We can approach the ecological structure developed over the past 75 years as an old house to be remodeled. Perhaps some beams were originally of improper material, or were improperly placed, and never functioned properly. Others were adequate in their time, now obsolete. In addition, perhaps materials that were not available then can now be used.

In retrospect, the evidence is overwhelming that the decision to use a systems model is the correct one. The systems model embodied in the ecological complex and the ecosystem concept has again been recently recommended not only by Poston, Frisbie and Micklin (1984, pp. 96-97), but also by Kasarda and Bidwell (1984) who use the system concept extensively.

Advantages

The systems models used previously in sociological ecology have a number of distinct advantages that we can build upon in the best tradition of cumulative science: (1) They are of sufficiently broad scope to deal with complex issues of ecological adaptation. (2) They are explicitly multivariate. (3) They focus explicitly on relationships. (4) They deal with systemic flows of energy, materials, and information.

Limitations

While these four important advantages of systems models in ecology insure that they will continue to be used, past models also displayed a number of visible limitations that should be rectified inasmuch as possible.

First, systems models in sociological ecology, particularly the earliest ones, relied heavily on the notion of equilibrium. Although equilibrium was widely in vogue when Park first used it and was rarely challenged at the time, now it is essentially obsolete and has been challenged extensively (see Bailey 1984; 1990a for extended discussion). Modern systems theory, following Prigogine (1955, 1962) and others (Dyke 1988; Wicken 1987), now routinely uses a nonequilibrium model. Thus, there is good reason to suggest that an ecological model for social systems should also be a model based not on equilibrium, but rather on nonequilibrium thermodynamics (NET).

Second, some past models have been under-bounded, or overly narrow. Such models did not include all relevant variables for the analysis of ecological adaptation. In fact, it appears that even the POET model is too narrow as it omits not only the information flows that Duncan (1964) emphasized in his ecosystems analysis but also the important variable of standard of living or level of living that Ogburn (1951) emphasized in his study, which was a precursor of the POET model.

Third, some past models have not had an adequate measure or operationalization of system state. Thus, there was no way to determine or measure whether the system was operating efficaciously. As long as the model was an equilibrium model, this point was less important. That is, the system was considered to be either in equilibrium, or in the process of returning to equilibrium, and that was really all it was necesary to know abut the system state.

There are a number of critical problems with such an equilibrium model (Bailey 1984). One is frequent conflation of heuristic and empirical models, and another is the discrete nature of equilibrium: The system is either in equilibrium or it is not. This is really *not* the best measure, or even an adequate measure, of system state for an ecological model. We need a model that measures all states of ecological adaptation from zero to maximum. Still another problem is that adequate empirical measures of ecological equilibrium were seldom if ever devised. But the biggest problem of all with equilibrium is that in thermodynamics (where the concept originated), equilibrium does not represent stability but rather the *opposite*—system death or maximum disorder (maximum entropy). Who would want this in an ecological model?

Neoclassical sociological ecologists often used the notion of population *survival* rather than population equilibrium as a criterion for analysis (see Poston, Frisbie, and Micklin 1984, p. 96). While this is an interesting theoretical question, it does not suffice as a measure of system state, as systems operating above mere survival levels require some further measure of system state. In other words, we *assume* that a society is surviving, but still need a measure of system states or ecological adaptation.

Fourth, an effective model should be broad enough to deal with all salient variables at all levels. Some past models were not. Specifically, they did not deal adequately with both biotic and sociocultural variables simultaneously. Our new model should do this. Not only must the biotic level be represented, with the inclusion of such variables as matter/energy and information, but also social and cultural variables.

ENTROPY

The task now is to construct an inclusive systems model of ecological adaptation. This can be done by eschewing reliance on obsolete concepts such as equilibrium, and stressing modern notions from nonequilibrium thermodynamics (NET) and from general systems theory.

The model rests on the First and Second Laws of thermodynamics. They are, first, energy is neither created nor destroyed, and second, entropy increases to a maximum. The Second Law holds for isolated thermodynamic systems in which neither matter, energy, nor information can be transferred across system boundaries. The thermodynamic concept of entropy is defined as inversely related to energy (in the form of heat). If we symbolize entropy by S, the degree of change in entropy dS is inversely related to q/T, where T is the temperature of the system and q is the amount of heat being added to the system.

Entropy can be interpreted as disorder. The Second Law simply implies that an isolated system, since it is receiving no inputs of energy will, *over the long run*, tend to run down and become increasingly disorderly (entropy will increase). The Second Law implies that entropy cannot decrease, but it does not have to increase much either. However, even a tightly sealed system can be expected to lose some energy and thus to increase its internal entropy, becoming increasingly disorderly. Equations written to describe equilibrium conditions for constant nonmaximum levels of entropy are mathematically equivalent to the equilibrium equations for maximum entropy. Thus, we can say that thermodynamic equilibrium occurs when entropy is maximized (Bailey 1984)—an equivalent of heat death for the system, hence disorganization.

The Second Law thus posed a great problem for social scientists and general systems theorists. It postulates that systems run down or become progressively disorderly over time. This is in direct contrast to the abundant empirical evidence that social systems (and living systems in general) are continually growing in complexity. While the Second Law postulates increasing disorder, increasing disorganization, and decreasing complexity, the social world displays an *opposite* trend. Fortunately, the work of Ilya Prigogine and others has solved the dilemma posed by this apparent contradiction.

The keystone of contemporary theory is the school of nonequilibrium thermodynamics, particularly the entropy equation of Prigogine. Central works by Prigogine are his *Introduction to Thermodynamics of Irreversible Processes* (1955) and his culminating and more popularized (but exceedingly valuable) *Order out of Chaos* (Prigogine and Stengers 1984).

Prigogine's work on linear nonequilibrium thermodynamics shows that linear systems can move to a stationary state of minimal entropy production *because* they evolve toward nonequilibrium conditions. (Remember that entropy production is zero, because $dS = 0$ at equilibrium by definition, as entropy has been maximized and, therefore, cannot be increasing or decreasing.) When boundary conditions prevent the system from going to a state of equilibrium, it goes to a state of minimum entropy production. In this stationary state, entropy processes do not change and so become "time invariant" and somewhat independent of the initial conditions of the system from which they evolved. As Prigogine and Stengers (1984, p. 139) say, "Whatever the initial conditions, the system will finally reach the state determined by the imposed boundary conditions. As a result, the reaction of such a system to any change in its boundary conditions is entirely predictable."

But while Prigogine stresses the principle of minimum entropy production, especially in his later work, the achievement that has had the most impact on general systems theory and on sociological systems theory is the Prigogine entropy equation:

$$d_t S = d_i S + d_e S \qquad (1)$$

where

$d_t S =$ total entropy change in the system,

$d_i S =$ change in internal entropy (entropy produced within the system), and

$d_e S =$ change in external entropy (entropy exported from outside the system).

In living and other open systems (including all human social systems), internal entropy buildup ($d_i S$) can be balanced through the importation of energy and information into the system from the environment, ($d_e S$). Some writers call this negative entropy (or negentropy). The tremendous significance of Equation (1) is that it shows how open systems such as social systems apparently violate the Second Law of Thermodynamics, which dictates an increase to maximum entropy (equilibrium) for all isolated systems.

In the case of equilibrium or a stationary state (minimal entropy production) of linear nonequilibrium systems, $dS = 0$. This implies that $d_eS = -d_iS$. In this case, the flow of negative entropy (d_eS) being exported into the system from the environment is *matched* by the internal entropy production (d_iS) so that total entropy is zero. When this occurs, no growth of organization or complexity is possible.

However, in living, open systems such as human groups, negative entropy or negentropy from outside the system *exceeds* the internal production of entropy. Negentropy can take the form of energy such as food and fuel (or information). In such a case, the system can grow in organizational complexity, and become *more* organized rather than less, in apparent violation of the Second Law. The difference is that while internal entropy production (d_iS) is still obeying the Second Law and, therefore, the system is "running down," burning up energy, and becoming less organized and complex, this is being *more than offset* by the energy and information imported from its external environment.

Equation (1) is, in a sense, the foundation for general systems theory. Without it, these theories would be still mired in the apparent contradiction of the Second Law, and would have the same problems with equilibrium as did social scientists such as Pareto, Spencer, and Parsons (see Bailey 1990a). With it, it can be seen that the Second Law holds for isolated systems only, and that the growth in organizational complexity of social systems is also easily explained.

Prigogine's nonequilibrium theory is foundational for most of contemporary social systems analysis. While not eschewing appropriate use of the concept of equilibrium, the theory addresses many instances of nonequilibrium systems behavior, which are the rule rather than the exception in sociological systems. Prigogine's Equation (1) is thus to contemporary social systems theory what Gibbs' prime equation was to nineteenth-century thermodynamics.

Prigogine has thus solved the riddle of society and the Second Law. Social systems *do not* violate the Second Law at all. It is only that, as open systems, they can import matter/energy and information so as to stave off the effects of the Second Law at least partially and temporarily, by staying far from equilibrium. Any system that does not effectively import matter/energy and information will quickly display the effects of the Second Law in the form of increases in internal entropy and increasing disorganization as it approaches equilibrium.

BOLTZMANN'S AND SHANNON'S ENTROPIES

Entropy was also given a statistical interpretation by Boltzmann, who defined it in terms of a probability:

$$S = -K \sum_{i=1}^{n} p_i \log p_i$$

(2)

where

$K =$ Boltzmann's constant, and
$p_i =$ the probability of occurrence of state i out of n possible states.

Subsequently, for nonthermodynamic problems concerning information transmission, Shannon (1949) proposed the H measure:

$$H = - \sum_{i=1}^{n} p_i \log p_i$$

(3)

where

$n =$ the number of categories in the variables, and
$p =$ the probability of occurrence of each category.

The minimum value of H is always zero. The maximum value is always log n, where n is the number of categories in the categorical variable.[1]

Generalizing the Concept of Entropy

To answer the question of whether entropy can be discussed outside of classical thermodynamics, let us set aside these measures for a moment and consider what entropy essentially is. Entropy is a basic system property inversely related to energy. It is, generically, a measure of disorder resulting from the loss of energy and the resulting inability to do work. The reality is that, in an isolated thermodynamic system, the system will run down and become increasingly disorderly over time unless free energy is imported into it or work is done in the system to overcome the tendency to disorder.

Now let us raise the question as to whether thermodynamics has some sort of patent or monopoly over the concept of entropy because the concept was first developed there. Is it even *proper* to discuss entropy in nonthermodynamic settings as an "extension" or "generalization" from thermodynamics? I think not. That procedure is backwards. I think, instead, that the real issue and point to take is that thermodynamic entropy itself cannot be interpreted as monolithic—that it is not the only kind of entropy that exists. Rather, thermodynamic entropy represents simply a *specific case* of the generalized entropy equation. The generalized entropy equation applicable to the real world is that *entropy is inversely related to energy* (however operationalized and wherever studied). The thermodynamic relationship between heat, temperature and entropy (q/T and dS) is only one specific measure of this. This limits entropy to isolated thermodynamic systems. *But entropy does not stop at the borders of the heat-bath system of classical thermodynamics.* Many of the basic system variables of thermodynamics (both extensive and intensive properties), such as volume pressure, and entropy were carefully studied in classical thermodynamical systems. However, this does not imply that these properties are found *only* in those systems. Pressure, volume, and entropy are more general properties, and are associated with energy and matter flows throughout ecosystems. The heat and temperature in a water bath is thus only a very limited and specific case—one of many within the open systems of the biosphere. So, the entropy that thermodynamics deals with is only a small part of the whole of entropy—the part limited to isolated thermodynamic systems.

Interpreting Measures of Entropy

Returning to H, I conclude that it is a good entropy measure and that, further, it is basically identical to Boltzmann's equation for entropy. Wicken (1987, p. 19) says this, discussing both Boltzmann's S and Shannon's H, "Since proportionality constants and logarithm bases are more matters of convenience and scaling than of substance, *the relationships among the variables in the two equations are identical*" (emphasis added).

Finally, we can make some sense of this semantic stew. The reality is that H is such a content-free measure of dispersion that it can measure *any* distribution, even a hypothetical one. Obviously it is not measuring entropy when it is applied to a nonentropic system, such as a set of hypothetical data, but this does not imply it is not an excellent measure when it is correctly applied.

So, on my interpretation H is an entropy measure (and is identical to Boltzmann's measure in its essential elements, as Wicken notes), and entropy is a property not only of isolated thermodynamic systems, but of larger ecosystems as well. It would indeed be strange if the entropy concept stopped at the boundary of the thermodynamic system. However, as Prigogine, Bertalanffy, and others have pointed out, open systems such as social systems handle entropy in different ways than isolated thermodynamic systems and this is, of course, to be expected.

SOCIAL ENTROPY THEORY

Although several controversies exist within entropy theory, the basic generic definition of entropy is clear. Increasing entropy is *always* interpreted as increasing disorder, whether applied to physical problems, to communication (Shannon 1949), or to social phenomena (Bertalanffy 1968; Miller 1978). There is relative consensus in general, that, regardless of the specific application, entropy is disorder.

Social Entropy Theory (SET) uses this basic consensus (Bailey 1990a). It begins with the premise that entropy is disorder and that it exists in various forms within society. How is this so? Another premise in SET, shared by many sociological human ecologists, is that humans are biological beings in a physical world. As such, all of their social actions and interactions (e.g., normative actions, network formations, exchange relations, and so forth) are conducted within a biological and physical context. Another way to view human action is that it rests on a thermodynamic foundation.

Social Entropy and Thermodynamic Entropy

SET deals with forms of entropy that are treated as hierarchically related. First I shall compare these two:

1. *Thermodynamic entropy.* This can be measured by Equation (2), as previously discussed. This includes other physical and biological entropies.
2. *Social entropy.* This is more complex. By social entropy I mean the *disorder* found in social relations. This can be measured by Equation (3).

The nexus between thermodynamic entropy (the foundation) and social entropy is energy. In each case, there is a direct inverse relationship between orderly energy expenditures and disorder. Without energy, disorder will prevail at *both* the thermodynamic and social levels. In both cases, however, energy is necessary but not sufficient. Energy dissipating randomly will not result in order, but in disorder. In both cases, entropy measures a *lack* of fixed structures or fixed energy assignments (Wicken 1987, pp. 25-26). Further, in both cases, entropy can be discussed in terms of macrostate-microstate relations, and is in fact restricted to such instances (Wicken 1987, p. 26).

Social entropy is disorder in social relations. It occurs when actions are not replicated. Replicated actions lead to order. As is shown below, order can be measured in relationships between objects and relationships between attributes, and these forms are related. Social entropy can be measured in both univariate and multivariate forms (see Bailey 1990a). The *difference* between social and thermodynamic entropy is that thermodynamic entropy is a measure of disorder in the physical world, while social entropy is a measure of disorder in human action and interaction. Both range from orderly (low entropy) to disorderly (high entropy). Both can be measured in probabilistic terms (respectively, by Shannon's H for social entropy and Boltzmann's S for thermodynamic entropy). Both are different in that the number of social interactions is different from the number of molecular actions or heat transfers.

Both are similar in that there *is* some number of social interactions, just as there is some number of heat transfers.

The relationship between social entropy and thermodynamic entropy can also be elucidated by examining the hierarchical relationship between thermodynamic equilibrium and various forms of physical equilibrium, including rotational equilibrium, stable equilibrium, and static equilibrium (see Bailey 1990a). *All of the latter are dependent upon thermodynamic equilibrium as a foundation and if it does not exist, they cannot either.* Similarly, the other forms of physical entropy, and also social entropy, all depend upon thermodynamic entropy. If thermodynamic entropy is high, then social entropy will be high. Conversely, a state of low social entropy (order) requires a foundation of low thermodynamic entropy (energy). Energy is the connection.

It is widely accepted (see Bertalanffy 1968; Buckley 1967; Miller 1978) that Prigogine's analysis of entropy in open systems applies to social systems, most all of which are open. Open systems, and therefore social systems, are dissipative structures in the energetic sense. Social entropy theory, accordingly, must accomodate all entropy processes that behave in social systems. These include thermodynamic entropy, other physical entropy, biological entropy, and social entropy. *Thermodynamic entropy*, strictly speaking, is about the dynamics of heat systems, such as hot-water baths. *Physical entropy* is about the dissipation of physical systems, such as the deterioration over time of tools and built environments. *Biological entropy* is about the deterioration of biological systems (such as death of the organism). *Social entropy* is about the deterioration of social structures, such as sustained patterns of social interaction (e.g., in voluntaristic associations). All of these forms of organization deteriorate if energy is lacking. Information is also important for the maintenance of some, especially for biological and social structures (see Miller 1978). But generically, entropy can be seen as dissipation, disintegration, or disorder that increases when energy is lacking or is not utilized properly. This is true for all forms of entropy, including the thermodynamic, physical, biological, and social.

Thus, it is misleading to view social entropy or biological entropy as an extension or analogue of thermodynamic entropy. It is not a question of extending a *concept*. The reality is that the tendency to dissipate (become more disorderly) exists *empirically and simultaneously* in structures in the physical, biological, and social worlds. Viewed so, there is nothing to extend and no way to conceive of social or biological entropy as an "analogue" of thermodynamic entropy. To do so is to pose a false problem. The issue is, rather, the relationship between measures of entropy (such as Boltzmann's and Shannon's). This is quite another matter, that has already been discussed. But while one measure may be an extension or analogue of another, the empirical action of entropy does not hinge upon the nature of its measurement. These are two separate issues.

Although it is false and misleading to say that social entropy is an extension of thermodynamic entropy or is derived from it (since they coexist simultaneously), we certainly can affirm that thermodynamic entropy is the foundation for the other forms and without it the other forms would not exist. Social and biological entropy depend upon thermodynamic entropy and rest on its foundation because low biological and social entropy are impossible in the face of high thermodynamic entropy. This fact goes back, of course, to the Second Law. Our point is that the functioning of human society encompasses all basic forms of entropy processes.

Entropy and Society

The interface between social entropy and biological and physical (including thermodynamic) entropy makes it possible to approach sociological human ecology through social entropy theory (SET). Humans, operating in open social systems, usually function so as to obstruct increases in entropy. If we fail to maintain a low entropy level, we and our societies cannot survive. So we routinely and mundanely perform activities designed to maintain low entropy, as when we heat our homes (thermodynamic or physical entropy), feed ourselves (biological entropy), and sustain our orderly social organizations and interactions (social entropy) by means of norms, rules, regulations, traditions, and customs. This orderly social interaction rests on a foundation of energy and information without which low social entropy is impossible.

However, though all forms of entropy rest on the thermodynamic, there is a sense in which social entropy is a foundation for the others. The sense is that human agents assume the responsibility of maintaining low entropy states that exist in the world. The Second Law insures that physical processes alone *will not* maintain these low entropy levels. So their maintenance (whether of thermodynamic, other physical, biological or social entropy) depends on social entropy. There is a basic circularity (a symmetrical relationship) between social entropy and physical entropy—something like a symbiotic relationship.

For example, bougainvillaea grows in Sweden in the winter, inside homes. This could not occur without human protection, as the water in the tender plants would freeze (lose heat), leading to an increase in thermodynamic entropy, and thus causing an increase in biological entropy to the point that the entire plant would perish. Without *organized* and *orderly* (low entropy) human action within societies, there could be no human life in cold climates (and certainly no bougainvillaea). Human climatic adaptations are possible only by the design and control of thermodynamic systems (heated houses) maintained by the humans.[2] Organized human society (low social entropy) produces heated houses (low thermodynamic entropy) that enable human life in cold climates (low biological entropy), which furthers the maintenance of organized human society (low social entropy). It is a circular process, and it continues indefinitely.

We may interpret ordinary social interaction in entropic terms because we may interpret it in statistical terms. Moreover, the connection with energy is direct: Humans use energy (and information) to perform their actions and conduct their interactions. When a replicated pattern of action is forthcoming, then *order* appears in a statistical system. For example, if only men receive high-paying jobs and only women receive low-paying jobs, then the correlation between sex and salary is 1.0. In this case we can *always* predict income (high or low) correctly when we know gender, and entropy is zero. What does entropy have to do with this? Simply that the energetically based, nonrandomly distributed interaction being measured is *orderly*. We know that high entropy is disorder. Here we have order rather than disorder, and so we interpret this as low social entropy. This entropy value of zero *can only result* from replicated human action that, in turn, can only result from the expenditure of energy. If there is no energy, then there is no human action, and no way to overcome entropy. In the total absence of replicated action, we would have only random and disorderly action (or maximum entropy). But, in fact, the opposite holds.

When humans do act randomly or nonorderly, the statistical pattern that they generate is one of maximum social entropy. This would be the "natural" or most probable statistical case, and would occur if there were no norms, laws, values, or cultural or social factors in general to guide human behavior. Since humans within society do have such guidance in various forms, they behave in distinctly nonrandom (although not totally nonrandom) patterns. When they engage in such replicated (orderly) action, they can be seen as engaging in social entropy—minimizing behavior, in the sense that the resulting statistical patterns that they generate are below maximum social entropy. Most social entropy values are intermediate between the minimum and the maximum. The results of these lower-entropy actions show up in statistical correlations that can be measured by Shannon's H. This is a true and legitimate measure of social entropy. The structures involved are *not* fixed or ordered structures. Rather, the number of alternatives is very large.

Note that the relationship between thermodynamic entropy and social entropy is not direct. Thermodynamic entropy is not the *cause* of social entropy, it is the foundation for it. Without energy sources, societies cannot engage in entropy-minimizing behavior. Energy (and information) provide the foundation for replicated (orderly) action that leads to patterns of low entropy. These entropy patterns can be adequately measured by Shannon's H (or by a modification of Boltzmann's S, because social entropic processes can alter thermodynamic entropic processes.

Human society is composed of biological beings operating in a physical world. They operate in such a way as to generate replicated social and cultural patterns (norms, values, and so forth). They process matter-energy and information in their day-to-day interactions (see Duncan's [1964] discussion of matter, energy, and information flows in the ecosystem). As such, they are processing matter and energy whose entropic process obeys the Second Law *when confined to isolated systems*. Nonisolated and open, social systems do not have the same relation to the Second Law, although the total configuration of open system plus environment does directly obey the Second Law (see Bertalanffy 1968).

A MODEL OF SOCIAL ENTROPY THEORY

I will now sketch a model of social entropy theory (SET) to be interpreted for ecological adaptation. A preliminary point concerns the relationship between equilibrium theory in general, as applied in classical ecology, and entropy (nonequilibrium) theory. SET simply wishes to study entropy in society *whatever* its form or "level" might be. If entropy remains relatively constant over time at a relatively low level, one may choose to call this a form of "equilibrium" (but not thermodynamic equilibrium), and I have no quarrel with this. SET accommodates the study of equilibrium very well but does not *require* the study of equilibrium, as did classical sociological human ecology and other equilibrium models. This is a crucial distinction. It is one thing to say that a condition of equilibrium may exist, and quite another thing to say that it *must* exist. The latter claim is dubious in social science; the former, much less so.

Another preliminary consideration is the metatheoretical world view of, and some terminology adopted by, Social Entropy Theory. SET considers society in its entirety (sui generis) as the basic unit. Society is not viewed as a set of individuals but as a concrete system, or organized population of individuals, interacting over physical space-time, within boundaries. This conception generates a set of supraindividual or *macrovariables*—social facts in Emile Durkheim's terms. They are *global variables* in Lazarsfeld's (1958) terms, meaning that they cannot be defined in terms of individual properties but only as units of a society. In the model to be presented below, social facts are macroscopic properties of the society treated as the system. In addition to global macrovariables, SET also distinguishes mutable distributions, and mutable and immutable variables.

THE PISTOL MODEL

I start with the premise that society is composed of a *population* that adapts ecologically to its environment, with particular adaptations conditioned by the *spatial area* in which the population resides. Adaptations require the expenditure of energy (the processing of matter/energy), and they are facilitated when the population's *organization* is such as to utilize *technology* and *information* to maximize the society's *level of living*. These are the elements of the model I call PISTOL.

They are appropriate variables to model a concrete system using SET. The semi-orderly ecological activity that results from their interaction exhibits a level of social entropy that is below the maximum, but above the minimum. The actual entropy level obviously varies empirically from society to society, and from time to time within a society.

Interpreting PISTOL Macroscopically

The first of the global macrovariables is evident from the above definition of a concrete system. I said that such a system operates in space-time. Thus, spatial area (S) within boundaries is one key macrovariable. Another, of course, is the population (P) of humans required to constitute the system. I said further that these humans must process matter/energy and information in order to maintain entropy levels below the maximum. If this is not accomplished, the society could not survive. While "matter/energy" could be listed as a global variable, I consider it to be included within the boundaries of the spatial area, and thus already included as part of (S). If not included as indigenous "natural resources," the needed matter/energy must be imported. Thus, space (S) in the model includes all area (land, water, air) within the boundaries and comprises what is often called the "environment." This environment contains matter/energy as raw materials (oil, coal, and so forth), including food.

However, available matter-energy cannot be properly processed without technology, which I define simply as organized tool development and use. These tools are not limited to primary extraction of matter/energy (as in mining or farming) but can also be used for secondary or tertiary manufacturing or distribution and, of course, technology is also used for processing information as well as matter/energy.

Thus, population (P), space (S), and technology (T) are all major macrostructural components of the system. The fourth major global macrovariable (already mentioned) is information level (I). For simplification, information may be operationally defined as any perception, conception, or knowledge that the society utilizes to make decisions. This definition is obviously very broad (and stated differently than in Bailey 1990a) and includes technical knowledge (physics, chemistry, medicine, and so forth), but also statements of fact of all sorts, as well as ideology, beliefs, values, norms, prejudices. Any cognitive content that guides societal functions may be included in this broad definition of information, including myths and erroneous information.

In addition to population, space, information, and technology, what other global variables are necessary for a society to operate? Obviously, all these other things have to be coordinated. A wealth of resources and a large spatial area are insufficient to maintain a population, particularly a large one, unless they can be properly organized. Thus, organization (O) is a crucial variable.

The last global variable is level of living (L). This can vary from zero (the society disappears) to some designated maximum. There are many ways to measure level of living, or standard of living, or quality of life. The most common socioeconomic measure is income or wealth. However measured, this is a crucial variable, and is a minimum (zero) when physical entropy is maximized.

Together, these six factors define PISTOL, the complete set of global macrovariables. A number of points about these six global macrovariables— I shall now call them globals—must be emphasized. By definition, as globals they cannot be defined in terms of characteristics of individuals. They are unitary macroproperties, and are not formed by aggregating or analyzing properties of individuals. There is one partial exception to this in the set. It is population (P), which elsewhere (Bailey 1990a) has been referred to as a "semiglobal." This is because (P) requires knowledge only of whether a person exists or not, but requires no other information. Thus, while (P) may be a "semiglobal" and not pure, it is still essentially global. The other five factors are full globals and require no information about (P) or about individuals in the system for their definition.

As global macrovariables, these are not distributions, "relational variables," or sociometric or network variables. Rather, they are sum totals of the amount of the entity in each case. They are ratio variables, with a minimum of zero and a maximum to be empirically determined, depending upon the particular application. For example, (P) is the sum total of all individuals (e.g., one million persons), (S) is the sum total of all spatial area (e.g., one million acres), (O) is the sum total of all occupation positions (e.g., one million jobs), (T) is the sum total of all tools, from spoons to lasers, (L) is the sum total of all optimal operational units measuring level of living (calories, dollars, and so forth), and (I) is the sum total of all information units (bits, books, and so forth).

The model is so general as to apply to all societies in the world regardless of level of development. Thus, all societies have some levels of each of the elements of PISTOL, although obviously appropriate empirical indicators for each will be much different for a small undeveloped society than for a large industrial society.

These six globals are all interrelated properties of the society taken as the basic unit of analysis. Although (L) may be sometimes conceived as a "dependent" variable and the others as independent, in fact, in systems terms, all are interdependently interrelated. We can express that condition with the following:

$$P = f(I,S,T,O,L) \tag{4}$$

$$I = f(P,S,T,O,L) \tag{5}$$

$$S = f(P,I,T,O,L) \tag{6}$$

$$T = f(P,I,S,O,L) \tag{7}$$

$$O = f(P,I,S,T,L) \tag{8}$$

$$L = f(P,I,S,T,O). \tag{9}$$

Thus, all six globals can alternatively be treated as "dependent variables" (in five of the equations) and as an "independent variable" in one equation. For example, while level of living (L) is certainly dependent upon a proper population size (P), spatial area (S), information level (I), technology (T), and organization (O), it in turn is necessary for the others. That is, population size (P) *cannot* be increased if the level of living is insufficient, for example, if (L) is at the subsistence level and there is simply no food for additional people. Similarly, technology (T) cannot be expanded if the level of living (L) is so low that resources for research or the purchase of technology are simply precluded.

The global macrovariables can also be interpreted in terms of process. Our discussion so far has interpreted all six as interrelated synchronic variables. So interpreted, they provide a structure for the social system. However, they can be analyzed diachronically, in terms of process, as well: Human agents, by design or not, change the levels of all six. For example, population-policy makers assess (P), politicians seek to maximize (L) and (I), and so forth. However, since the six are interrelated, the level of each imposes process constraints upon the others, thereby affecting the levels of the others. (This is one reason social planning cannot be done piecemeal, but ideally should take all six variables into account simultaneously.)

If viewed superficially, the PISTOL formulation may appear to be somewhat similar to the POET model (Duncan and Schnore 1959). However, holistically it is quite different, as it includes level of living and information—both crucial, but missing in POET. Also keep in mind that as systems theorists we are not analyzing six individual variables piecemeal, but are studying the *relationships* among the six. Thus, while the POET model has only six relationships (*PO, PE, ET, OE, TO, PT*), the PISTOL model has 15—all crucial to the model. We will consider further comparisons with the POET model shortly.

Interpreting PISTOL Microscopically

I have said that the six globals are sums of units. As such, they form six dimensions along which individuals can be distributed. Each individual, at a given point in time, occupies a position not only as a member of the population (P) but also in the information structure (I), spatial area (S), technology (T), organization (O), and level of living (L). One of the most crucial questions in SET is the issue of how individuals are allocated into this multidimensional structure. Allocation cannot be random, or there would be no social order and no predictability. In that case multidimensional entropy (H) would be maximum. It is a postulate of SET that the entropy level is always below the maximum. It has to be, because there are orderly processes by which individuals are allocated—processes regulated by norms of various types, from federal or international laws, to local regulations, to folkways, mores, customs, and precedents.

The six global macrovariables obviously serve as constraints for any individual. An individual's life style, life chances, and life choices are very different in a small, poor, technologically underdeveloped society than in a large, bureaucratic society with the latest technology from computers to lasers. Within a given society, the life chances of an individual vary with the relations between the structural globals. For example, if (P) is less than (O), there are fewer people than organizational positions, and vacant jobs exist. But if (P) is greater than (O), there are more people than jobs and competition for available positions may be fierce.

Within the context formed by global structure, the individual nevertheless has personal characteristics, which we may conceive as variables, that also greatly affect his or her life chances. Many of these personal characteristics are *immutables*, meaning that they cannot be changed. They are microscopic properties, with the individual taken as the unit of analysis. Among notable immutable microscopic properties are race, ethnicity, sex, and age (birth date).

One of the chief ways that individuals are selected for allocation into different dimensions of the structure and process of PISTOL is through their immutable variables. Characteristics such as race, age, and sex are ideal for use by the powerholders who make societal decisions regarding allocation. Such immutables are immediately visible and cannot be changed. Thus, decisions to allocate can be made quickly, without extensive prior research, and require only perusal of the person's salient immutables. After the decision is made, power is not threatened by any alteration of the characteristics, for the individual cannot do that. If an individual is dissatisfied with his or her allocation (say, a particular job), he or she has little recourse through changing immutables. For instance, a woman stuck in a "woman's job" cannot change her sex. She must either work for "social change" in the form of change in the norms, change of designation of the job as "women's work," or change in her position on some other variable such as residence.

Matters of the allocation and reallocation of individuals to various levels raise a question: How can the interaction of the macroscopic properties of a society and the microscopic properties of individuals be accomodated within the PISTOL model?

There is a third class of variables in PISTOL besides the globals and immutables—the *mutables*. Globals, we said, are purely macroscopic. They are defined only for societies and do not require information about individual characteristics such as race or sex (the special case of population has been discussed). Immutables, on the other hand, are purely microscopic, and are definable only for individuals (societies do not have race or gender). Mutables are intermediate. They have both macro and micro qualities and so in the PISTOL model provide a true micro-macro link.

Mutable variables take the form of distributions. There are five basic mutable distributions in PISTOL, and they are formed by allocating or distributing the population of individuals (P), a semi-global, into the other five globals. That is, each individual has a value for (L), (S), (I), (T), and (O). Since each individual in the system has a set of mutable characteristics, the system as a whole therefore possesses a *mutable distribution*. This distribution is a macroscopic property of the society, but it is not a global. It cannot be defined without information on the characteristics of individuals. Rather, it is an analytical property in Lazarsfeld's (1958) terms, as it is formed from aggregating individual mutable properties, such as occupation, into a distribution. While mutable microscopic characteristics are each a property of an individual (e.g., his or her occupation), the mutable macroscopic distribution is a property of the society (e.g., the occupational division of labor). A distribution such as an occupational division of labor cannot be defined for an individual (by definition), but it can be defined for subsystems of the society such as an organization or group.

Thus, there are three main types of variables in PISTOL: globals, which are macrovariables only; immutables, which are microvariables only; and, mutables, which take the dual form of both *macro* mutable distributions and *micro* mutable individual properties. Since mutables have dual micro-macro properties, they serve as the link to connect the microscopic and the macroscopic.

IMPLICATIONS FOR HUMAN ECOLOGY

Social entropy theory is based on certain principles from nonequilibrium thermodynamics (NET), as well as other sociological and ecological principles. It will be worthwhile to discuss the relationship of SET to entropy theory, including (NET), and to relate SET to classical human ecological theory.

SET and NET

SET is a nonequilibrium model. Equilibrium and nonequilibrium models both focus on order. However, equilibrium models assume that order is a given and will continue unless disturbed. Further, they assume that if order is disturbed, it will reappear. This is evident in classical human ecological theory in sociology (e.g., Park 1936) and in other forms of functionalist theory in the social sciences (Parsons and Shils 1979).

In contrast, nonequilibrium theory makes no such assumption about order. It does not assume that order necessarily is at a high and constant level of "equilibrium" but, rather, that the magnitude of order varies and is always potentially changeable. Further, nonequilibrium theory that is based on thermodynamic principles (NET) assumes that order obeys the Second Law and will erode over time unless forces are activated to reverse this tendency.

SET shares this latter view. The PISTOL model of SET assumes that some degree of order can exist in relationships among the three major sets of variables. However, this order is not established in a tendency to "equilibrium," but order is fragile and will disappear unless maintained. In entropy language, its order consists of low entropy levels and its disorder of high entropy levels. According to SET, the maintenance of orderly, low entropy levels is necessary for societal functioning. However, this is contrary to the Second Law. Necessary levels of order are maintained through human action and interaction, chiefly goal-oriented behavior governed by norms the effect of which is to limit entropy increase.

The key to this process is energy (see Miller 1978), which maintains certain levels of order. Thus, energy maintains certain intercorrelated levels of the global macrovariables—population, information, spatial area, technology, organization, and level of living. Energy is also used to allocate individuals into mutable distributions—their level of living, organization, technology, information, and space. Societies operate upon a foundation of thermodynamic entropy processes. They must first control thermodynamic entropy (heat) and assure proper physical energy levels. Then they must supply organic energy (food) for the human soma, in order to stave off an increase in biological entropy. These foundational entropy processes—thermodynamic (and other physical) and biological—are the foundation for social entropy. Given the foundations, human actors work to establish social order (low entropy levels). Thus, social order *is not automatic* but is achieved only through concerted human action resting on the foundation of thermodynamic and biological entropy. The human action works through the three levels—global, mutable, and immutable, described earlier. (For further discussion, see Bailey 1990a.)

SET and POET

Probably the most visible ecological feature of the PISTOL model of SET is the addition of two variables to the classic POET model. Both models affirm that populations (*P*) organize (*O*) to effectively utilize technology (*T*) in the course of their adaptations. These three variables are identical in each model.

Population has been treated at length (see Duncan and Schnore 1959; Micklin and Choldin 1984; and Bailey 1990a). It is definitional in macroecology that a population is adapting to a spatial environment and, thus, population will virtually always be central to any ecological model. So will the other two common components, organization and technology, always be central, and they also have been widely discussed (see Duncan and Schnore 1959; Bailey 1968, 1990a, 1990b; Micklin and Choldin 1984).

There is a fourth component that overlaps but is labeled differently in the PISTOL and POET models, and thus deserves discussion. In PISTOL, it is spatial areas (S); in POET, it is environment (E). In my opinion, these are essentially the same, whether labeled S or E, and I treat them as virtually identical in the two models. Further, in systems theory, environment refers to all factors outside of (external to) the system boundary that impact the system or are impacted by it. Thus, if the system were the United States of America, in *systems terms* the environment would be the area *outside* of the United States of America's boundaries, rather than the area within the boundaries as the term "environment" is usually used.

To eliminate confusion engendered by terminological differences between systems theory and ecological theory, I use the term spatial area rather than environment for PISTOL, but I mean the same thing as environment. In system's terms, (S) is a variable of the concrete ecological system, while all factors outside the system that impinge upon it are still labeled the environment. The two uses of the term environment should not be confused. Spatial area includes all land, resources, vegetation, air space, water space, and so forth, within the system boundaries (see Bailey 1990a for extended discussion). This usage is consistent with how Hawley uses environment (see Poston, Frisbee, and Micklin 1984; Hawley 1986).

The remaining two components of PISTOL—(I) and (L)—were entirely missing in POET. Since I have argued elsewhere (Bailey 1990a) that the six PISTOL variables constitute the *minimum* satisfactory sociological model of macroecological adaptation, the question arises as to why information (I) and level of living (L) were excluded from POET. It was probably more or less an oversight, since both of these components were recognized in ecological theory prior to the conceptualization of POET. Information was widely recognized as an important variable by such diverse authors as Parsons (Parsons and Shils 1979) and Duncan (1964). The exclusion of level of living (L) from POET is a little harder to explain since POET was based rather explicitly on prior work by Ogburn (1951), and is also evident in the work of Park (1936).

Social entropy theory (Bailey 1990a) implies that all six PISTOL components are essential in a model of macroecological adaptation. They all are symmetrically interrelated, and emphasis is placed not only on the variables, but also on their relationships, as advocated by Poston, Frisbee, and Micklin

(1984). Each in turn can be considered a dependent variable, and all six are alternatively independent variables for each of the other five.

While it seems clear that POET is too narrow, the question remains as to whether even PISTOL is sufficiently inclusive. As it is, it can be summarized thus: A *population* (*P*) *organizes* (*O*) so as to effectively utilize *information* (*I*) and *technology* (*T*) in adapting to its *spatial* environment (*S*) in such a way as to optimize its *level of living* (*L*). But, should energy specifically be added to the model, considering the important role energy plays in ecosystems as a companion to information (see Miller 1978; Duncan 1964)? Should we expand PISTOL to something like PISTOLE, with energy as the seventh component? For now, I find this unnecessary. Energy and information have a different role in ecological adaptation, with energy being more fundamental. If information is lacking, ecological action is still possible, although it may well be random and highly entropic (and may lower rather than raise the level of living). But without energy, no change in *any* of the other six components is possible. There can be no change in population size, technology, organization, spatial boundaries, information generation, or level of living without expenditures of energy. Indeed, there can be no change in anything at all.

Because energy is crucial to limiting increases in entropy, energy is interpreted in SET to be a necessity for change in all ecological components. Energy is assumed to be gotten from the spatial areas controlled by the given ecological system (primarily the area within system boundaries), or else imported from outside. To the degree that societies can effectively secure and utilize energy, social entropy can be decreased. However, if desired, the role of energy could be explicitly introduced into the model as a seventh component.

Thus, one contribution of SET is to expand POET to PISTOL (or PISTOLE). A second contribution is the explicit inclusion of social and cultural variables in the ecological model. Neoclassical and sociocultural approaches to human ecology (see Theodorson 1982) acknowledge the need for the explicit inclusion of cultural variables in ecological models. The SET approach includes them.

A third contribution of SET is the explicit focus on micro-macro linkages in the form of the global-mutable-immutable distinctions. This has been generally lacking in past human ecological models developed for social systems, and is an important topic in contemporary sociological theory (see Ritzer 1990).

A fourth contribution of SET is its explicit utilization of the systems approach, which is explained in much greater detail in Bailey (1990a). The systems approach is useful for ecology for a number of reasons. For one, the notion of an ecosystem is strongly ingrained in ecology, and the systems approach has been used almost throughout the history of ecology. For another, the systems framework adds rigor and facilitates operationalization. For yet another, the systems approach links ecology with related approaches such as general systems theory (Buckley 1967; Bertalanffy 1968) and ecologically oriented systems approaches, such as those of Miller (1978) and Odum (1983).

The fifth contribution of SET to human ecology is its emphasis on ecological entropy. The inverse relationship between energy and entropy in SET is clear, and is consistent with thermodynamics. Since ecosystems include thermodynamic variables, it behooves human ecology to continue to study the relationships between energy and entropy, and the ways in which these relationships affect ecological adaptation.

In a real sense, social entropy theory is not detracting from the accomplishments of classical sociological ecology, but is merely augmenting them. The two variables added to POET to get PISTOL provide additional theoretical power. Similarly, the entropy approach used in SET retains the possibility for classical equilibrium analysis, while also providing for nonequilibrium analysis. Much more work needs to be done in this area. I hope that others will join me in developing the richness of entropy theory as applied to human ecological problems.

NOTES

1. Shannon's H and Boltzmann's entropy equation are the same, except for Boltzmann's constant (K). There is some confusion regarding the interpretation of each measure and of the relationship between them. Let us first consider H alone. There is a plethora of symbols to contend with, leading to symbolic confusion. The measure has been symbolized not only by H, but also by E (for entropy), S (the thermodynamic symbol for entropy), and U (for uncertainty). In addition to the symbolic confusion, there is confusion over exactly what H measures, and how to interpret it. Some writers say that H measures information (Miller 1978), while others say it measures entropy (Shannon and Weaver 1949), and still others call it a measure of uncertainty (Horan 1975).

It is misleading to interpret H as an information measure, as maximum H is complete randomization. Such a state of chaos is *not* maximum information. This mater is discussed at length elsewhere (Bailey 1990b). While H varies inversely to information, it is also not a measure of thermodynamic entropy, or a concept generalized from thermodynamics (see Dyke 1991; Wicken 1987; Campbell 1982). However, H clearly is a measure of uncertainty and also of disorder. Maximum H is maximum disorder (randomization) while minimum H is minimum disorder (complete predictability that all cases are in a single category).

2. Classical analysis of thermodynamic systems assumes an isolated system. We are generalizing the notion of a thermodynamic system to include empirical systems involving heat exchanges. Not all of these are isolated systems, but all of them exhibit classical irreversible properties of heat exchange.

REFERENCES

Aldrich, H.E. 1979. *Organizations and Environments*. Englewood Cliffs, NJ: Prentice-Hall.
Alihan, M.A. 1938. *Social Ecology*. New York: Columbia University Press.
Bailey, K.D. 1968. "Human Ecology: A General Systems Approach." Unpublished Ph.D. dissertation, University of Texas, Austin.

_____. 1984. "Equilibrium, Entropy and Homeostasis: A Multidisciplinary Legacy." *Systems Research* 1: 25-43.

_____. 1990a. *Social Entropy Theory*. Albany: State University of New York Press.

_____. 1990b. "Why H Does Not Measure Information: The Role of the 'Special Case' Legerdemain Solution in the Maintenance of Anomalies in Normal Science." *Quality and Quantity* 24: 159-171.

_____. 1990c. "From POET to PISTOL: Reflections on the Ecological Complex." *Sociological Inquiry* 60: 386-394.

Berry, B.J.L. 1964. "Cities as Systems Within Systems of Cities." P. 34 in *Papers and Proceedings of the Regional Science Association*.

Berry, B.J.L., and J.D. Kasarda. 1977. *Contemporary Urban Ecology*. New York: Macmillan.

Bertalanffy, L. von, 1968. *General System Theory*. New York: G. Braziller.

Brooks, D.R. and E.O. Wiley 1988. *Evolution as Entropy*. 2nd ed. Chicago: University of Chicago Press.

Buckley, W. 1967. *Sociology and Modern Systems Theory*. Englewood Cliffs, NJ: Prentice-Hall.

Burgess, E.W. 1925. "The Growth of the City." Pp.47-62 in *The City*, edited by R. E. Park, E. W. Burgess, and R. D. McKenzie. Chicago: University of Chicago Press.

Campbell, J. 1982. *Grammatical Man: Information, Entropy, Language, and Life*. New York: Simon & Schuster.

Carroll, G.R. 1987. *Publish and Perish: The Organizational Ecology of Newspaper Industries* (Monographs in Organizational Behavior and Industrial Relations, Vol. 8). Greenwich, CT: JAI Press.

_____, ed. 1988. *Ecological Models of Organizations*. Cambridge, MA: Ballinger.

Davie, M.R. 1938. "The Pattern of Urban Growth." In *Studies in the Science of Society*, edited by G.P. Murdock. New Haven, CT: Yale University Press.

Delacroix, J., A. Swaminathan, and M.E. Solt, 1989. "Density Dependence Versus Population Dynamics: An Ecological Study of Failings in the California Wine Industry." *American Sociological Review* 54: 245-262.

Duncan, O.D. 1959. "Human Ecology and Population Studies." Pp. 678-716 in *The Study of Population*, edited by P.M. Hauser and O.D. Duncan. Chicago: University of Chicago Press.

_____. 1961. "From Social System to Ecosystem." *Sociological Inquiry* 31: 140-149.

_____. 1964. "Social Organization and the Ecosystem." Pp. 37-82 *Handbook of Modern Sociology*, edited by R.E.L. Faris. Chicago: Rand-McNally.

Duncan, O.D., and L.F. Schnore. 1959. "Cultural, Behavioral, and Ecological Perspectives in the Study of Social Organization." *American Journal of Sociology* 5: 132-146.

Dyke, C. 1988. *The Evolutionary Dynamics of Complex Systems: A Study in Biosocial Complexity*. New York: Oxford University Press.

_____. 1992. "From Entropy to Economy: A Thorny Path." Pp. 149-176 in *Advances in Human Ecology*, Vol. 1, edited by L. Freese. Greenwich, CT: JAI Press.

Firey, W.I. 1947. *Land Use in Central Boston*. Cambridge, MA: Harvard University Press.

Frisbie, W.P., and C.L. Clarke. 1979. "Technology in Evolutionary and Ecological Perspectives: Theory and Measurement at the Societal Level." *Social Forces* 58: 591-613.

_____. 1980. "Further Notes on the Conceptualization of Technology." *Social Forces* 59: 529-534.

Frisbie, W.P., and D.L. Poston, Jr. 1978. "Sustenance Differentiation and Population Redistribution." *Social Forces* 58: 591-613.

Gettys, W.E. 1940. "Human Ecology and Social Theory." *Social Forces* (May 18): 469-476.

Gibbs, J.P., and W.T. Martin. 1959. "Toward a Theoretical System of Human Ecology." *Pacific Sociological Review* 2: 33.

————. 1962. "Urbanization, Technology and the Division of Labor: International Patterns."
    American Sociological Review 27: 667-677.
Hannan, M.T., and J. Freeman. 1977. "The Population Ecology of Organizations." *American
    Journal of Sociology* 82: 929-964.
————. 1988. "Density Dependence in the Growth of Organizational Population." Pp. 7-31
    in *Ecological Models of Organizations*, edited by G.R. Carroll. Cambridge, MA: Ballinger.
Hawley, A.H. 1968. "Human Ecology." Pp. 328-337 *International Encyclopedia of the Social
    Sciences*, Vol. 4, edited by D.L Sills. New York: Macmillan.
————. 1981. *Urban Society: An Ecological Approach*. Rev. ed. New York: Ronald.
————. 1986. *Human Ecology: A Theoretical Essay*. Chicago: University of Chicago Press.
Horan, P.M. 1975. "Information-Theoretic Measures and the Analysis of Social Structures."
    Sociological Methods and Research 3: 321-340.
Kasarda, J.D. and C.E. Bidwell. 1984. "A Human Ecological Theory of Organizational
    Structuring." In *Sociological Human Ecology: Contemporary Issues and Applications*,
    edited by M. Micklin and H. M. Choldin. Boulder, CO: Westview Press.
Lazarsfeld, P.F. 1958. "Evidence and Inference in Social Research." *Daedalus* 87: 99-130.
Michelson, W.H. 1970. *Man and His Urban Environment*. Reading, MA: Addison-Wesley.
Micklin, M. 1984. "The Ecological Perspective in the Social Sciences: A Comparative Overview."
    Pp. 51-90 in *Sociological Human Ecology: Contemporary Issues and Applications*, edited
    by M. Micklin and H. M. Choldin. Boulder, CO: Westview Press.
Micklin, M., and H.M. Choldin, eds. 1984. *Sociological Human Ecology: Contemporary Issues
    and Applications*. Boulder, CO: Westview Press.
Miller, J.G. 1978. *Living Systems*. New York: McGraw-Hill.
Odum, H. 1983. *Systems Ecology*. New York: Wiley.
Ogburn, W.F. 1951. "The Ecological Perspective in the Social Sciences: An Overview." *American
    Journal of Sociology* 56: 314-319.
Park, R.E. 1936. "Human Ecology." *American Journal of Sociology* 17: 1-15.
Parsons, T., and E.A. Shils, eds. 1979. *Toward a General Theory of Action*. New York: Harper
    & Row.
Poston, D.L., Jr., W.P. Frisbie, and M. Micklin. 1984. "Sociological Human Ecology: Theoretical
    and Conceptual Perspectives." Pp. 91-123 in *Sociological Human Ecology: Contemporary
    Issues and Applications*, edited by M. Micklin and H. M. Choldin. Boulder, CO: Westview
    Press.
Poston, D.L., Jr., and R. White. 1978. "Indigenous Labor Supply, Sustenance Organization, and
    Population Redistribution in Nonmetropolitan America: An Extension of the Ecological
    Theory of Migration." *Demography* 15: 637-641.
Prigogine, I. 1955. *Introduction to Thermodynamics of Irreversible Processes*. Springfield, IL:
    C. C. Thomas.
————. 1962. *Non-equilibrium Statistical Mechanics*. New York: Interscience Publishers.
Prigogine, I., and I. Stengers. 1984. *Order Out of Chaos*. New York: Bantam Books.
Ritzer, G. 1990. *Frontiers of Social Theory: The New Syntheses*. New York: Columbia Univeristy
    Press.
Russett, C. 1966. The Concept of Equilibrium in American Social Thought. New Haven, CT:
    Yale University Press.
Schnore, L.F. 1960-1961. "Social Problems in the Underdeveloped Areas: An Ecological View."
    Social Problems 8: 182-201.
Shannon, C.E., and W. Weaver. 1949. *The Mathematical Theory of Communication*. Urbana,
    IL: University of Illinois Press.
Sly, D.F. 1972. "Migration and the Ecological Complex." *American Sociological Review* 37: 615-
    628.

Theodorson, G.A., ed. 1882. *Urban Patterns: Studies in Human Ecology* Rev. ed. University Park, PA: Pennsylvania State University Press.

Weber, B.H., D.J. Depew, and J.D. Smith, eds. 1988. *Entropy, Information, and Evolution.* Cambridge, MA: MIT Press.

Weiner, A.M., and H. Hoyt. 1939. *Principles of Urban Real Estate.* New York: The Ronald Press.

Wicken, J.S. 1987. *Evolution, Thermodynamics, and Information.* New York: Oxford University Press.

SUSTAINABLE REGIONAL DEVELOPMENT:
A PATH FOR THE GREENHOUSE MARATHON

Carlo C. Jaeger

ABSTRACT

Since 1973, total carbon dioxide emissions from economically advanced countries have not increased. This partial decoupling of economic from physical growth is based, among other things, on a new dynamic of sociotechnical innovation, focused no more on increases in physical productivity but on improvements in product quality. By using this dynamic, economically advanced countries can first reduce and then stabilize greenhouse emissions per capita. Under these conditions, developing countries can first increase and then stabilize greenhouse emissions per capita without ever reaching the exorbitant levels of today's advanced regions. Eventually, economic growth may be decoupled from physical growth in the whole world economy. Also, people may then discover that they can enjoy further improvements in product qualities without economic growth. The overall transition we are discussing would last for several generations. A major requirement for such a transition is a successful evolution of social rules in which various social agents, including business firms, learn to solve problems

Advances in Human Ecology, Volume 2, pages 163-190.
Copyright © 1993 by JAI Press Inc.
All rights of reproduction in any form reserved.
ISBN: 1-55938-558-8

in a cooperative mode. Currently such forms of rule evolution are taking place in different highly innovative economic regions. These regions offer important opportunities for policies aiming at solving the greenhouse problem.

INTRODUCTION

The total amount of greenhouse gases contained in the atmosphere fluctuates in the course of time. As long as the order of magnitude of anthropogenic emissions of such gases is smaller than the one of natural fluctuations in atmospheric greenhouse gas levels, anthropogenic emissions present no problem at a global scale. In particular, carbon dioxide by itself is not a pollutant, but simply one of the many chemical substances involved in the metabolism of the biosphere.

However, it is beyond doubt that at very low or very high levels of carbon dioxide in the atmosphere, the earth would cease to sustain the life of plants and animals. Even without considering these limit cases, massive fluctuations of carbon dioxide contained in the atmosphere could create tremendous adjustment problems for the global civilization of our times. In particular, rapidly increasing carbon dioxide levels would lead to serious consequences. Climatic change would foster extreme events like hurricanes and droughts. Persistent global warming would lead to increased sea levels, thereby inundating many coastal regions of the world. Agricultural regions could become deserts while it might be difficult to achieve fast increases of agricultural production elsewhere. Large-scale migrations, military conflicts and severe cultural crisis should be expected. Beyond some critical level, carbon dioxide becomes a very dangerous pollutant, indeed. The greenhouse problem consists in a situation where humankind risks to cross this critical level. Vellinga and Swart (1991) compare the task of solving this problem to a marathon race stretching over several decades. The metaphor is quite appropriate as it stresses the perseverance and stamina that will be required to tackle the problem.

A few generations ago, humankind began to increase the carbon dioxide content of the atmosphere to a significant degree by burning fossil fuels. This process lies at the very core of humankind's present life form: The energy provided by fossil fuels is used to keep buildings at the temperatures required for human well-being, to transport people and all kinds of things in the amazing system of spatial mobility without which contemporary human life would be impossible, to produce food and clothes, cars and computers, dwellings and freeways, as well as to provide services ranging from education to health care and entertainment. Humankind has learnt to control energy flows which are much larger than the ones involved in the metabolism of human organisms, and it has developed a planetary civilization relying on such energy flows.

Today, fossil fuels are the single most important source of energy tapped by human beings.

In the early 1970s, the first oil crisis was seen by many as evidence that the world economy was reaching ecological limits to growth. The zero-growth advocates, however, were heavily criticized, among other things for neglecting the situation of developing countries which desperately need economic growth. The tension between this need for growth and global environmental problems became the subject of lively international debates at the United Nations conference on "Human Environment" in 1972 in Stockholm. An important contribution to tackle this tension was made by human ecologists elaborating the notion of ecodevelopment (Glaeser 1984). The notion of sustainability was introduced in the debates about environment and development by the publication of the "World Conservation Strategy" (IUCN, UNEP, and WWF 1980).[1] By the end of the 1980s the theme of limits to growth had given way to themes of global change (Buttel, Hawkins, and Power 1990) and sustainable development (WCED 1987).

However, the notion of sustainable development remains highly ambiguous. To some, it means the possibility of reconciling economic growth and environmental protection forever, to others it is a will-o'-the-wisp making people believe that environmental problems can be solved without challenging existing distributions of power and wealth. In the present paper, we will try to clarify the notion of sustainable development with regard to the greenhouse problem by using Max Weber's method of ideal types.[2]

Ideal types are often considered as synonymous to scientific abstractions. They are then seen to include frictionless motion, ideal gases, as well as perfect competition. To Weber, however, ideal types meant a specific method appropriate for the moral sciences only. In a nutshell, with this concept he tried to organize the search for historical possibilities which are morally relevant for some human community. An ideal type relates historical facts and moral norms in such a way as to enable the researcher to understand major causal links in human history. In this sense, researchers interested in ancient Greece may try to elaborate an ideal type of democracy as well as one of tyranny. In the present paper, our interest in the human dimensions of the greenhouse problem will lead us to discuss four ideal types which we will designate as quantitative growth, qualitative growth, sustainable development and economic bliss.

In order to elaborate these ideal types, the next section sketchs a minimal notation for the analysis of problems lying at the interface between economics and ecology. The following section analyzes quantitative growth by clarifying the distinction between economic and physical growth. This distinction enables us, in the next section, to identify an ideal type of qualitative growth based on continuous innovations in product quality. Then, the ideal type of sustainable development is presented as a form of social transition that is limited in time and relies on qualitative growth taking place simultaneously in advanced world regions. If the transition of sustainable development was succesfully completed economic growth could actually give way to the ideal type of economic bliss discussed in the penultimate section. These, however, are matters for the remote future. For the present, a more urgent question is how to bring about the forms of cooperation required to combine sustainable growth and sustainable development. The final section argues that this might best happen in the context of regional developments both in advanced and in developing world regions.

A FRESH LOOK AT ECO-ECO PROBLEMS

The greenhouse problem is a major example of an eco-eco problem, that is, a problem situated at the interface between economy and ecology (Folke and Kåberger 1991). Such problems can be analyzed by trying to include ecological phenomena into the highly elaborated theoretical apparatus provided by the discipline of economics. This is the strategy usually followed by environmental economists (e.g., illustrated by Archibugi and Nijkamp 1989). Conversely, economic phenomena can be included in the framework of ecological analysis, especially in conjunction with systems theory. This is the way of thinking which has led to the well-known debate about limits to growth. Both approaches have their merits and will no doubt stimulate much further research. However, the challenge presented by today's eco-eco problems is so formidable that there is also a need for a line of research that does not try to study these problems as special cases within an already established theoretical scheme but takes them as starting points for the development of a new conceptual network.

This option, which corresponds well to the spirit of human ecology (Young 1983), provides the perspective adopted in this paper. In this perspective, we first need a minimal notation for the description of interlocked human activities taking place in a physical setting. This notation should, as far as possible, be compatible with the conceptual schemes used by economists and ecologists dealing with eco-eco problems. A notation fulfilling this requirement has been proposed by Haegerstrand (1970) in a seminal paper on so-called time-geography and has been elaborated in the context of human ecology by Carlstein (1982). The basic idea behind this approach is to trace the spatial trajectories which human beings and human artifacts follow in the course of time. In many cases, this can be done by means of two-dimensional diagrams, with vertical lines indicating that an entity keeps its place and diagonal lines indicating spatial movements. Horizontal lines are impossible because movement takes time.

Figure 1 gives an example for a business firm. The firm is situated in buildings equipped with machinery, and its site remains unchanged during the period

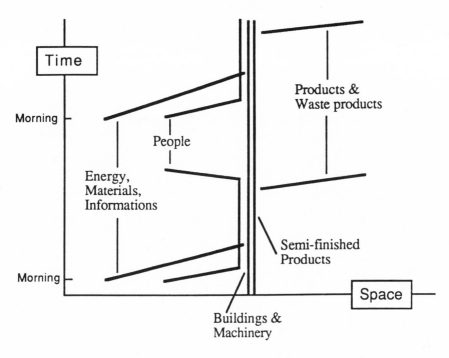

Figure 1.   A Business Firm

under consideration. People enter the plant in the morning and leave it in the evening. Moreover, energy, materials, and information are fed into the plant on a regular basis. These inputs are continuously transformed into the plant's stock of semi-finished products and then into its final output, which includes products as well as waste products.

A highly significant aspect of patterns like the one displayed in Figure 1 is the fact that they are often reproduced again and again, thereby providing pathways for routinized action. If this is the case, we call such a pattern a human ecological structure. Such structures are not static entities but relatively stable features of highly dynamic processes which can reproduce themselves in a recursive fashion. This recursive character of social practices is a major theme of recent social theory, illustrated by the work of Giddens (1984), who also draws on the notation of time-geography.

Economic life involves plenty of human ecological structures as defined above. In particular, any technique for the production of industrial products, like cars, computers and so forth, usually implies a whole set of such structures. However, as Luhmann (1986) emphasizes in his analysis of ecological communication, contemporary economic institutions draw a crucial distinction between two different components of human ecological structures. By their reliance on rules of business accounting, these institutions make visible all those events which directly affect the profitability of business firms. This is the case with events that modify the monetary value of a firm's assets and liabilities, including modifying the firm's stock of semi-finished goods by producing new ones. But from the point of view of the economic system, other aspects of human ecological structures, in particular their embeddedness in a biophysical environment which is not reckoned as part of the firm's assets, are hidden.

The difference between visible and hidden aspects of a human ecological structure can be expressed with a simple algebraic notation if we consider such a structure during a fixed time span. Given the recursiveness of these structures, we can choose this time span so that the situation at its beginning is equal to the one obtaining at its end. In the case of Figure 1, this can be done by considering the period from one morning to the next. For the chosen time span we can list all the inputs of the structure as a vector $\mathbf{d}$ and the outputs as a vector $\mathbf{b}$. The structure can then be represented by a mapping from the input vector into the output vector.

The economically visible part of the structure is then a submapping that maps the economically visible inputs $\mathbf{d}_v$ into the economically visible outputs $\mathbf{b}_v$. We will treat the input of human labor separately and designate it with a vector for human activities, $\mathbf{a}_v$. Each element of this vector indicates the amount of time which people with the same kind of vocational skills have contributed to the process under consideration.

Such a mapping can be defined not only for single human ecological structures but also for sets of such structures, including the world economy as a whole. If the (row) vectors for the different structures are written one below the other, we get an input and an output matrix, $\mathbf{D}_v$ and $\mathbf{B}_v$, together with a human activity matrix, $\mathbf{A}_v$. However, in an aggregated system like the world economy, single structures can be combined in very different proportions and older structures can be replaced by newer ones. The three matrices are time dependent and therefore we mark them with a time index t:

$$\mathbf{D}_{v,t},\ \mathbf{A}_{v,t} => \mathbf{B}_{v,t} \qquad (1)$$

The sums of the columns of the three matrices form an input vector, $\mathbf{d}_{v,t}$, a human activity vector, $\mathbf{a}_{v,t}$, and an output vector, $\mathbf{b}_{v,t}$. An important advantage of this notation is its affinity to the notation of input-output analysis which is well established in economics. In the latter framework the ecological relevance of the distinction between visible and hidden processes has been analyzed by Perrings (1987).

The economically visible output for a given period consists of all the goods and services which business firms have sold during that period plus the goods which they own at its end. These goods and services include capital equipment which is not yet written off, and they also include rights to use land and other natural resources for the period considered as well as land and other natural resources themselves, as far as they are owned or sold by business firms.

The economically visible output excludes natural resources which are owned by private households or by public authorities as well as those for which no specific property rights are defined. Clearly, for many purposes it is essential to consider the economically invisible outputs, too. But in order to analyze the interface between economy and ecology, it is extremely important to be aware of the distinction between what is economically visible and what is not. This distinction does not depend on how some statistical office estimates GNP and similar measures of economic performance. It depends on the rules of accounting applied by business firms in their operations.

For our subsequent discussion, we next need to consider briefly a simple accounting relation which necessarily holds for the world economy as a whole. If we multiply the output vector for a given time span with the average prices ruling in this time span, we obtain the value of total output. If we multiply the input vector (which includes fixed capital) with the same prices, we obtain total input costs. In the actual world economy, output value exceeds input costs. The difference feeds total wages, total profits, and total taxes. If we divide total profits by the value of total capital, K_t, we obtain the rate of profits, σ_t; if we divide total taxes by the value of the net product, Y_t, we obtain the share of taxes in value added, τ_t. Total wages are the product of the human activity vector, $\mathbf{a}_{v,t}$, with the vector of wage rates for different kinds of labor, $\boldsymbol{\omega}_t$. We can then write:

$$\mathbf{b}_{v,t}\mathbf{p}_t = \mathbf{d}_{v,t}\mathbf{p}_t + \mathbf{a}_{v,t}\,\boldsymbol{\omega}_t + K_t\sigma_t + Y_t\tau_t \tag{2}$$

The rate of profits is crucial for the analysis of eco-eco problems because it serves as a guideline for management decisions in a market economy. In such an economy, the decision about which human ecological structures are reproduced and which ones are displaced by new ones is taken at the level of individual firms, in particular, in the form of decisions about gross and net investment. The multitude of management decisions results in the dynamic process in which the input and output matrices are modified in the course of time. This modification can be described by a decision matrix, $\mathbf{M}_t$, which maps the block matrix consisting of the input and output matrices of one period in a similar, but usually different block matrix for the next period:[3]

$$[\mathbf{D}_{v,t+1};\ \mathbf{B}_{v,t+1}] = [\mathbf{D}_{v,t};\ \mathbf{B}_{v,t}]\mathbf{M}_t \tag{3}$$

UNDERSTANDING QUANTITATIVE GROWTH

Equation (3) describes the dynamics of the economic system. It should be noted that the rank of $\mathbf{D}_{v,t}$ and $\mathbf{B}_{v,t}$ can change as new products are invented and old ones are displaced. For our present purposes, the most important property of the decision matrices that have characterized the world economy so far is the fact they have led to positive economic growth. More precisely, under conditions of positive profits, usually a positive fraction of these profits is used for net investment and thereby leading to economic growth. Therefore, the positive profits which have prevailed in the history of the world economy have consistently led to a positive rate of economic growth, $g_{e,t}$, that is, the rate of growth of net output valued at constant prices:[4]

$$g_{e,t} = (\mathbf{b}_{v,t+1} - \mathbf{d}_{v,t+1})\mathbf{p}_t \, / \, (\mathbf{b}_{v,t} - \mathbf{d}_{v,t})\mathbf{p}_t - 1 \qquad (4)$$

This rate of growth as such does not yet tell us much about the ecological implications of economic growth. In order to analyze these implications, we must be able at least to some degree to describe the relation between the economically visible part of human ecological structures and their hidden part. For this purpose, we need some measure of environmental impact for the various components of economic output. In the case of the greenhouse problem, such measures can be estimated, for example, in the form of greenhouse gas emissions coefficients, which indicate how much greenhouse gas emissions (expressed as carbon dioxide-equivalents) are generated by the production and consumption of one unit of various goods. If and only if a vector $\mathbf{i}_t$ of such impact factors can be at least roughly estimated, an environmentally meaningful rate of physical growth, $g_{p,t}$, can be defined for the economic system:

$$g_{p,t} = (\mathbf{b}_{v,t+1} - \mathbf{d}_{v,t+1})\mathbf{i}_t) \, / \, (\mathbf{b}_{v,t} - \mathbf{d}_{v,t})\mathbf{i}_t - 1 \qquad (5)$$

In the case of the greenhouse problem, we know that there is a positive impact vector of greenhouse gas emission coefficients, even if its components can be estimated only very roughly. It is important to notice that the impact coefficient associated with a gallon of gasoline indicates not only the carbon dioxide emitted when the gasoline is actually burned down. The impact coefficient also includes the greenhouse gas emissions (CO_2 and other) associated with the refinery where the gasoline was produced and with the transportation of the gasoline to the point of sale. Also, we must include the emissions associated with the processes of building the refinery, the gas station, and so forth.

In the actual world economy, fossil fuels are basic goods in the sense that they are used at least indirectly for the production of every good and service. Therefore, the greenhouse impact vector is strictly positive because even goods that do not contain a single molecule of carbon cannot be produced without using fossil fuels. For decades the average physical growth rate associated with this vector according to Equation (5) has been strictly positive.

To say that quantitative growth is not sustainable basically means that there is a limit G which the world economy's greenhouse impact should not exceed for a given period.[5] Actually, that limit may decrease as past greenhouse emissions persist in the atmosphere, but for our purposes it is sufficient to consider G as an upper bound for all time-dependent limits which may be additionally specified. It is then obvious that if the average rate of physical growth defined by the greenhouse impact vector is positive without converging to zero, there always is a period t^* after which greenhouse emissions exceed the limit G by an increasing margin. Sustainability with regard to the greenhouse problem, however, would be defined as the state of affairs described by the formula in Equation (6):

$$(\mathbf{b}_{v,t} - \mathbf{d}_{v,t})\mathbf{i}_t \leq G, \text{ for all } t \tag{6}$$

In the case of the greenhouse problem, the claim that a quantitative limit of sustainability exists relies on properties of the climate system. However, this does not mean that such a limit could not be crossed—quite the opposite. The claim is that the limit should not be crossed for economic, political, and moral reasons, although it is actually possible to do so. The present paper does not evaluate the evidence for and against such a claim. Rather we acknowledge that it cannot be easily dismissed and try to investigate some of its consequences.

In particular, we ask how the rate of physical growth defined by the greenhouse impact vector can become negative or at least zero under conditions of a market economy and without waiting for technological miracles. The answer depends mainly on the decision matrix representing the outcome of management decisions taken at the level of business firms. These decisions are oriented by social rules, the simplest of which requires managers and entrepreneurs to avoid their firms going bankrupt. In the past decades, management decisions also followed the rule to increase physical production while keeping the amount of raw materials and capital goods needed per unit of product more or less constant. While the former rule is a necessary element of the institutional setting of a market economy, the latter is much more contingent and may be specific for a limited phase in the evolution of market economies.

In this view, a solution to the greenhouse problem could depend on the future evolution of the rules which orient management decisions within a market economy. These rules can be thought of as the cultural dimension of economic reality, which complements the structural dimension considered above. Recently, different authors have proposed conceptions of cultural evolution which may help to understand the evolutionary dynamics of social rules (e.g., Boyd and Richerson 1985). However, until now these models have not been applied to current possibilities of economic change. I will therefore not try to insert the analysis of such possibilities in the framework of a theory of rule evolution, although the last section returns to this theme. The next sections are limited to considering some ecological implications of different rules which can orient economic decisions in the setting of a market economy.

QUALITATIVE GROWTH

In the period from 1950 to 1973, carbon dioxide emissions[6] from economically advanced (i.e., highly industrialized) countries increased steadily at an annual rate of more than 4%. As we will discuss in the next section, emissions continue to grow in developing countries. It is a remarkable fact, however, that after 1973, emissions from advanced countries have not increased for at least two decades. An important reason for this new situation is the fact that the average rates of economic growth in advanced countries have been substantially lower since 1973 than they were in the postwar period. Our present purposes do not require a detailed analysis of the processes which led to the end of the "golden age" of economic growth (e.g., for such analyses see Marglin and Schor 1988; Jaeger and Weber 1988); it is enough to recognize the shift to lower growth rates as an important reason for the stabilization of carbon emissions from advanced countries. A second reason is the structural change toward an increasing share of services in total output. Service provision requires fossil fuels, too, but in general less so than the production of manufacturing goods.

Finally, the various measures by which OPEC since 1973 limited oil production are a third, very important reason. As a result of production limitations, oil became more costly and, thereby, carbon saving innovations were fostered.[7] These innovations include changes in automobile technology leading to increased energy efficiency of cars, changes in manufacturing technology leading to decreased energy requirements for heat generation in industrial production processes, and changes in construction technology which lower the energy used for the heating of buildings. The dynamics of these innovations are closely related to the development of new materials and to the emergence of new information technologies.

Fuel price increases due to production limitations should not be confused with a possible substitution effect. If fuel prices rise, we may expect private households to reduce fossil fuel consumption, for example, by reducing car trips in the evening and amusing themselves with video tapes instead. Similarly, within the range of known technologies, firms may find it profitable to shift toward technologies that use less fossil fuels but that were not profitable at lower fuel prices because they use greater amounts of some other inputs. Such substitution effects modify the overall pattern of demand and the quantities of goods produced so as to induce a shift from goods requiring large amounts of fossil fuel toward goods requiring smaller amounts. Substitution effects do not expand the range of known technologies, they just lead to a different choice among the technologies available for the satisfaction of given preferences.

Although some such substitution effects probably have taken place as a consequence of rising oil prices, they are by no means as widespread as might be expected and surely are far less important than the innovation processes which have led to a partial decoupling between economic growth and use of energy in general (Kuemmel 1989) and use of fossil fuels in particular.[8] The relevant innovations include the development of technologies whose intended effect is a reduction in energy requirements per unit of production but also many innovations where such a reduction is an unintended effect. The latter case is especially relevant in service industries where in many cases—for example, software development or with psychotherapy—the economic value of a product can be increased from period to period while the flows of energy and materials involved remain more or less unchanged.

In such cases, the new products rely on fossil fuels no less but also no more than the old ones. Waste production as well as input flows of energy and materials are more or less constant while the increase in product quality is due to improved information inputs. The greenhouse impact vector can then be constant and in terms of this impact vector[9] no physical growth occurs:

$$(\mathbf{b}_{v,t+1} - \mathbf{d}_{v,t+1})\mathbf{i}_{t+1} = (\mathbf{b}_{v,t} - \mathbf{d}_{v,t})\mathbf{i}_t \tag{7}$$

In the absence of physical growth, product innovation can be successful only if it leads to higher quality for the new products. On the other hand, if this is the case, these products may well be more expensive than the older ones. Under such conditions, even with constant or decreasing total greenhouse gas emissions economic growth can be generated:

$$(\mathbf{b}_{v,t+1} - \mathbf{d}_{v,t+1})\mathbf{p}_t > (\mathbf{b}_{v,t} - \mathbf{d}_{v,t})\mathbf{p}_t \tag{8}$$

Clearly, if there was only one output good this situation could not obtain. If Equation (7) holds for a single output good with a positive greenhouse emission coefficient, it follows immediately that physical output does not change from one period to the next and therefore Equation (8) cannot be true. This case has been taken for granted in many discussions about ecological limits to economic growth. But in reality the world economy produces a myriad of different goods and services and product innovation is continuously modifying the composition of this multidimensional output.

The conditions under which positive economic growth can go on without generating positive physical growth as measured by the greenhouse impact vector can be stated by considering the difference between the net output in period t and period $t + 1$. This difference consists of a semipositive vector, $\mathbf{b}_{g,t}$, of goods and services which is added to the former output and of another semipositive vector, $\mathbf{b}_{z,t}$, which is subtracted from that output. It then follows that the formulas in Equations (7) and (8) hold if:

$$\mathbf{b}_{g,t}\mathbf{p}_t > \mathbf{b}_{z,t}\mathbf{p}_t \quad \text{and} \quad \mathbf{b}_{g,t}\mathbf{i}_t = \mathbf{b}_{z,t}\mathbf{i}_t \tag{9}$$

The remarkable fact about this condition is that the greenhouse impact coefficients do not need to diminish in the course of time in order to achieve sustainable economic growth. It is sufficient if technical innovations lead to improved product quality with nonincreasing impact coefficients. This process may be described as an ideal type of qualitative growth.

According to this analysis, a highly innovative world economy could continue to grow indefinitely without increasing carbon dioxide emissions, even if fossil fuels should not be replaced by other energy sources. The basic mechanism of the ideal type of qualitative growth would be the introduction of new goods of better quality than older ones but with similar greenhouse emissions per physical unit. If the higher quality of new goods results in higher prices per physical unit the effect would be to lower greenhouse emissions per monetary unit of output while keeping them constant per physical units.

Qualitative growth requires a different kind of technological progress than the one which was dominant in the golden age of economic growth after World War II. Fortunately, this new kind of technological progress is already operating quite successfully in economically advanced countries. Therefore, technological dynamics and structural change presently offer serious opportunities for a pattern of economic growth with stabilized greenhouse emissions from advanced countries.

Until now we have considered the possibility of a non-increasing impact vector without exploring the possibility of actual decreases. But if carbon emissions from advanced countries can be stabilized, it is crucial to consider the level at which this might happen in the long run. Presently, annual carbon emissions per capita range from 5 metric tons in the United States to 3 tons in Germany, to 2 tons in Japan. These differences indicate that there is a considerable potential for reducing emissions from advanced countries.

With suitable incentives, such reductions could be achieved in two complementary ways. First, business firms could develop technological innovations in order to reduce greenhouse emissions. Second, consumer demand could shift toward goods that generate relatively little greenhouse emissions. These two processes are no doubt essential in order to realize a reduction of emissions. Without the basic mechanism of qualitative growth—improving product quality while keeping emissions constant—they would, however, sooner or later be offset by the effects of persistent economic growth.

Reducing greenhouse emission coefficients to zero will hardly be possible in the setting of highly industrialized countries. But in fact, there is no reason to try to reach such an unrealistic goal. Carbon dioxide and most other greenhouse gases are not pollutants per se. They become a threatening problem only if their production grows indefinitely. Stabilizing greenhouse emissions at a relatively low level seems quite compatible with economic growth in advanced countries, if such growth is characterized by ongoing product innovations rather than by continuous increases in physical output. Until some day in the future when this low emission level will actually have been reached by all advanced countries, substantial decreases in greenhouse emissions can still be achieved by these countries as a group.

SUSTAINABLE DEVELOPMENT

Economic growth was defined in Equation (4) as the ratio between today's economically visible net output and yesterday's visible net output, both valued at constant prices. Equation (5) defined physical growth by multiplying physical vectors not with the price vector but with the greenhouse-impact vector. Without such an impact vector, the notion of physical growth would make little sense, at least in the context of the greenhouse problem. The same impact vector is used in Equation (6) to define the notion of sustainability in terms of a given limit for total emissions of greenhouse gases per period. The next step is to introduce the notion of development in the context of our analysis.

Let us therefore distinguish between an advanced and a developing part of the world economy, with labor productivity being much larger in the former than in the latter. For our present purposes, we can then define development as the process by which this difference disappears after some period t^* as a result of faster economic growth in developing countries than in advanced ones.

According to this definition, economic growth is a necessary, but not a sufficient, condition for development. Successful development means that developing economies actually grow faster than advanced ones. This requires labor productivity to be dramatically improved in developing countries. Such improvements cannot be achieved without profound social and cultural changes in which the technical knowledge, the vocational skills, and probably even the meaning of personal identity which for generations has evolved in the context of today's advanced economies, are shared with developing economies.

This implies a huge cultural transfer process in which highly complex systems of rules and beliefs are made accessible to developing economies. An important vehicle for this process is the export of capital goods from advanced to developing economies. For investors from advanced countries, the prospect of higher economic growth in developing countries would no doubt provide a strong incentive in favor of this kind of capital flow. Capital accumulation in developing economies then would not depend only on net investment by these economies, but also on foreign investment from advanced economies.

However, for the purpose of successful development an inflow of foreign finance is useful only to the extent to which it helps to organize an inflow of capital goods that become vehicles of "international learning" (Pasinetti 1988). This proviso is crucial because the difficulties of developing economies are not caused simply by lack of capital but rather by a situation of low and only slowly increasing labor productivity, owing to complex social and cultural reasons.

If actual development requires that both economic growth and capital accumulation proceed faster in developing than in advanced economies, it is very likely that greenhouse emissions from developing countries will increase. As a matter of fact, although carbon dioxide emissions from advanced countries have been more or less constant since 1973, emissions are still increasing in the rest of the world. This is quite understandable in view of the fact that emissions per capita are at least ten times smaller in China and Brazil than in the United States.[10]

In 1991, humankind produced annual carbon emissions at a level of nearly 1 metric ton per capita with a total population tending toward 6 billion people. The average level for developing countries lies well below this level while, as we have seen, the U.S. level is about 5 tons per capita. It is perfectly clear that developing countries will strive to emulate the standard of living of the richest countries on planet earth and that this is a highly legitimate effort. But there seems to be a very reasonable answer to the problems of global environmental change, which are inevitable if the contemporary life-form of the richest countries spreads over the whole planet: These countries should develop a sustainable life-form, a life-form that can actually be generalized to the whole planet.

As we have seen, in Japan annual carbon emissions per head amount to less than half the U.S. level, namely, to 2 metric tons per capita. If the richest countries of the world undertake a substantial effort to reduce their carbon emissions, they have a fair chance of attaining the level of 1 metric ton per capita, which is the present world average. Setting this level as a goal for the whole world would slow down the increase in world emissions to the speed of world population growth. This would still increase carbon emissions in the coming decades by a factor between two and four, but not by the factor between ten and twenty which would result from a generalization of present U.S. levels. We therefore may specify the ideal type of qualitative growth introduced in the preceding section by stating that total carbon emissions from industrialized countries should be reduced to a level of less than 1 metric ton per capita.

However, the ideal type of qualitative growth does not fit the situation of developing countries. These countries, to which the majority of humankind belongs, urgently need a physical increase of their capital equipment. This immediately rules out our model of qualitative growth. Moreover, developing countries need to achieve growth rates above the average rate of the world economy as a whole. Both goals will no doubt require an increase in per capita emissions from developing countries. Therefore, development can hardly fulfill the condition of qualitative growth which we have described in Equation (9). In each period, the greenhouse impact of additional output must be expected to be considerably greater than the greenhouse impact of whatever output is not produced any longer as a result of ongoing development.

This means that successful development will require at least some physical growth in terms of greenhouse impact. Obviously, we could not label as sustainable a kind of development that would try to emulate present emission levels of advanced countries. But even if developing countries would aim from the outset at the reduced emission levels that advanced countries will hopefully achieve within several decades, in most developing countries this would still imply an increase of greenhouse emissions above current levels. If development is to be sustainable, then the positive rate of physical growth in developing economies must be offset by negative rates of physical growth in advanced economies.

As we have seen in the preceding section, at least for a limited time-span this seems compatible with positive economic growth in advanced countries. However, a moment will come when advanced economies may still be able to experience economic growth with stable greenhouse emissions, but not to reduce their greenhouse emissions any further. A process of sustainable development, then, requires that by this time developing economies will have caught up with the advanced ones, so that physical growth will no longer be required in either part of the world economy.

In the context of the greenhouse problem, sustainable development must then fulfill two conditions: The physical growth of developing countries must be compensated by reducing emissions in advanced countries, and development must be successfully completed before the potential for such reductions is exhausted. If by development we mean that developing countries achieve levels of labor productivity similar to advanced countries, then sustainable development is not a process of infinite duration. Rather, it is a process that *in a finite time span* achieves a specific social goal in a way that is compatible with specific ecological conditions.

In the greenhouse marathon, sustainable development does not mark the goal, but marks an essential part of the distance to cover. Also, qualitative growth in the industrialized countries is essential precisely to support the process of sustainable development. This support consists, on the one hand, of reducing greenhouse emissions in advanced countries so that a moderate increase from developing countries can be tolerated, and on the other hand in providing foreign investment so as to foster international learning in developing countries. However, as discussed in the next section, once the task of sustainable development has been completed, a very different kind of socioeconomic dynamics become feasible.

AN ECONOMIC "STATE OF BLISS"

The ideal type of qualitative growth elaborated two sections back can easily be generalized beyond the case of greenhouse emissions. In theory, impact vectors and limits like the ones used in Equation (6) could be defined for all kinds of pollution and depletion problems. However, in most cases specific limits could be subsumed under a limit for energy use. All human activities involve energy transformations and these can be described by an energy impact vector. If the total amount of energy so transformed could be limited at a sufficiently low level, most disruptive effects of humankind on the biosphere would gradually disappear. It could therefore be argued that, ultimately, the efforts toward sustainable development should lead to a situation of endless economic growth under the condition of limited energy use.

Obviously we are talking about a rather distant future, because stabilizing worldwide energy use will hardly be possible for several decades. But even then there is an important reason to consider ongoing economic growth only as a transitory pattern: In a situation characterized by innovations leading to improved product quality but without physical growth, people will sooner or later realize that they can enjoy exactly the same quality improvements without economic growth. In order to analyze this possibility we next specify the accounting relation in Equation (2) for all the firms that together constitute the world economy. For this purpose, we consider an input matrix, $D_{v,t}$, a human activity matrix, $A_{v,t}$, and an output matrix, $B_{v,t}$, with each row corresponding to a single firm. If we write ω_t for the vector of wage rates for different kinds of labor, s_t for the vector of profits made in different firms,[11] and t_t for the taxes paid by these firms we can rewrite Equation (2) as follows:

$$B_{v,t}p_t = D_{v,t}p_t + A_{v,t}\,\omega_t + s_t + t_t \qquad (10)$$

This is a system of inhomogeneous linear equations, and if it describes an actual state of the world economy it has a positive solution for the price vector:

$$p_t = (B_{v,t} - D_{v,t})^{-1}(A_{v,t}\,\omega_t + s_t + t_t) \qquad (11)$$

Equation (11) is a linear system that maps the positive vector for value added, $(A_{v,t}\,\omega_t + s_t + t_t)$, into a positive price vector. The derivative of the magnitude of p_t, the price level, with respect to the magnitude of ω_t, the general wage level, is a positive constant. Therefore, if profits, taxes, and available technologies are fixed, wage increases will lead to inflation. However, even with a given array of possible technologies, the increase in prices could be offset by lowering profits and taxes. Relative prices would then change somewhat, but the price level would be constant and the purchasing power at the disposal of wage earners would increase.[12]

However, because Equation (11) is a linear system, the derivative of any specific price with respect to wages, profits, and taxes is always a constant. Therefore, for any given set of possible technologies there is a finite upper bound for the range of wage increases whose inflationary effect can be offset by reducing both taxes and profits to zero. If we write π_t for the price vector resulting from that situation and w_t for the vector of wages paid in different firms (i.e., for $A_{v,t}\ \omega_t$) we obtain:

$$\pi_t = (B_{v,t} - D_{v,t})^{-1}\ w_t \qquad (12)$$

Suppose now that for some product a successful product innovation leads to improved quality without changing the amounts of inputs required for production or the pattern of wage costs. In the situation described by Equation (10), the new product could have a bigger or smaller price than the old one depending on changes in profits and taxes. But in the situation described by Equation (12), the new product would have the same price as the old one. The difference in quality with equal price would then lead to rapid displacement of the old product by the improved version.

In physical terms, this is the same process that we discussed in the context of qualitative growth. But now not only the rate of physical growth but also the rate of economic growth is zero. Obviously, it might be wondered whether an economy with zero profits would be viable at all. To clarify this point, we need a minimal understanding of the role of profits in a market economy.

In the course of time, the rate of profits of a given firm varies considerably, and may well turn negative in difficult years. Clearly, avoiding persistent losses is vital if the firm is to stay in business. But avoiding losses is not enough in today's economy. In a given business, there is usually some positive rate of profits that is considered the normal rate. Empirically, rates of profits are distributed according to a probability distribution akin to the one depicted in Figure 2, with r^* as the normal rate. A firm that regularly fails to meet this rate will encounter great difficulties in trying to withstand its competitors.

Normal rates of profits enter the rules that orient decisions by managers and entrepreneurs. These rules cannot be described adequately as aiming at maximizing profits in a generic sense. Rather, investment decisions will be oriented by the rule that a project must not be realized if it is expected to yield less than the normal rate of profits.[13] The amazing efficiency and flexibility of a market economy depends on the use of profitability as a basic criterion for investment decisions, but this criterion can be defined for very different levels of normal rates of profit—including a zero level.

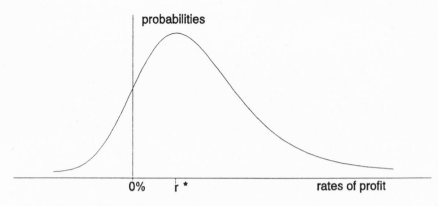

Figure 2. Probability Distribution of Rates of Profit with
Positive Normal Rate

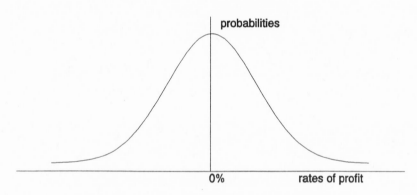

Figure 3. Rates of Profit in a "State of Bliss"

In an economy where the profitability criterion would refer to a zero rate of profit, firms would simply be trying to avoid losses. Their rates of profits might then be distributed according to a symmetrical probability distribution, as represented in Figure 3. Such a pattern would be appropriate for an economy in which the pursuit of happiness would no more take the form of economic growth—a situation that was described in a classical paper by Ramsey (1928) as an economic "state of bliss."

In several respects, the "state of bliss" specifies the economic dimension of what Milbrath (1990) calls a sustainable society. It is obviously a very similar concept to what a venerable tradition in economics has called the stationary state, and to what Daly (1973) has designated as a steady state economy. Investigating these concepts in detail would lead us into the analysis of profound questions about the motives and goals of economic activities and finally about the nature of human agency and cultural evolution. Such questions lie beyond the scope of our present analysis.

What should be emphasized, however, is the fact that our ideal type of a state of bliss is characterized by ongoing technical progress aimed not at further improvements in labor productivity but at the perfection of product quality. There is a remarkable similarity between this kind of progress and the dynamics of artistic production. The efforts of poets, for example, are not directed at reducing the time needed to write a poem, but at perfection in the practice of poetry. Although such perfection has been reached many times in the past, the way to achieve it again is not simply to reproduce old styles of poetry but to develop new ones.

Another important aspect of the state of bliss is the fact that it is differentiated from qualitative growth by the rules specifying normal rates of profits, but not necessarily by the general shape of firms and markets. However, there is a basic difference in the role of markets for natural resources. Consider a piece of land or some other natural resource whose use yields an annual rent of one million dollars. From the point of view of an investor operating under contemporary economic conditions, this piece of land is roughly equivalent to a capital asset yielding a profit of the same amount. Therefore, the value of land depends not only on the size of the rent but also on the level of the normal rate of profit.[14] At a rate of 10% the land is worth 10 million dollars, while at a rate of 5% its value is twice as high. At a zero rate, however, the value of rent-yielding assets becomes infinite.

This result is important because many people who understand that environmental destruction is the logical outcome of situations where environmental goods are free still feel that there is something deeply wrong with attempts to define positive prices for these goods. It is true that today many environmental goods are too cheap, but they will remain too cheap as long as their price falls short from infinity.[15] There is an economic arrangement that implies infinite prices for natural resources, namely the "state of bliss" beyond positive rates of profit and of economic growth.

To say that the price of land is infinite does not mean that land is traded for infinite sums of money. Rather, land is not traded at all, because no sum of money is big enough to be considered equivalent to the absolute and exclusive ownership of land. What can be traded under such conditions are usufructuary rights that entitle their owner to use a piece of land for a limited time without deteriorating the land in question.

An elegant way to organize such a state of affairs would be an institutional setting in which the use of natural resources would be regulated by freely tradeable usufructuary rights for these resources. These usufructuary rights could be offered by public authorities in annual auctions and the income generated by these auctions could then make the more traditional systems of taxation obsolete. In this context, it is worth noticing that two of the most influential economists of all times, David Ricardo and Léon Walras, were strongly convinced that rent incomes should be partially or totally at the disposal of public authorities.

The idea of a state of bliss offers an ideal type that might be described as a sustainable use of natural resources. Such a situation is the goal of the greenhouse marathon—and it will no doubt be impossible to reach it in less than several generations' time. Therefore, at the present moment, we can be satisfied with very tentative descriptions of this goal. We have also seen that its attainment could be prepared by a combination of qualitative growth in advanced countries with sustainable development in developing countries. Only after this combination has led to an end of the tremendous inequality between advanced and developing countries could we expect both qualitative growth and sustainable development to give way to economic bliss. But this transition will be a task for our grandchildren, and next we better consider the tasks of the present.

THE SPATIAL EVOLUTION OF COOPERATION

In order to analyze the possibility of sustainable development with regard to the greenhouse problem, we have considered economic processes as causes of global environmental change, but also as components of two broad social contexts. The first context was given by highly industrialized countries, the second by developing countries. We have suggested that a combination of qualitative growth in advanced countries with sustainable development in developing countries could lead in a distant future to a global state of economic bliss, in which humankind would take care of the biosphere instead of disrupting it. But obviously, humankind has other options as well. To say that the kind of quantitative growth analysed four sections back is unsustainable does not at all preclude its continuation for decades.

If we knew for certain that further growth of global greenhouse emissions would lead to terrible catastrophe, quantitative growth of such a kind might well be avoided. After all, awareness of the destructive power of nuclear weapons has induced highly antagonistic states to avoid nuclear war for several decades. If the destructive power of greenhouse emissions was of the same kind, effective agreements to limit these emissions might turn out to be feasible on similar grounds. But, in fact, one of the salient features of the greenhouse problem is the lack of straightforward certainty about the dangers humankind actually faces (Schneider 1989).

It seems that until now nature has been patient with us: So far, no actual climatic change has been shown to be a clear effect of increasing greenhouse emissions, and nature may still be patient in the future. In many respects, humankind has become much less dependent on climate than it used to be in the past (Ausubel 1990), and it is not certain that nature will react to greenhouse emissions in ways which will hurt humankind severely. Even if global warming should occur as a consequence of anthropogenic greenhouse gases, it is by no means certain that the overall effects on human well-being, and especially on agricultural productivity, would be disastrous (Idso 1991).

But even if we do not know whether nature will be patient or impatient with us in the future, there is a strong case to be made for prudence now. The argument can be illustrated with a simple game-theoretic pattern represented by Figure 4. The four cells of the table indicate the four possible outcomes if nature can be patient or impatient while humankind can be prudent or imprudent. The plus and minus signs indicate preference orderings between different outcomes. It may be useful to notice this: To say that an outcome is preferable to another is quite sensible even where no quantitative level of "utility" can be assigned to the different outcomes.

Presently, humankind seems to follow an imprudent strategy with regard to the greenhouse problem. This strategy, which corresponds to the pattern of quantitative growth discussed earlier, yields considerable gains as long as nature is patient, but it may lead to frightening problems if nature should become impatient. By contrast, a combination of qualitative growth und sustainable development may exploit less drastically the opportunities offered by nature as long as she is patient. However, such a strategy deserves to be called prudent because it could lead to substantial improvements in welfare even if nature's patience with regard to the greenhouse problem came to an end.

Obviously, we are using metaphorical language here. What the metaphor should emphasize is the fact that as long as we cannot be sure that nature will actually be patient with regard to future greenhouse emissions, an imprudent strategy is plainly irrational. As such a strategy is actually pursued, we must ask why humankind does not make the rational choice of becoming prudent.

Before trying to answer that question, we better pause a moment to wonder whether humankind does make any choices at all. To attribute a choice to some human collectivity makes sense if its members can legitimately say: "We made such and such a choice." And such reference to one's collectivity is legitimate if this collectivity shares a set of rules for procedures of deliberation and decision, and if these procedures have been followed so as to lead to a definite conclusion. Even if we acknowledge that often the rules in question are quite informal, it is obvious that so far what may be called the conversation of humankind has rarely, if ever, shown these features.

With regard to the greenhouse problem, a major obstacle to procedures of shared deliberation and decision is the division between advanced and developing regions of the world. We prefer talking about regions here because we want to avoid the assumption that nation-states are the most important

Nature

	patient	impatient
prudent	+	+
imprudent	++	--

Human-kind

Figure 4. Possible "Strategies" of Humankind and Nature

building blocks for procedures of global decision making. This may or may not be the case; but in any case, what we have described as an irrational strategy for humankind as a whole can be analyzed as the outcome of strategies that may seem quite rational for advanced world regions or for developing ones.

A prudent strategy for humankind as a whole, namely, combining qualitative growth in advanced world regions with sustainable development in developing ones, would require mutual cooperation between the two. But such cooperation is difficult to achieve. Imagine, for example, that developing world regions deliberately renounced to reach the levels of carbon emissions which are common in advanced regions, while the latter did not really reduce their emissions. As a consequence, the chances of developing regions to catch up in economic terms with advanced regions would be seriously impaired. Imagine, on the other hand, that advanced regions actually reduced their carbon emissions to a large extent, while developing regions continued with current rates of physical growth in terms of greenhouse impact. As a consequence, advanced regions might face slower economic growth than developing ones without being able to reap the ecological benefits of sustainable growth.

This situation is represented in Figure 5. In the present context, the alternative to cooperation is not competition but ruthlessness. Actually, highly innovative competitive markets would be an essential component of a cooperative solution for the greenhouse problem involving qualitative growth and sustainable development. However, the current situation may be characterized as one where competitive markets operate in a ruthless way both with regard to nature's greenhouse effect and to the relation between advanced and developing world regions.

The preference ordering of different outcomes is represented by symbols in brackets, the "D" or "A" symbols before the brackets indicating whether the preference refers to developing or to advanced world regions. Different typefaces may help to remember that in economic terms, advanced regions enjoy much larger outcomes than developing ones. However, for both

**Advanced
world regions**

		cooper- ative	ruth- less

**Developing
world regions**
	cooperative	D(++)
		
		    A(++)
			D(--)
			
			    A(+)

	ruthless	D(+)
		
		    A(--)
			D(0)
			
			    A(0)

Figure 5.   Humankind in a Prisoner's Dilemma

advanced and developing regions, the situation of mutual ruthlessness has been labelled with a zero because this is the point of reference for both parties: It is the world we live in. Figure 5 indicates a classic prisoners' dilemma because a situation of mutual cooperation would be preferable for both parties, but each party must try to avoid a situation where it behaves cooperatively while the other party remains ruthless.

If two parties get stuck in a prisoners' dilemma once and for all, they have little chance of reaching the optimum outcome of mutual cooperation. However, things are different if the game can be repeated again and again (e.g., a situation analyzed by Axelrod 1984). In the iterative case, rules of cooperation can evolve, and eventually these rules can stabilize situations of mutual cooperation. The positive outcome of such situations in turn then stabilize cooperative rules.

It may well be that political measures to control carbon emissions at a global scale will be far too weak to achieve significant results in the forseeable future. Such failure would actually be inevitable if political measures were to be introduced in a single step. In reality, however, the implementation of such measures can and must be broken down into a long series of small steps. The crucial problem then will be whether these steps will trigger an innovation process in which economic agents gradually develop new technologies and new courses of actions, thereby modifying the alternatives among which they can choose.

In order to envisage this possibility, it is no longer sufficient to consider humankind as split in the two large camps of advanced and developing world regions. It is very unlikely that the greenhouse problem will offer the opportunity for a long series of trial and error at this level of aggregation. With regard to climatic change, the time needed to assess whether a global decision was actually an error or not may be so long that rules of cooperation could hardly evolve in less than several centuries. Moreover, cooperation between advanced and developing world regions will hardly be successful if cooperative rules are absent from the relations between the myriad of actors within these camps.

If, however, we ask how cooperative rules can evolve in settings where large numbers of human agents are involved, two questions arise. First, we may ask how such rules come about in the first place. For the purposes of our present analysis, however, we can be satisfied with acknowledging that the existence of cooperative rules is a fact of life no less than the experience of ruthlessness.[16] Second, we may ask under what conditions cooperative rules can successfully evolve in settings with large numbers of actors.

Obviously, mutual cooperation must yield some kind of advantage if it is to be positively selected. But there is a second condition referring to the odds ratio that an actor who is following a cooperative rule will meet a similar partner rather than a ruthless one. Only if this ratio is relatively favorable can the potential advantages of cooperative rules be realized so as to stabilize the rules. Therefore, given the fact that human agents are embodied beings spending the greatest part of their lives on the surface of the earth, we may expect cooperative rules to be stabilized more easily in relatively compact territorial settings than in spatially dispersed social systems.

Interestingly, recent research on economic restructuring has shown that cooperative milieus, in which firms and public authorities as well as other institutions engage in cooperative processes of sociotechnical innovation, often emerge at a regional level (Sabel 1987). This innovation potential offers a remarkable opportunity for the greenhouse marathon.[17] Rayner (1989, p. 174) has argued in a similar vein that communication about the risks of climate change must lead to a complex pattern of social learning, not to a top-down enforcement of global solutions: "Participants in such a many stranded, loosely coupled network are free to innovate in many small ways, without facing the challenge of accepting or rejecting a single big treaty." However, he does not consider the territorial dimension of social networks, which has been stressed by research on innovative milieus in the contemporary world economy.

Environmental policy could gain in efficiency if it would be developed in a cooperative dialogue with such milieus. Current research on societal responses to regional climate change (Glantz 1988) can be of great help for this purpose. But it is also necessary to focus on the ways in which global climatic risks are perceived at a regional scale. Political authorities can contribute to improve such perception, and they can encourage innovation processes by which regional milieus react to perceived risks. This should not be understood only in the narrow sense of expected regional damage from global climate change.[18] Rather, regional economies may as well seize new opportunities that they associate with the prospect of such change. An example would be the implementation of a less-energy-intensive system of spatial mobility in a given region with the explicit intent to export some of the technology involved.[19] Or a region with important insurance services may seize the opportunity to develop new insurance schemes for damages related to climate change,[20] and thereby contribute to greater awareness of climatic risks.

It is possible that the ideal types of qualitative growth and of sustainable development will never be even approximated. But there is also a definite possibility to start a process oriented to these ideal types if a vision of a global goal, which we have sketched with the notion of economic bliss, is linked with determined action in the context of today's regional economies both in industrialized and in developing countries.

ACKNOWLEDGMENTS

In writing this paper I have profited from discussions with R. Clemençon, G. Hirsch, L. Scherer, I. Schmid, K. Timmel, and B. Truffer, as well as from comments by Lee Freese, editor of this series, and by two anonymous referees. The responsibility for remaining errors is mine.

NOTES

1.   Adams (1990) offers an excellent account of the debates which led to the contemporary interest in sustainable development.

2.   See Weber ([1903-06]1951, [1904]1951) and Burger (1978). My understanding of ideal types owes much to Hirsch (1990). Recently, the methodology of ideal types has been advocated by Morishima (1990) for the purposes of integrating sociological and economic analysis, a task which is no doubt essential for the interdisciplinary analysis of human dimensions of global change (Price 1990).

3.   In principle, the dynamics of decision matrices through time could be reconstructed ex post by observing the input and output matrices of various periods and solving Equation (3) for M_t. However, forecasting the interdependent outcome of future management decisions is hardly a sensible exercise except for narrowly limited time horizons of maybe two or three years. But even if decision matrices cannot be specified in detail, it may still be possible to indicate certain general properties of such matrices. Two such properties are the tendency to increase labor productivity by means of technical progress and the tendency to shift production toward more sophisticated goods as incomes increase.

4.   In order to obtain vectors of the same number of components for both periods, we consider a vector space witth a separate dimension for every kind of goods and services produced in at least one of the two periods. The output vectors then contain zero components for the goods and services not produced in the period to which they refer. The components of the price vector indicate prices prevailing in period t except for the goods and services which are produced only in period $t + 1$.

5.   This notion of lacking sustainability can be generalized to other environmental problems for which a sensible impact vector can be defined. This is the case, for example, with the problem of the ozone hole and with many problems of waste products. However, there are other environmental problems, for example, with regard to biodiversity, for which an impact vector can hardly be defined in a meaningful way. We therefore use Formula (6) to define the notion of sustainability in the context of the greenhouse problem only and leave open the question of how this notion should be understood in other contexts.

6. The figures about carbon emissions used in the present paper are from UNEP and The Beijer Institute (1989, p. 45) and from Flavin (1989, p. 25f).

7. This efect was enhanced by a series of political measures to increase energy efficiency.

8. For an early identification of this possibility, which meanwhile is confirmed by actual developments, see Mazur and Rosa (1974).

9. With the procedure describe in note 4 for the price vector, we can keep the number of components of the impact vector constant, too.

10. Emissions have also dramatically increased in the USSR, where they are already higher than in Germany. Until recently, it seemed plausible to associate the United States with a first world, the USSR with a second one, and Brazil and maybe China with a third one. Meanwhile, the breakdown of centrally planned economies in the USSR and Eastern Europe marks the end of the "second world." The nations which are experiencing this breakdown obviously hope to become part of the first world. But this hope actually is the common denominator of developing countries. Therefore, in today's world economy, there are good reasons to draw a broad distinction between advanced and developing countries, with Russia still being a developing country, even if its nuclear armament makes it a military superpower.

11. For many purposes it is helpful to interpret s_t as a vector of expected values of probability distributions like the ones depicted in Figures 2 and 3. For a probabilistic analysis of profits, see Farjoun and Machover (1983).

12. The shifts in relative prices could induce some technological change, as the rank ordering of profitability for different technologies depends on relative prices. Such technological change would occur in particular in cases where wage increase would otherwise drive some specific price toward zero or even turn it negative. Obviously, with a constant price level such cases can never occur for all prices at once.

13. Such a rule does not determine which investment projects will actually be designed in detail and which projects will finally be realized. These decisions will depend on a multitude of factors ranging from carefully elaborated business strategies to chance events.

14. Conceptually and numerically, there are important differences between rates of interest and rates of profit, and a more detailed discussion of the state of bliss would have to analyze these differences. This would be especially relevant for the argument that lower rates of interest lead to higher amounts of investment, which may jeopardize sustainability. This argument presupposes a constant normal rate of profit; if both rates fall, no effect of investment should be expected.

15. An example of the alternative view which would be satisfied with finite prices for all environmental goods is offered by Barbier, Markandya, and Pearce (1990).

16. It is worth stressing that the biological helplessness of human babies would bring the reproduction of the species to a rapid end if ruthlessness was the dominant experience in the early years of life.

17. The relationships between regional innovative milieus and environmental awareness are explored in Jaeger (1990).

18. For a recent attempt to assess such damage, see Johnson and Stabler (1991).

19. This could become the case of southern California if it should acquire possible first-mover advantages in the production of electric cars (Morales et al. 1991).

20. Peele (1988) discusses some relations between insurance and the greenhouse effect.

REFERENCES

Adams, W.M. 1990. *Green Development. Environment and Sustainability in the Third World.*
    London: Routledge & Kegan Paul.
Archibugi, F., and P. Nijkamp, eds. 1989. *Economy and Ecology: Towards Sustainable Development.* Dordrecht, The Netherlands: Kluwer.

Ausubel, J.H. 1991. "Does Climate still matter?" *Nature* 350: 649-652.

Axelrod, R.M. 1984. *The Evolution of Cooperation*. New York: Basic Books.

Barbier, E.P., A. Markandya, and D.W. Pearce. 1990. "Environmental Sustainability and Cost-Benefit Analysis." *Environment and Planning A* 22: 1259-1266.

Boyd, R., and P.J. Richerson. 1985. *Culture and the Evolutionary Process*. Chicago: University of Chicago Press.

Burger, T. 1978. *Max Weber's Theory of Concept Formation. History, Laws, and Ideal Types*. Durham, NC: Duke University Press.

Buttel, F.H., A.P. Hawkins, and A.G. Power. 1990. "From Limits to Growth to Global Change. Constraints and Contradictions in the evolution of environmental science and ideology." *Global Environmental Change* 1: 57-66.

Carlstein, T. 1982. *Time Resources, Society and Ecology*. London: George Allen & Unwin.

Costanza, R. 1989. "What is Ecological Economics?" *Ecological Economics* 1: 1-7.

Daly, H., ed. 1973. *Towards a Steady-State Economy*. San Francisco, CA: Freeman.

Farjoun, E., and M. Machover. 1983. *Laws of Chaos. A Probabilistic Approach to Political Economy*. London: Verso.

Flavin, C. 1989. *Slowing Global Warming: A Worldwide Strategy*. Washington, DC: Worldwatch Institute.

Folke, C., and T. Kåberger, eds. 1991. *Linking the Natural Environment and the Economy: Essays from the Eco-Eco Group*. Dordrecht, The Netherlands: Kluwer.

Giddens, A. 1984. *The Constitution of Society. Outline of the Theory of Structuration*. Berkeley, CA: University of California Press.

Glaeser, B., ed. 1984. *Ecodevelopment: Concepts, Projects, Strategies*. Oxford: Pergamon Press.

Glantz, M.H., ed. 1988. *Societal Responses to Regional Climatic Change. Forecasting by Analogy*. Boulder, CO: Westview Press.

Haegerstrand, T. 1970. "What about people in regional science?" Papers of the Regional Science Association 24: 7-21.

Hirsch, G. 1990. *Biographie und Identität des Lehrers. Eine typologische Studie über den Zusammenhang von Berufserfahrungen und beruflichem Selbstverstndnis* [*Biography and Identity of Teachers. A Typological Study*]. Munich: Juventa.

Idso, S.B. 1991. "Carbon Dioxide and the Fate of Earth." *Global Environmental Change* 1(3): 178-182.

IUCN (International Union for the Conservation of Nature and Natural resources), UNEP (United Nations Environmental Programme), and WWF (World Wildlife Fund) 1980. *World Conservation Strategy: Living Resource Conservation for Sustainable Development*. Gland, Switzerland: World Wildlife Fund.

Jaeger, C.C. 1990. "Innovative Milieus and Environmental Awareness." *Sociologia Internationalis* 28: 205-216.

Jaeger, C.C., and A. Weber, 1988. "Lohndynamik und Arbeitslosigkeit" [Wage Dynamics and Unemployment]. *Kyklos* 41: 479-506.

Johnson, S., and J.C. Stabler. 1991. "An Approach to Estimating the Economic Impact of Climatic Change on a Regional Economy." *Environment & Planning A* 23: 1197-1208.

Kuemmel, R. 1989. "Energy as a Factor of Production and Entropy as a Polution Indicator in Macroeconomic Modelling." *Ecological Economics* 1: 161-180.

Luhmann, N. 1986. *Oekologische Kommunikation* [*Ecological Communication*]. Opladen, FRG: Westdeutscher Verlag.

Marglin, S.A., and J. Schor (eds.). 1988. *The Golden Age of Capitalism. Reinterpreting the Postwar Experience*. Oxford: Oxford University Press.

Mazur, A., and E. Rosa. 1974. "Energy and Life-Style." *Science* 186: 607-610.

Milbrath, L.W. 1989. *Envisioning a Sustainable Society: Learning Our Way Out*. Albany, NY: State University of New York Press.

Morales, R., M. Storper, M. Cisternas, C. Quandt, A.J. Scott, J. Slifko, W. Thomas, M. Wachs, and S. Zakhor. 1991. *Prospects for Alternative Fuel Vehicle Use and Production in Southern California: Environmental Quality and Economic Development*. Working Paper No. 2, Lewis Center for Regional Policy Studies, University of California—Los Angeles.

Morishima, M. 1990. "Ideology and Economic Activity." *Current Sociology* 38: 51-77.

Pasinetti, L. L. 1988. *Structural Change and Economic Growth. A Theoretical Essay on the Dynamics of the Wealth of Nations*. Cambridge: Cambridge University Press.

Peele, B.D. 1988. "Insurance and the Greenhouse Effect." Pp. 588-601 in *Greenhouse: Planning for Climate Change*, edited by G.J. Pearman. Leiden, The Netherlands: Brill Publishing Company.

Perrings, C. 1987. *Economy and Environment*. Cambridge: Cambridge University Press.

Price, M. 1990. "Humankind in the Biosphere: The Evolution of International Interdisciplinary Research." *Global Environmental Change* 1: 3-13.

Ramsey, F.P. 1928. "A Mathematical Theory of Saving." *The Economic Journal* 38: 543-559.

Rayner, S. 1989. "Risk Communication in the Search for a Global Climate Management Strategy." Pp. 169-176 in *Risk Communication*, edited by H. Jungermann, R.E. Kasperson, and P.M. Wiedemann. Jüelich, FRG: Kernforschungsanlage Jülich.

Sabel, C.F. 1989. "Flexible Specialisation and the Re-emergence of Regional Economies." Pp 17-70 in *Reversing Industrial Decline? Industrial Structure and Policy in Britain and Her Competitors*, edited by P. Hirst, and J. Zeitlin. Oxford: Berg.

Schneider, S.S. 1989. "The Greenhouse Effect: Science and Policy." *Science* 243: 771-781.

UNEP (United Nations Environment Programme), and The Beijer Institute. 1989. *The Full Range of Responses to Anticipated Climatic Change*. Geneva: UNEP.

Vellinga, P., and R. Swart. 1991. "The Greenhouse Marathon: A Proposal for a Global Strategy." *Climatic Change* 18: vii-xii.

WCED (World Commission on Environment and Development). 1987. *Our Common Future*. Oxford: Oxford University Press.

Weber, M. (1904) 1951. "Die 'Objektivitae' sozialwissenschaftlicher und sozialpolitischer Erkenntnis" [The 'Objectivity' of Sociological and Sociopolitical Knowledge]. Pp. 146-214 in *Gesammelte Aufsätze zur Wissenschaftslehre*, by M. Weber, Tübingen, Germany: J.C.B. Mohr.

————. (1903-06) 1951. "Roscher und Knies und die logischen Probleme der historischen Nationalkonomie" [Roscher and Knies and the Logical Problems of Historically Oriented Economics]. Pp. 215-290 in *Gesämmelte Aufstäze zur Wissenschaftslehre*, by M. Weber. Tübingen, Germany: J.C.B. Mohr.

Young, G.L., ed. 1983. *Origins of Human Ecology*. Stroudsburg, PA: Hutchinson Press.

MINIMUM DATA FOR COMPARATIVE HUMAN ECOLOGICAL STUDIES:
EXAMPLES FROM STUDIES IN AMAZONIA

Emilio F. Moran

ABSTRACT

The proliferation of approaches to human ecology provides a rare opportunity to explore a range of problem-oriented methods that disciplinary-based methods no longer permit. This positive scenario has some potentially negative risks. If comparison between different human ecological settings is to be workable, it will be necessary to agree on minimal data sets that ought to be collected, if there are to be comparable data in human ecology. This paper proposes criteria for minimum data that are consistent with the research goals of several types of human ecology. The criteria are developed from the kinds of questions posed by researchers working in rural settings (about climate, soils, flora, and fauna), some of which may prove generally applicable in human ecological studies (of social organization, demographic structure, health, and nutrition). This is done in the context of the ecology of Amazonian populations to provide a demonstration of how such minima may fit in with larger questions asked by researchers. These minima are not intended to reduce our current diversity in methods but, rather, to ensure that our data can contribute to the comparative understanding of the human condition on this planet.

Advances in Human Ecology, Volume 2, pages 191-213.
Copyright © 1993 by JAI Press Inc.
All rights of reproduction in any form reserved.
ISBN: 1-55938-558-8

INTRODUCTION

For the past 40 years, the Amazon Basin has been a testing ground for human ecological theories, and it is likely to remain so in the foreseeable future. The reasons why are worth examining, as well as how we might be able to advance the quality of hypothesis testing and generalizations coming from research in this part of the world. Initial interest in the area was rooted in its vast lushness, and extremes of opinion were expressed by early travellers to the region: some argued that the region was undoubtedly "a rich realm of nature," while others asserted that the lush greenness was a cover-up for a depauparate landscape.

One of the central points of discussion has been the quality of the soils in the region. Amazonian soils have been a point of controversy for a good part of this century. Late-nineteenth-century travellers' opinion that the soils of the region must be very rich given the lushness of the vegetation were followed by severe criticisms suggesting they were so poor that they could not support complex cultures or intensive cultivation. No one stated this view more coherently and firmly than Betty Meggers (1954). In a now classic article, she set out to demonstrate that the poor and acidic soils could only support small-scale societies living by swidden cultivation, because soil fertility could only be sustained from the nutrients released by burning the forest, and these would be leached by the second or third year of cultivation. It did not take long for critics of this view to appear. Carneiro (1957) suggested that the Kuikuru of the Upper Xingu could sustain populations of up to 2,000 people over the long term without requiring village movement. For him, the limiting factor was not the fertility of the soils but weed invasion. His suggestion has turned out to be correct—for very rich soils only. In alfisols, for example, the vigor of weed invasion is greater than in acid, nutrient-poor soils, where soil fertility becomes a limiting factor first (Sanchez, Bandy, Villachica, and Nicholaides 1982). Ferdon (1959) added the point that the notion of static carrying capacity overlooks human capabilities for modifying the environment and changing the limiting conditions to cultural development. He provided examples from several Asian civilizations in the humid tropics as evidence of the human capacity for overcoming limiting constraints. Recent studies tend to emphasize that the soils of the Amazon are among the richest and the poorest in the world, with many soils along the middle of such a fertility continuum. Thus, future research in the area will need to include an understanding of the soil patchiness present in order to give due attention to the variability present in human uses of variable soil resources.

In this paper, I hope to briefly show that some of the obstacles to improved understanding of the region may be related to the persistent dependence on a simple dichotomous environmental distinction between floodplain and upland ecosystems. I also suggest a couple of ways in which it might be possible to develop future research in ways that go beyond trying to answer the simple question, "Can complex social systems develop in humid tropical environments?" While useful as a broad breakdown of the region, it is necessary at this stage in scientific development to move beyond distinguishing floodplains from upland ecosystems and use more elaborate classes to characterize areas being studied. Some of these classes of environments are discussed. Moreover, if comparison among regions is to be viable, it will be necessary to arrive at some agreement on the minimal data sets that ought to be collected at most study sites to create an accumulation of comparable data in categories generally relevant to human ecological study. This minimum data may also prove useful in areas other than the humid tropics and if this is the case, comparisons could be extended more generally in human ecological studies.

In comparative terms, the area occupied by the Amazon is equivalent to the continental United States of America, or to both Eastern and Western Europe combined (without the Soviet Union), or about 6 million square kilometers. The Amazon is a region not only of rain forests. It also has semi-evergreen forests, flooded forests, savannas of various types, montane forests, and palm forests. The rivers have very distinct qualities, with some having clear, limpid waters, and others having a muddy appearance, reflecting important differences in the amount and quality of alluvium they transport.

Recent evidence contradicts many of the views espoused until recently that only small, politically disconnected settlements may be present in Amazonia. It now seems that the ancestors of contemporary indigenous peoples have inhabited the Amazon Basin for at least 12,000 years (Roosevelt 1989, p. 3). They may be among the first to have produced ceramics in the New World, 6,000 to 8,000 years ago (Roosevelt 1987). By 5,000 years ago, they seem to have had a set of domesticated crops and art forms very similar to those of contemporary indigenous populations (Roosevelt 1987). By 2,000 years ago, there is evidence of the rise of larger settlements with more complex political organization and art forms such as polychrome pottery. These seem to have been more common in the more fertile areas of the floodplain and to have been supported by the cultivation not only of manioc but also of cereals such as corn (Roosevelt 1987).

The heterogeneity of the populations that inhabit the Amazon reflects the diversity of the physical environment and their diverse historical experiences (Oliveira 1988, p. 66). The European explorers of the sixteenth-century found an Amazon with large populations inhabiting the riverbanks of the larger rivers, capable of organizing themselves in self-defense and of conquering territory (Roosevelt 1989; Porro 1989; Whitehead 1989). Chroniclers of the time described the existence of chiefdoms capable of mobilizing thousands of warriors and of offering an abundance of food to visitors, with towns extending for hundreds of kilometers along the riverbanks (Herrera 1856; Simon 1861; Porro 1989; Myers 1989; Whitehead 1989). According to ethnohistoric sources, the land of the Omagua in the sixteenth century included between 23 and 34 villages along a 700 km continuous stretch of riverfront, from the lower Napo river to the mouth of the Javarí and Içá rivers (Myers 1989, p. 6). Some of these villages have been estimated to have had at least 8,000 inhabitants (Porro 1989, p. 7). The Omagua population persisted until the seventeenth-century, although its numbers declined and its settlements covered by then only 300 kilometers of riverfront (Porro 1989; Myers 1989). There is evidence, too, for pre-Columbian chiefdoms in the upland forests of the Amazon which Whitehead (1989, p. 9) suggests depended more on control over regional commerce than on local habitat productivity to sustain their complex polities.

In the sixteenth- and seventeenth-centuries, the principal impact felt by the indigenous people came from epidemic diseases, the presence of missionaries, and the wars of conquest along the major rivers (Fritz 1922; Figueroa 1904; Uriarte 1952; Hemming 1978). By the beginning of the Rubber Era, which began in the middle of the nineteenth-century, the native peoples were already a minority. It is by this time that there appear the beginnings of the more detailed ethnographic reports upon which many of our views have been based. What was observed were the shreds and patches of past societies, small populations seeking to escape from the arm of the state and its deleterious influence on their health and well-being. The mad search for rubber led to the violent expulsion of native peoples from their territories. Instead of being a necessary, even essential, labor force, as they had been up to this point, the Indians began to be seen as an obstacle to the region's development, and outside labor was brought in to take on productive tasks (Weinstein 1983; Oliveira 1988, p. 68). Today, only 220 ethnic groups survive with a total population of about 230,000, 60% of them living in the Amazon (Gomes 1988, p. 24).

One of the important objectives of human ecology is to discover strategies of resource use that permit conservation (Denevan and Padoch 1988). The adaptive strategies of indigenous and folk Amazonian populations constitute riches that human ecology, and non-Amazonian societies, ought to value since they offer solutions to the dilemma of how to obtain resources and yet preserve the biotic diversity of Amazonia.

THE ECOSYSTEMS OF THE AMAZON BASIN

Despite the explosion of research in the Amazon in the past 20 years, which has shown just how variable the habitats can be, comparative studies persist in the aggregating of results. Findings from one site are viewed as generalizable to the entire region or, conversely, treated as site-specific. Most people accept the dichotomy between uplands (*terra firme*) and floodplain (*várzea*) as adequately separating the important differences present in this vast region, which is equivalent to the continental United States in area. The distinction between uplands and floodplains glosses over important ecological differences,

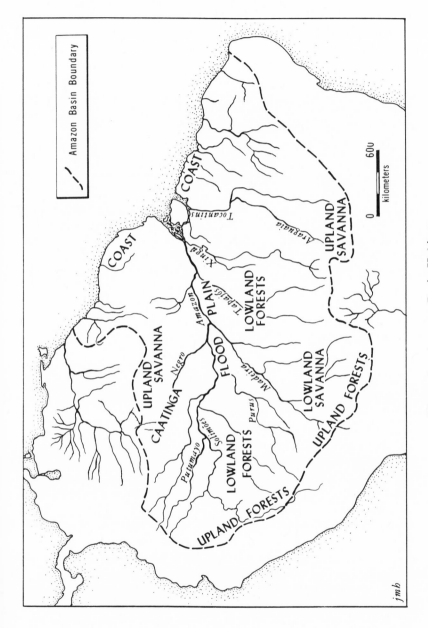

Figure 1. Amazon Basin Habitats

Table 1.   Types of Vegetation in Amazonia

Upland Forests of Terra Firme

a. dense forest	b. open forest
c. liana forest	d. bamboo forest
e. caatinga on spodosols	f. palm forests
g. dry forests	h. pre-montane forests

Floodplains and Flooded Forests

a. forests over clay soils
b. floodplain forests of the lower Amazon
c. floodplain forests of the upper Amazon
d. forests of the estuary
e. pantanal of the Rio Branco
f. flooded forests in blackwater rivers

Upland Savannas of Terra Firme

a. campo sujo	b. campo cerrado
c. cerrado	d. cerradao
e. campo rupestre	f. savanna of Roraima
g. coastal savanna	h. flooded savannas

Restricted Vegetations

a. mangroves
b. levees
c. buriti-dominated areas (*Mauritia sp.*)

Sources: Adapted from Prance (1978) and Pires and Prance (1985).

as we shall see below. The dependence of scholars on this dichotomous distinction is no accident. It is broad enough to speak across the biological and social sciences, allowing the integration of findings from each. It has considerable value in distinguishing areas enriched by Andean sediments and having highly productive fisheries from areas less well endowed (Lathrap 1970).

The floodplains of the Amazon are not homogenous but need to be differentiated further into at least three distinct habitats: the estuary, the lower floodplain, and the upper floodplain. The estuary of the Amazon differs from the lower floodplain by the important role played by the daily fluctuations of the tides. Here we do not find the once-a-year rise of 10 to 20 meters for several months that exists further upriver, but a twice daily rise and fall. The estuary runs from the mouth of the Xingú river to the island of Marajó at the mouth of the Amazon river. This type of floodplain is associated with clayish soils on which grow an abundance of palms adapted to the estuary's cycles. The estuary resembles a system experiencing constant early secondary succession, thrown back constantly to earlier stages of succession by the dynamic action of the river system. Carrying capacity is high when properly managed. It may be better managed by sustained-yield extractive activities than by intensive farming (Lima 1956; Anderson and Ioris 1989). These were the areas that supported large Amazonian populations before the Europeans' arrival, and which experienced the most devastating depopulation during the first century of contact. Only in recent years, with the growth of cities, have these areas once again become centers of intensive economic activity, due to the growth of nearby urban populations.

A second type of floodplain occurs upstream from the estuary, and is known as the lower floodplain or lower Amazon. This is the area described most often as typical of the floodplain as a whole—with annual deposition of alluvium rich in nutrients from the Andes, with pH near neutral, and with rich and varied fish populations (Junk 1984, p. 215). Despite the high potential it offers—it supported large pre-Columbian populations, such as the Omagua (Myers 1989)—its potential has not been fully exploited for several centuries. The highly variable annual flood levels make water control difficult and costly. Although it covers only 64,000 square kilometers or 1.6% of the Basin, its significance is many times greater. This is an area of dynamic morphology, where rivers continuously cut and modify the landscape, annually carrying whole river banks to be deposited downstream as sediment (Sternberg 1975, pp. 17-18).

The third kind of floodplain, known as the upper floodplain or upper Amazon, is the most internally diverse. Depending on the geological formations it may be acid or basic, rich or poor. Soils with headwaters in the eastern Peruvian Cordillera (e.g., the Rio Mayo) are generally nutrient rich, with pH values between 6.5 and 8.5. Those developing in sediments eroded from the calcareous sedimentary deposits of the Andean foothills of Ecuador and Peru (e.g., the drainage area of the Rio Cashiboya) tend to be slightly acidic, with pH between 5.0 and 6.5, but have no serious chemical deficiencies. By contrast, upper floodplain alluvial soils (usually thought to be uniformly excellent) originating in the eastern portion of the Peruvian Basin (e.g., the Rio Yavarí watershed) tend to be strongly acidic. Some of them may be blackwater watersheds, with pH of 4.0 to 5.0, and have toxic levels of aluminum saturation exceeding 85% (Hoag, Buol and Pérez 1987, pp. 78-79). Thus, it is necessary to approach all floodplains with considerable care in establishing their physical characteristics and the human strategies for dealing with and modifying those physical differences.

The uplands, an area constituting 98% of the Basin, contain a diverse array of habitats. We can minimally distinguish between blackwater river watersheds, lowland savannas, montane forests, and upland forests.

Lowland savannas are characterized by a marked dry and wet season, highly acid soils deficient in phosphorus, and patches of richer gallery forests along riverbanks. Until very recently, agriculture was very uncertain and of relatively low productivity. The lowland savannas were areas favored for human occupation because of the ease of hunting in this grassland habitat, the proximity to forested areas for other resources, and the abundance of ecotones for different resources (Gross, Eiten, Flowers, Leoi, Ritter, and Werner 1979; Posey 1985; Anderson and Posey 1985). Some are poorly drained (such as the Llanos de Mojos in Bolivia and Marajó Island at the mouth of the Amazon river), while others are well-drained, such as the cerrado of Brazil. The former are quite extensive in Amazonia and are believed to have supported large prehistoric populations that practiced intensive agricultural techniques, such as raised fields (Denevan 1966; Erickson 1988).

Blackwater watersheds were labelled very early as "rivers of hunger," given their sparser vegetation which resembles a semi-arid scrub forest more than an Amazonian landscape. From the viewpoint of nutrients, these are the most limited and fragile regions of the Amazon (Jordan and Herrera 1981). Rainfall is high, and soils are white sands of near-pure quartz that are extremely acid and devoid of nutrients. Plants have a high content of secondary compounds that serve to reduce herbivory and, thus, loss of nutrients. Plants have adaptations to drought (e.g., sclerophylly) as well as to flood (e.g., above ground fine roots). Many of the allusions to the perfection of nutrient cyclying in Amazonia refer to the processes found in this region—and not found in better endowed areas of Amazonia. Human populations lived in these extremely poor habitats by depending on highly toxic cultivated plants like bitter manioc varieties and by profound knowledge of local habitats ensured by territorial control over prime fishing areas and patches of slightly better soils for horticulture (Moran 1991).

Upland forests remain to this day a catchall category that includes a wide variety of habitats. In this region, we find what appear to be anthropogenic vegetations such as liana or vine forests, bamboo forests, palm forests, and brazilnut forests (Balée 1989). The vine or liana forests alone cover over 100,000 square kilometers of the Basin and are found near or on sizable outcroppings of high base status soils, in areas with a characteristic dry season and associated often with anthropogenic black earths.

The montane forests of the western Amazon have been the focus of many studies. They are different in having lower tree biomass but more epiphytes. There is a noticeably lower animal biomass but better soils in some watersheds. The lowland populations depended on trade relations with the Andean highlands with which they maintained regular interactions. This area has been profoundly affected by oil exploration in Ecuador and Peru, and more recently by the activities of cocaine interests.

In short, what this brief outline of the differences to be found in the uplands and the floodplains suggests is that the ecosystems of Amazonia are far more diverse than people have been willing to admit. In the process of human ecological study or in the efforts at ecosystem protection and conservation, it is important that the goal be not to conserve some vague notion of floodplain habitat and upland habitat but the much richer biotic and human variation present in this vast region. To preserve this cultural and biotic richness, it is important to rely on the native peoples of the region, whose knowledge reflects the regular use of such resources. A fuller discussion of native uses of Amazonian ecosystems can be found in *The Human Ecology of Amazonian Populations* (Moran 1990, 1993).

MINIMUM HUMAN ECOLOGICAL DATA

Which variables of an ecosystem are the object of a human ecological study will depend on the objectives. Therefore, it is impossible to be all-inclusive about which data ought to be collected. If this is the case, is it ever possible to collect data that is systematic enough to permit rigorous comparison across sites? One possible way to proceed is by developing generally agreed-upon minimum data of such fundamental importance to the understanding of human ecologic relations that its collection does not detract from the more specific goals of a particular study but, in fact, provides a necessary basis for any generalization that may be made.

In studying human ecological processes, attention needs to be paid both to human perception of the environment and individual human behavior towards environment. Our perception of the environment is as influential as the physical reality of the environment. Ethnoecological data collection focuses attention on dimensions that we might overlook if we presumed that a population has the same perceptions as we have. Of interest, too, should be the fit between those perceptions and some measurable behavioral treatment of the environment. The perception of environment is influenced by other components of an individual's social experience, such as the population's demographic structure, social organization, health and nutritional status, and historical experience in a region, and thus does not stand alone and unrelated to the feedback processes experienced by individuals. Whether one begins with collecting data on perception or on behavior is less important than ensuring that both dimensions are studied and compared.

In ethnoecology, the investigation begins by asking about what names a population gives to items in a given domain of importance to it—for example, "fish" among a population where fishing is a major occupation. Thus, one would ask the informant: "How many kinds of fish are there around here?" He or she might respond by saying: "Well, there are many...there are acarí, tamuatá, bacú, pirarucú, traíra, arraia, puraqué, mandubí...." For each of these type of fish, one would subsequently ask, "Are there several kinds of, for example, acarí?" For each fish named, one would seek to arrive at the maximum number of named distinctions made by the informant. After that, one would proceed one-by-one and compare each one with the other, asking: "How can one tell an acarí boi from an acarí naná?" This process gradually leads to the definition of distinctive criteria used in making such discriminations. For example, while they both have a roundish head, Acari naná has distinctively pointy scales and Acarí boi does not (having instead a larger head than Acarí naná). Table 2 illustrates one such ethnoecological classification collected among fishermen in the central part of Marajó Island, at the mouth of the Amazon Basin. Sometimes an important criterion will be differences in color, which tend to suggest age differences rather than species or variety differences. Such a distinction might be indicative of the importance of age discrimination to fishermen in how and when they catch fish. This possibility would have to be investigated by other means, such as detailed interviews and observation of use. From these cognitive dimensions of environment, it is possible to move to the collection of other social and environmental data that permit discussion of the ecosystem.

The strategy of human ecology is a complex one that relies on methods from a large number of disciplines. In the subsections that follow, a brief discussion of some minima that can be used in human ecological assessment is presented. The goal is to begin the process of dialogue among human ecologists so that some minimum standards in data collection might be agreed upon in the near future to enhance efforts in comparative human ecological studies. This discussion uses examples from Amazonia to give specificity to the discussion and to highlight problems that are present in data collection, in what is generally considered one of the most poorly understood regions of the world from both an environmental and cultural perspective.

Climate

One of the basic parameters in the understanding of ecosystem structure and function is climate. Climate affects organic decomposition, nutrient cycling, seasonality, and so forth. Amazonian climate was cited for some time as one of the reasons for the region's underdevelopment. It still looms as one of the alleged "problems" posed by the region to outsiders (i.e., hot and humid). Given how complex climate research can be, it is necessary to select some indices that can be productively used. The most necessary information for human ecological study is to know the *daily precipitation and maximum and minimum daily temperature* in the area of interest (Wilken 1988). With this data, it is possible to estimate other indices, such as number of days of continuous rain, evapotranspiration rates, (Bordne and McGuinness 1973), and indices of available soil moisture (Baier, Chaput, Russelo, and Sharp 1972), among others. Monthly or annual means are insufficient for an adequate assessment of the role of climate on local ecosystems. The above data should represent a 20-year time-series, minimally, if they are to have any chance of reflecting the effects of year-to-year fluctuations. At present, the number of climatological stations in Amazonia is insufficient, and more attention to the collection of climate data is needed, if we are ever to be able to take proper account of

Table 2.   Fish Ethnoecology (Marajó Island)

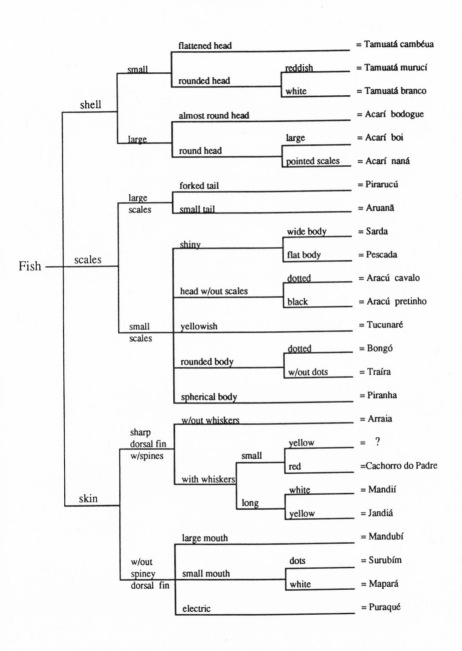

Source: Fábio de Castro and Emilio Moran, Field notes, 1989

the role of climate in human decisions. Until such time as more inclusive data is available for the immediate area under study, it may be wise to collect the folk systems of climate prediction (i.e., the ethnoclimatology, if you will) that represent long-term observations by local people (cf. Stigter 1986), and to take with a dose of skepticism the data from climatological stations of only a few years' duration.

Soils

Ecosystem characterization cannot go far without a description of the variation in soil types in an area. In the Amazon, it is rare to find soil maps at a scale appropriate for management decisions at the level of the farm (i.e., 1:10,000). Most maps are at the FAO scale of 1:5,000,000 or at best at 1:1,000,000 (Radam 1974-1979). To get around this limitation, most investigators may need to take soil samples. To be able to integrate this data into human ecological investigation, it is ideal to begin by collecting the local population's means of classifying soils (see the earlier discussion of ethnoecology). By asking, for example, "How many kinds of soils do you name?," it is possible to begin to construct a taxonomy that reflects locally important criteria. This might be followed by collecting the indicators used by the population to locate each type of soil. Figure 2 illustrates the good and bad soils in the area near Altamira, along the Transamazon Highway of Brazil, using vegetation indicators recognized by local Amazon peasants. This system of illustrating soil fertility is an effective way of visualizing the degree of fertility in tropical soils (Alvim and Cabala 1974) and has broad applicability. To construct such a summary view of a soil's fertility, it is necessary to have soil samples. In general, one soil sample is composed of 10-15 cores taken randomly from a homogenous field at a depth of 0-20 centimeters. In some cases, it may be useful to take deeper soil samples if the use of the land involves rooting processes at deeper levels in the soil profile or if the goal is to classify soils in a formal fashion, rather than simply to assess their potential fertility. The nutrients illustrated in Figure 2 are commonly the most telling in Amazonian soils.

Flora

The composition of a forested area is commonly sampled using transects, commonly of areas of 100 or 200 square meters. Another method is to sample the vegetation 5 meters to the right and left of a 50 meter tape placed on the forest floor until one arrives at 100 individuals. The manual of Nueller-Dumbois and Ellenberg (1974) is considered the standard (cf. Cain and Castro 1959) for work in the tropics. Other, often more sophisticated, manuals are available for temperate zones, given their better-studied status and less diverse

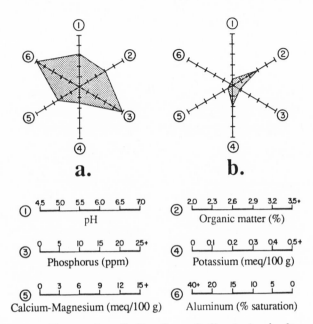

b.

① $\overset{4.5 \quad 5.0 \quad 5.5 \quad 6.0 \quad 6.5 \quad 7.0}{\rule{2cm}{0.4pt}}$
 pH

② $\overset{2.0 \quad 2.3 \quad 2.6 \quad 2.9 \quad 3.2 \quad 3.5+}{\rule{2cm}{0.4pt}}$
Organic matter (%)

③ $\overset{0 \quad 5 \quad 10 \quad 15 \quad 20 \quad 25+}{\rule{2cm}{0.4pt}}$
Phosphorus (ppm)

④ $\overset{0 \quad 0.1 \quad 0.2 \quad 0.3 \quad 0.4 \quad 0.5+}{\rule{2cm}{0.4pt}}$
Potassium (meq/100 g)

⑤ $\overset{0 \quad 3 \quad 6 \quad 9 \quad 12 \quad 15+}{\rule{2cm}{0.4pt}}$
Calcium-Magnesium (meq/100 g)

⑥ $\overset{40+ \quad 20 \quad 15 \quad 10 \quad 5 \quad 0}{\rule{2cm}{0.4pt}}$
Aluminum (% saturation)

a. Forest Vegetation Indicative of Good Agricultural Soils

Local Term	Scientific Name
Pau d'arco or ipé (yellow variety)	*Tabebuia serratifolia*
Pau d'arco or ipé (purple variety)	*Tabebuia vilaceae*
Faveira	*Piptadenia* spp.
Mororó	*Bauhinia* spp.
Maxarimbé	*Emmotum* spp.
Pinheiro preto	(unidentified)
Babaçú	*Orbignya martiana*
Açaí	*Euterpe oleraceea*

b. Forest Vegetation Indicative of Poor Agricultural Soils

Local Term	Scientific Name
Acapú	*Vouacapoua americana*
Jarana	*Holopyxidium jarana*
Sumaúma	*Ceiba pentandra*
Melancieira	*Alexa grandiflora*
Sapucaia	*Lecythis paraensis*
Piquí	*Caryocar microcarpum*
Cajú-Açú	*Anacardium giganteum*
Massaranduba	*Manilkara huberi* (or *Mimusops huberi*)

Source: Moran (1977).

Figure 2. Soil Selective Using Vegetarian Criteria

species array. Biomass production is estimated most often by placing about 10 one-meter-square screens to catch leaf fall, placed randomly in the area of forest to be studied. Leaf fall must be collected every one or two weeks to avoid losing the collection to the natural process of decomposition. Most human ecologists also collect floral specimens given the richness of the flora of Amazonia and the importance of identifying new species. Leaves, flowers, and fruits are necessary for accurate identification by systematists working with major collections such as are found, for example, at the New York Botanical Gardens, Kew Gardens (United Kingdom), the Missouri Botanical Gardens, the Goeldi Museum in Belem, Brazil, and the National Institute for Amazonian Research in Manaus, Brazil.

Fauna

Some scholars have argued that it was not soil quality but the availability of game that kept the size of settlements small in Amazonia (Lathrap 1968). Gross (1975) suggested that the consumption of animal protein varied between 15 and 63 grams per capita per day, and that to maintain such levels it was necessary to relocate settlements often. Implicated in this process of village mobility was the taboo against hunting some of the larger mammals, as noted by Ross (1978), because their incidence was so low that it was more effective to focus cultural attention on smaller game than on the large animals. A whole generation tried to prove or disprove this proposition, each one arguing based upon their single study site the rightness or correctness of the formulation (e.g., Gross 1975; Beckerman 1979; Chagnon and Hames, 1980; Hames, 1980; Vickers 1979).

Despite a now considerable body of information, we still do not have systematic studies of animal biomass in Amazonia. One of the most detailed studies pointed out that it was precisely the meat yield of tapir and peccaries that accounted for the bulk of the meat hunted in the western Amazon (Vickers 1984), and that taboos are specific to ethnic groups and need to be explained in microecological rather than regional terms. Vickers also noted that the meat yields drop in tropical forests beyond 600 meters altitude above sea level, as would be expected in montane forests, and that yields are higher in the lowland forests. One careful analysis suggests what may be behind the assumption of low faunal availability: of the 41 most hunted species, 39% were of less than 5 kilograms total weight, 73% were nocturnal, 54% were solitary, and 44% were arboreal (Sponsel 1981). The lack of long-term studies continues to limit human ecological formulations of how people use faunal resources. In small-scale populations, the data for a single year may represent an outlying point in a long-term average, and the average may not be estimable from that single year. To this day, there is an excessive dependence on the two studies made in the neotropics: one in Barro Colorado, Panama (Eisenberg and Thorington 1973) and the other near Manaus, Brazil (Fittkau and Klinge 1973). The study by Fittkau and Klinge, for example, is beginning to be seen as having seriously underestimated animal biomass (Eisenberg and Redford 1979; Eisenberg, O'Connell and August 1979; Emons 1984).

Faunal data collectors must ask hunters about the various kinds of habitats used in hunting, and about sampling from each habitat used in hunting, as well as those that have been abandoned. The most common method is to scan an area of 100 square meters for visual accounting (Eberhardt 1978; Brower and Zar 1984; Seber 1986). To determine the efficiency of hunting, data should be obtained from hunters about the distance travelled, how many animals were seen, how many killed, how much meat was consumed on the spot and how much brought back, together with data reporting basic morphometric measurements that permit the sex and age determinations of animals the hunted (Redford and Robinson 1987).

Social Organization

Human beings, as social animals, organize in ways that permit them to effectively obtain needed resources. Their social organization, especially among populations depending on the immediate physical environment, often reflects solutions to problems presented by those environments. Among the basic dimensions (adapted from Netting, Stone, and Stone 1988) that need to be described are the activities associated with resource use, the calendar of activities, and the local forms of organizing labor. One can begin by informal interviews about goods produced, including a list of cultivated plants, domesticated animals, fish caught, and wild food sources obtained. Then one can inquire into the seasonal division of labor in the various activities. The utilization of products for subsistence, exchange, sale, and the proportions going to each kind of use need to be accounted for, as does the nature of these activities (i.e., their names, the technologies used, and the relationship between the technology management and the resource).

Who participates in the subsistence activities is important basic data, and includes the division of labor by sex, age and status, the units of production (household, clan, phratry, etc.), types of mutual obligation created, the role of wage labor, sharecroppers, and so forth. The existing residential subsistence units may be isomorphic in many cases, but there may be important contrasts between work units and kin units. Finally, the problems perceived by the population, such as seasonal problems with climate, with crops, with getting enough labor, and with transportation give a baseline of what constraints the population may face that affects its forms of organization for subsistence.

Demographic Structure

As part of the collection of data on environmental perception and social organization, it is often necessary to do a census. A census permits the collection

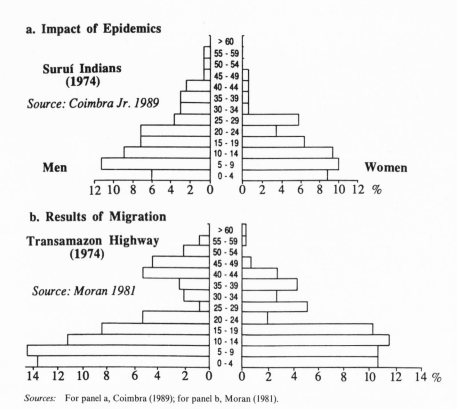

a. Impact of Epidemics

Suruí Indians (1974)

Source: Coimbra Jr. 1989

Men   Women

12 10 8 6 4 2 0   0 2 4 6 8 10 12 %

b. Results of Migration

Transamazon Highway (1974)

Source: Moran 1981

14 12 10 8 6 4 2 0   0 2 4 6 8 10 12 14 %

Sources: For panel a, Coimbra (1989); for panel b, Moran (1981).

Figure 3.   Impact of Epidemics and Migration on Age-Sex Distribution

of demographic data and an estimate of the population's fecundity, mortality, and other changes. Getting a census down in size is always difficult, and the following suggestions may help. The most telling demographic indicator is the age-sex distribution illustrated commonly in the form of a pyramid. A sex-age pyramid serves as a synthesis of a population's history. A young population will have a broad base, while an aging one will be almost rectangular. If a significant gap exists in a given sex or age group, it suggests the occurrence of some notable event that led to the loss of population—for example, outmigration or epidemic deaths. Figure 3 illustrates the impact of epidemic disease on the Suruí Indians of Rondônia. During epidemics, not only is there high mortality but there is also a fall in fecundity (Coimbra 1989; Feldman 1977, p. 29; Peters 1980; Netter and Lambert 1981), confounding the demographic collapse and crimping the pyramid in telling ways.

Following a major decline in fecundity, a population may experience periods of catch-up fertility, which Coimbra (1989) observed among the Suruí. Figure 4

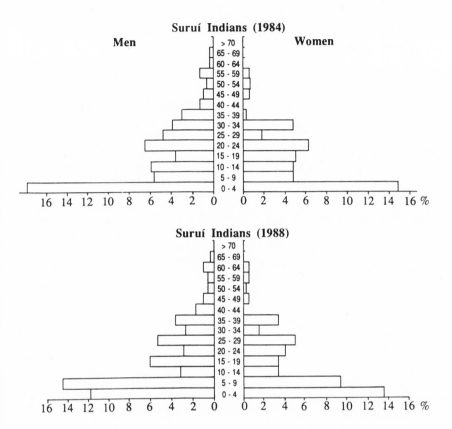

Source: Coimbra (1989).

Figure 4. Catch-up Fertility After Epidemic

illustrates the rapid increase in the number of children in the 1984(4a) and 1988(4b) censuses. Between these two censuses, the population grew at an annual rate of 5.6%, a rate that would permit it to double every 14 years. Given that they are recovering from a 75% mortality from the first decade of epidemics, such rates are entirely justified to ensure their biological survival.

Because of the difficulties in studying fertility in populations with high child mortality, one of the useful indices that can be used is the ratio between the total number of children aged 0-4 to the number of women of reproductive age (15-45). The child/woman ratio has a high correlation with more traditional indices such as the gross rate of fecundity ($p = 0.961$), the general rate of fecundity ($p = 0.975$) and the rate of total fecundity ($p = 0.970$), and can be used as a rapid assessment measure of a population's fecundity.

Another useful demographic measure is the infant mortality rate. This index refers to the number of deaths in the 0-1 years age group per 1,000 births. At present, the rates of infant mortality among many Amazonian indigenous groups are extremely high, due in large part to the lack of medical assistance and neglect of their needs. A rate of more than 100 per 1,000 births is considered very high, from 50 to 100 is considered high, 25 to 50 is considered mid-level, and below 25 is considered low. Among the Suruí of Rondônia, for example, recent rates have been 232.2 per 1,000 births (Coimbra 1989). This means that 23.2% of all children die in their first year of life! The rate among the Xavante in the 1980s was 242 per thousand (Flowers 1983). It has been noted to be 97.5 per thousand among the Shipibo of the Peruvian Amazon (Hern 1977, p. 360), suggesting that access to health care may be more precarious in the Brazilian than in the Peruvian Amazon.

Health and Nutrition

There is a close relationship between a population's demographic structure and its health and nutritional status. Native Amazonians' health status is generally good before contact, with high prevalence but low levels of morbidity and mortality. Following contact with national society, they experience epidemic mortality, which eventually stabilizes itself at a low level, and then they increase their numbers. With greater integration into national society, indigenous societies become increasingly affected by metabolic and chronic diseases rather than infectious or epidemic diseases.

Nutritional status can take any number of directions, depending on the degree of dislocation and transformation felt by the population's food production system. Signs of undernutrition increase with the intensification of contact. During periods of high mortality, there is a near total abandonment of farm work because of the loss of organization for production brought about by high adult mortality. The subsidies provided by government agencies and missionaries during this stage lead gradually to the population's loss of autonomy and to their growing dependence on subsidies. The contribution of these new sources of nutrition has rarely been positive. Most often, the products made available include refined sugar, table salt, and alcoholic drinks (associated with chronic and metabolic disorders such as goiter (Vieira Filho 1981) and diabetes (Vieira Filho 1977). Efforts to sedentarize Amazonian populations, without improving their access to better medical attention, could result in the spread of serious diseases such as Chagas' disease, which has never been reported for lowland South America but is endemic in the Andean region. Coimbra (1989) suggests that freedom from Chagas may be tied to the pattern of mobility and the type of housing materials used, which do not provide a favorable environment to the vector of the disease. This could change as they are restricted in their mobility and forced to sedentarize. Given the presence of the vector in their environment, the situation could become critical very quickly.

The most accurate and efficient measurements of the nutritional status of a population are obtained by body measurements or anthropometry. The minimum data to be collected are the height, weight, and age of each person (especially children under 12). Anthropometric measurements address the two principal causes of undernutrition: nutritional deficiencies and infection. Three indices are commonly used: height-for-age, weight-for-age, and weight-for-height. In general, a *chronic* deficiency of adequate nutrition will be reflected in height-for-age (i.e., stunting). Acute deficiencies may be reflected in below normal weight-for-age, but it may be hard to separate these from the effects of chronic undernutrition. For monitoring populations, the age-dependent indices are very sensitive to chronic deficiencies. When weight-for-height is abnormally low, we have a sensitive index to individuals in emergecy need of supplements due to *acute* forms of malnutrition (i.e., wasting) (Martorell 1982; Coimbra 1989). These indices can be supplemented with the measurement of subcutaneous fat using calipers. Most often used are the triceps skinfold and the subscapular skinfold. To estimate the muscular area and the fat-to-muscle proportion, the skinfold measurements are related to the circumference of the upper arm.

CONCLUSIONS

The object of study in human ecology is the interactive behavior of people toward their surroundings. The orientation is essentially interdisciplinary, concerned not only with people but also with the characteristics of the physical environment with which people interact. Both behavior and perception need to be studied in their context.

To explain human ecological relations, we need to account for a large number of possible implicated factors. The effective environment of an individual or a population is all-encompassing, and the effective pressures may come just as easily from the physical as from the political environment. Each population of Amazonia has a unique historical experience that makes it different from all others; each has suffered a specific impact from epidemic contact with outsiders that has resulted in a distinctive yet patterned age-sex distribution; each has been exploited by outsiders in particular ways; each has a given set of resources in their territory that they exploit in ways that reflect their seasonal availability and conflicting demands on the populations's time. They find themselves today in a particular situation that reflects all of these experiences. The solutions that each population, and individuals within the population, finds will also reflect all of these experiences, and some will be more effective than others. The interdisciplinary approach of human ecology constitutes a first step in rethinking research and action towards our relations with the physical environment. I hope that the suggestions on minimum data will prove useful in coming to grips with the need to produce comparable data without regard to which specific disciplines our human ecology derives from. I hope that these minima prove useful not only to other Amazonian human ecologists but to others working in very different ecosystems. Although we can live without standards, we also need them—to ensure consistency in quality, fairness in evaluating various work produced, and to allow comparisons over time. Standards do not prevent innovation. In fact, it can be argued that standards promote change, by setting up a clear canon against which to match the gifts of individuals who are challenged to best the current standard. There is plenty of room in these minima for creativity and imagination. Human ecology, because of its disparate definitions and multidisciplinary foundations, is in particular need of seeking a common ground. Various efforts have been attempted at the level of theory, with mixed results. Perhaps a no less profitable avenue may be offered by agreement at the level of method and baseline data in what could be called human ecological minima.

REFERENCES

Alvim, P.T., and F.P. Cabala. 1974. "Um novo sistema de representação gráfica da fertilidade dus solos para cacau." *Cacau Atualidader* 11(1): 2-6.

Anderson, A., and E.M. Ioris, 1989. "The Logic of Extraction: Resource Management and Income Generation by Extractive Producers in the Amazon Estuary." Paper presented at Conference on Traditional Resource Use in Neotropical Forests, Gainesville, Florida.

Anderson, A., and D. Posey, 1985. "Manejo de Cerrado pelos Indios Kayapó." *Boletim do Museu Paraense Emilio Goeldi* (Botánica) 2(1): 77-98.

Baier, W., D.Z. Chaput, D.A. Russello, and W. Sharp. 1972. *Soil Moisture Estimator Program System.* Technical Bulletin 78. Ottawa: Agrometry Section, Canada Department of Agriculture.

Balée, W. 1989. "The Culture of Amazonian Forests." *Advances in Economic Botany* 7: 1-21.

Beckerman, S. 1979. "The Abundance of Protein in Amazonia." *American Anthropologist* 81: 533-560.

Bordne, E.F., and J.L. McGuinness, 1973. "Some Procedures for Calculating Potential Evapotranspiration." *Professional Geographer* 25: 22-28.

Brower, J.E., and J.H. Zar. 1984. *Field and Laboratory Methods for General Ecology.* 2nd. ed. Dubuque, IO: Wm. C. Brown.

Cain, S., and G.M. de Oliveira Castro. 1959. *Manual of Vegetation Analysis.* New York: Hafner.

Carneiro, R.L. 1957. "Subsistence and Social Structure: An Ecological Study of the Kuikuru." Ph.D. Dissertation, Department of Anthropology, University of Michigan.

Chagnon, N., and R. Hames. 1980. "La Hipótesis Protéica y la Adaptación Indígena a la Cuenca del Amazonas." *Interciencia* 5(6): 346-358.

Coimbra, C. 1989. "From Shifting Cultivation to Coffee Farming: The Impact of Change on the Health and Ecology of the Surui Indians." Ph. D. dissertation, Department of Anthropology, Indiana University.

Denevan, W. 1966. *The Aboriginal Cultural Geography of the Llanos de Mojos, Bolivia.* Berkeley, CA: Department of Geography, University of California.

Denevan, W., and C. Padoch, eds. 1988. *Swidden Fallow Agroforestry in the Peruvian Amazon.* Economic Botany Monograph. New York: New York Botanical Garden.

Eberhardt, L.L. 1978. "Transect Methods for Population Studies." *Journal of Wildlife Management* 42(1): 1-31.

Eisenberg, J.F., M.A. O'Connell, and P.V. August. 1979. "Density, Productivity, and Distribution of Mammals in Two Venezuelan Habitats." Pp. 187-207 in *Vertebrate Ecology in the Northern Neotropics*, edited by J.F. Eisenberg. Washington DC: Smithsonian Institute Press.

Eisenberg, J.F., and K. Redford. 1979. "A Biogeographic Analysis of the Mammalian Fauna of Venezuela." In *Vertebrate Ecology in the Northern Neotropics*, edited by J.F. Eisenberg. Washington DC: Smithsonian Institute Press.

Eisenberg, J., and R. Thorington. 1973. "A Preliminary Analysis of a Neotropical Fauna." *Biotropica* 16(3): 210-222.

Erickson, C. 1988. "An Archeological Investigation of Raised Field Agriculture in the Lake Titicaca Basin of Peru." Ph.D. dissertation, Department of Anthropology, University of Illinois.

Emmons, L.H. 1984. "Geographic Variation in Densities and Diversities of Non-Flying Mammals in Amazonia." *Biotropica* 16(3): 210-222.

Feldman, J. 1977. "Effects of Tuberculosis on Sexual Functioning." *Medical Aspects of Human Sexuality* 11: 29.

Ferdon, E. 1959. "Agricultural Potential and the Development of Cultures." *Southwestern Journal of Anthropology* 15: 1-19.

Figueroa, A. 1904. *Relación de las Misiones de la Compañía de Jesús en el País de los Maynas.* Madrid: Librería F. de V. Suarez.

Fittkau, E., and J. Klinge. 1973. "On Biomass and Trophic Structure of the Central Amazonian Rain Forest Ecosystem." *Biotropica* 5(1): 2-14.

Flowers, N. 1983. "Seasonal Factors in Subsistence, Nutrition, and Child Growth in a Central Brazilian Indian Community." Pp. 357-390 in *Adaptive Responses of Native Amazonians*, edited by R. Hames and W. Vickers. New York: Academic Press.

Flowers, N. et al. 1982. "Variation in Swidden Practices in Four Central Brazilian Indian Societies." *Human Ecology* 10(2): 203-217.

Fritz, S. 1922. *Journal of the Travels and Labors of Father Samuel Fritz in the River of the Amazons between 1686 and 1723.* London: Hakluyt Society.

Gomes, M.P. 1988. *Os Indios e o Brasil.* Petropolis, Brazil: Vozes.

Gross, D. 1975. "Protein Capture and Cultural Development in the Amazon Basin." *American Anthropologist* 77: 526-549.

Gross, D., G. Eiten, N. Flowers, F. Leoi, M. Ritter, and D. Werner. 1979. "Ecology and Acculturation among Native Peoples of Central Brazil." *Science* 206: 1043-1050.

Hames, R., ed. 1980. *Studies of Hunting and Fishing in the Neotropics.* Working Papers on South American Indians No. 2. Bennington, VT: Bennington College.

Hemming, J. 1978. *Red Gold: The Conquest of the Brazilian Indians.* Cambridge, MA: Harvard University Press.

Hern, W. 1977. "High Fertility in a Peruvian Amazon Indian Village." *Human Ecology* 5: 355-368.

Herrera, A. de. 1856. *The Voyage of Francisco de Orellana down the River of the Amazons, A.D. 1540-1541.* London: Hakluyt Society.

Hoag, R., S.W. Buol, and J. Pérez. 1987. "Alluvial Soils of the Amazon Basin." Pp. 78-79 in *Tropsoils: Technical Report 1985-86*, edited by N. Caudle and C. McCants. Raleigh, NC: North Carolina State University.

Jordan, C., and R. Herrera. 1981. "Tropical Rain Forests: Are Nutrients Really Critical." *American Naturalist* 117: 167-180.

Junk, W.J. 1984. "Ecology of the Várzea of Amazonian Whitewater Rivers." Pp. 215-244 in *The Amazon: Limnology and Landscape Ecology of a Mighty Tropical River and its Basin*, edited by H. Sioli. Dordrecht, The Netherlands: Junk.

Lathrap, D. 1968. "The Hunting Economics of the Tropical Forest Zone of South America." Pp. 23-29 in *Man the Hunter*, edited by R. Lee and I. deVore. Chicago: Aldine.

_____. 1970. *The Upper Amazon*. New York: Praeger.

Lima, R.R. 1956. "A Agricultura nas Várzeas do Estuário Amazónico." Boletim Técnico do Instituto Agronómico do Norte. Belém: IAN.

Martorell, R. 1982. *Nutrition and Health Status Indicators*. LSMS Working Papers, No. 13. Washington, DC: The World Bank.

Meggers, B. 1954. "Environmental Limitations on the Development of Culture." *American Anthropologist* 56: 801-824.

_____. 1971. *Amazonia*. Chicago: Aldine.

Moran, E.F. 1977. "Estratégias de subrevivéncia: O uso dos recursos ao Longo da Rodovía Transamazônica." *Acta Amazänica* 7: 363-379.

_____. 1982. "Ecological, Anthropological, and Agronomic Research in the Amazon Basin." *Latin American Research Review* 17: 3-41.

_____. 1990. *A Ecologia Humana das Populações da Amazônia*. Petrópolis, Brazil: Vozes.

_____. 1991. "Human Adaptive Strategies in Amazonian Blackwater Ecosystems." *American Anthropologist* 93: 361-382.

_____. 1993. *Through Amazonian Eyes: The Human Ecology of Amazonian Populations*. Iowa City: University of Iowa Press.

Mueller-Dumbois, D.M., and H. Ellenberg. 1974. *Aims and Methods of Vegetation Ecology*. New York: Wiley.

Myers, T. 1989. "The Expansion and Collapse of the Omagua." Paper presented at Wenner Gren Foundation Conference on "Amazonian Synthesis," Nova Friburgo, Brazil.

Netter, A., and A. Lambert. 1981. "Iatrogenic and Environmental Factors in Human Reproduction." Pp. 117-128 in *Research on Fertility and Sterility*, edited by J. Cortes-Prieto et al. Baltimore, MD: University Park Press.

Netting, R., P. Stone, and G. Stone. 1988. "The Social Organization of Agrarian Labor." Paper presented at the AAAS meeting, Boston.

Oliveira, A.E. de. 1988. "Amazonia: Modificações socials e culturals decorrentes do processo de ocupação humana." *Boletim do Museu Paraense Emilio Goeldi* 4(1): 65-115.

Peters, J.F. 1980. "The Shirishana of the Yanomami: A Demographic Study." *Social Biology* 27: 272-285.

Pires, J.M., and G. Prance. 1985. "The Vegetation Types of the Brazilian Amazon." Pp. 109-145 in *Amazonia*, edited by G. Prance and T. Lovejoy. Oxford: Pergamon Press.

Porro, A. 1989. "Social Organization and Power in the Amazon Floodplain: The Ethnohistorical Sources." Paper presented at Wenner-Gren Foundation Conference on "Amazonian Synthesis," Nova Friburgo, Brazil.

Posey, D. 1985. "Indigenous Management of Tropical Forest Ecosystems: The Case of the Kayapo Indians of the Brazilian Amazon." *Agroforestry Systems* 3: 139-158.

Prance, G. 1978. "The Origin and Evolution of the Amazon Flora." *Interciencia* 3(4): 207-222.

RADAM. 1974-79. *Levantamento da Regiao Amazônica*, Vols. 1-12. Rio de Janeiro: Min. das Minas e Energia.

Redford, K., and J. Robinson. 1987. "The Game of Choice: Patterns of Indian and Colonist Hunting in the Neotropics." *American Anthropologist* 89: 650-667.

Roosevelt, A.C. 1989. "Natural Resource Management in Amazonia before the Conquest." *Advances in Economic Botany* 7: 30-62.

Ross, E. 1978. "Food Taboos, Diet and Hunting Strategy." *Current Anthropology* 19: 1-36.

Sanchez, P. et al. 1982. "Amazon Basin Soils: Management for Continuous Crop Production." *Science* 216: 821-827.

Seber, G.A.F. 1986. "A Review of Estimating Animal Abundance." *Biometrics* 42: 267-292.

Simon, P. 1861. *The Expedition of Pedro de Ursua and Lope de Aguirre in Search of El Dorado and the Omagua.* London: Hakluyt Society.

Sponsel, L. 1981. "The Hunter and the Hunted in the Amazon." Ph.D. dissertation, Department of Anthropology, Cornell University.

————. 1986. "Amazon Ecology and Adaptation." *Annual Review of Anthropology* 15: 67-97.

Sternberg, H. 1975. *The Amazon River of Brazil.* Wiesbaden, Germany: F. Steiner.

Stigter, K. 1986. "In Quest of Tropical Micrometeorology for On-Farm Advisors." *Agricultural and Forest Meteorology* 36: 289-296.

Uriarte, M. 1952. *Diario de um Misionero de Maynas.* Serie A, No. 7. Madrid: Institute Sto. Torigio de Mongrovejo.

Vickers, W. 1984. "The Faunal Component of Lowland South American Hunting Kills." *Interciencia* 9(6): 366-376.

————. 1988. "Game Depletion Hypothesis of Amazonian Adaptation: Data from a Native Community." *Science* 239: 1521-1522.

Vieira Filho, J.P.B. 1977. "O Diabetes mellitus e as glicemias de jejum dos indios Caripuna e Palikur." *Revista da Associação Medica Brasileira* 23(6): 175-178.

————. 1981. "O Bocio entre os Indios Brasileiros." *Revista da Associação Medica Brasileira* 27: 285-287.

Weinstein, B. 1993. *The Amazon Rubber Boom, 1850-1920.* Stanford, CA: Stanford University Press.

Whitehead, N.L. 1989. "The Ancient Amerindian Polities of the Lower Orinoco, Amazon, and Guayana Coast." Paper presented at Wenner-Gren Foundation conference on "Amazonian Synthesis," Nova Friburgo, Brasil.

Wilken, G.C. 1988. "Minimum Climate Data for Comparative Analysis in Agriculture." Paper presented at the AAAS meeting, Boston.

THE ELEMENTARY FORMS OF
THE FIRST PROTOHUMAN SOCIETY:
AN ECOLOGICAL/SOCIAL
NETWORK APPROACH

A. R. Maryanski

ABSTRACT

Data from primates are used to assess the plausibility of various hypotheses about the nature of the first protohuman or hominid societies. These data indicate that social structure among primates is related to mating and transfer systems as these are affected by ecological pressures and conservative ancestral characters. The result is a typical pattern of social ties among age and sex classes for a particular species in a given environment. Thus, to the extent that we are willing to speculate on the nature of the first hominid societies on the basis of data from contemporary primates, we might consider the social network ties among those species closest to humans and assess which ones could serve under savanna-like conditions as the basic building blocks for hominid social structure. Such an analysis lends credence to the hypothesis that the first hominid societies were built from strengthened adult male-female bonds with a patri-focal emphasis.

Advances in Human Ecology, Volume 2, pages 215-241.
Copyright © 1993 by JAI Press Inc.
All rights of reproduction in any form reserved.
ISBN: 1-55938-558-8

INTRODUCTION

Efforts to reconstruct the first "human" societies are longstanding among social scientists. During the nineteenth century, such giants as Herbert Spencer, Henry Morgan, Henry Maine, and Friedrich Engels speculated on the origin of the family and its development, with classic evolutionary debates focused around two main issues: (a) whether the first "human" societies were constructed around a promiscuous, polyandrous, polygynous, or monogamous mating system, and (b) whether these mating practices laced societies together through male or female blood lines (Maine 1874; McLennan 1865; Post 1875; Lubbock 1889; Bachofen 1861; Giraud-Tevlon 1884; Morgan 1870; Westermarck 1891; Engels 1902). Despite the great labor expended by these early classical thinkers and the far-reaching consequences of reconstructing the origin of society, nineteenth-century evolutionary conjecture was greatly flawed and, as a result, social evolutionary thinking was deemphasized for a good portion of this century.

In recent times, research into the evolution of humans has reawakened interest in reconstructing the first hominid societies.[1] Beginning with the Plio-Pleistocene fossil record of four million to one million years ago, the physical features of early hominids are now becoming evident (Johanson and White 1979; Leakey and Lewin 1977; Rak 1983; Blumenberg 1985; Grine 1988). Drawn with broad strokes, these data tell us that early hominids had ape-like facial features, walked upright long before developing a larger brain, evidenced a large sexual dimorphism in body size, and had already carved out a niche on the African plains before making stone tools (Lewin 1987a, 1987b; Leakey and Hay 1979; Johanson 1985; Tobias 1985; Wolpoff 1976; Rapp and Vonda 1981; Stringer 1984; Campbell 1988; Clark 1985).

While a physical picture of early hominids provides a clear starting point for understanding human biological evolution, the fossil and archaeological records for this time are still of limited use when constructing a portrait of human *social* evolution. This limitation has prompted scholars to use another approach: If our hominid ancestors are descendants of African apes, and hence distant cousins to present-day monkeys and apes, then the study of the physical and organizational features of nonhuman primates may offer clues to the origins of human society (Hooton 1955; Reynolds 1966, 1968; Kinzey 1987). This mode of inquiry has taken at least three tacks. One has been to determine how early hominids became differentiated from apes through such forces as ecological change (Lovejoy 1981; Bartholomew and Birdsell 1953; Kortlandt 1972), dietary specialization (Lucas, Corlett, and Luke 1985; Jolly 1970, 1978; Isaac and McCown 1975; Goodall and Hamburg 1975), and technological innovation (DeVore 1964; Washburn 1963). A second tack has been the detailed study of such open-range primates as baboons (Papio) who are seen as the closest "ecological counterparts" to early hominid populations (Wolpoff

1978; and see Strum 1987). These models focus on the ecological context and the adaptive problems faced by savanna-living primates, with the presumption that hominid ancestors faced similar adaptive problems (DeVore and Washburn 1963; Washburn and DeVore 1961). A third tack has been the study of apes who are genetically closest to humans. Phyletic models typically study the Great apes, particularly the chimpanzee (Pan) and gorilla (Gorilla), with an eye to uncovering their common affinities with each other and early hominids (Wrangham 1987). These models usually assume that those behavioral features shared by phyletically close species, especially when they live in different environments, are likely to be contemporary manifestations of characteristics retained from a common ancestor. When similar attributes are found among apes and humans, then it is considered likely that early hominids also evidenced these same traits (Goodall 1975; Goodall-Van Lawick 1975; Goodall and Hamburg 1975; Reynolds 1968; McGrew 1981; Tanner 1987; Lancaster 1968; Kortlandt 1972; Zihlman and Lowenstein 1983; see the edited volume of Kinzey 1987).

The reconstruction of hominid lifeways through the analysis of fossil and archaeological evidence and the behavioral study of nonhuman primates offers promise for the reconstruction of early hominid organization. The purpose of this paper is to consider a further strategy: a social-network perspective put to use with the nineteenth-century insight that, until very recently, human societies were structured around mating and blood ties. Wanting to avoid the pitfalls of the nineteenth-century evolutionists, however, this analysis will not begin with present-day kinship patterns, drawn from band and tribal societies, to then project backward into time. But, in a sense, we can look back by considering the social relationships of less complicated nonhuman primate societies to then project forward to the first hominid societies. While nonhuman primates lack kinship terminology, marriage rules, and cultural definitions of "legitimate" offspring, they do have preferred mating and blood-tie connections. Such is the rationale for the data and analysis presented in this essay. Below, some basic properties of primate organization are outlined, along with the social network perspective.

A FRAMEWORK FOR APPROACHING THE ORIGIN OF SOCIETY

Most primates are organized into stable heterosexual groups. For slowly maturing, intelligent animals with relatively long lifespans, such permanent social arrangements require the integration of a variety of age and sex classes—not just the adult males and females. As a result, the social orders of primates are complex and flexible, although most species reveal a modal group size and a typical ratio of age and sex classes (for discussions see Eisenberg,

Muckenhirn, and Rudran 1972; Southwick and Siddiqi 1974; Clutton-Brock 1974; Clutton-Brock and Harvey 1977; Jolly 1985, p. 115). While primate organization is still not well understood, the available data strongly support the premise that varying environmental pressures and the innate predispositions primate species have for particular kinds of social and sexual relations, restrict and regulate the movements of individuals (Carpenter 1942; Hinde 1979, 1983; Clutton-Brock and Harvey 1977). Drawing from these data, this papers focuses on a rather limited aspect of primate organization—the strength of social bonds in association with mating and patterns of movement or transfer—in an effort to assess how these processes are implicated in creating and maintaining particular kinds of social structures among a small sample of Old World anthropoids. The ultimate goal, of course, is to speculate on the implications of these mating and social ties for understanding the structural base of the first hominid societies.[2]

The Nature of the Data

The argument to be presented is drawn from the following tendencies in the data. Mating patterns among Old World monkeys and apes are of three generic types: (1) one male and female pair (a "monogamous" arrangement); (2) one male and multiple females (a "polygynous" or "harem" arrangement); and (3) multiple male and multiple female (a nonexclusive and unstable mating arrangement) (Southwick and Siddiqi 1974). Moreover, each species of higher Old World primate with one of these mating patterns also evidences a pattern of transferring a specific age and sex class out of the social unit in which mating occurs. These transfer patterns, in which males, or females, or both, leave the natal unit at puberty, are not caused by the mating pattern, but a transfer pattern is associated with a mating system for a given primate species (Packer 1979; Greenwood 1980; Drickamer and Vassey 1973; Demarest 1977). In turn, the system of mating and transfer among primate species is connected to a pattern of social bonding within and between the age and sex classes. Social bonding can be seen in such behaviors as social grooming, embracing (but often excluding sexual contact), food sharing, aiding and protecting, continual close proximity, cooperative alliances, and when possible, the length and intensity of a social relation.[3] These patterned relations reflect inherent social predispositions, as most studied primate species show a propensity for preferential relationships among and between age and sex classes, with wide variation (see Hinde 1979, 1983; Cheney, Seyfarth, and Smuts 1986). Since these relations are associated with mating and transfer patterns, each probably reveals some inertia that will limit the kinds of structural transformations possible in a given habitat.[4]

These tendencies in the existing data, however, require some procedures for ordering them if they are to be useful in speculating about the structural base of the first societies. Hence, the following procedures are followed: First, attention is focused on how primate relations reveal a specific social structure, with the concept of social structure used here in a narrow way to denote the social-network pattern for a given primate species. This analysis, then, is concerned only with structural regularities in the patterning of relations among conspecifics and the emergent properties that characterize these relations.[5] Second, primate bonding patterns are assumed to be reciprocal and positive interactions. Negative and asymmetric relations also occur among primates, but mutually reinforcing and friendly interactions among dyads form the core of any primate group. Third, a simple scale of tie strength will be constructed. The scale ranges from absent (nonexistent or negligible interactions) to weak (occasional interactions), to moderate (close affiliation for a time but without great intensity or endurance over time), to strong (very high rates of interaction, extensive physical contact and a stable relationship that may last a lifetime). The variation in tie strength ranges, therefore, from little attraction to binding intimacy. While the weights attached to each measure of affinity cannot be quantified, the scaling of tie strength is an uncomplicated procedure because primate investigators are in agreement on the attraction among and between most age and sex classes, especially for the well-studied species detailed here. Thus, the social bonds outlined are drawn from the primate literature and are the tie patterns for a given primate species in their normal habitat. However, to avoid unnecessary complexity, only the following classes of social ties will be used: (1) adult male-adult male ties; (2) adult female-adult female ties; (3) adult male-adult female ties; (4) adult male-daughter ties; (5) adult male-son ties; (6) adult female-daughter ties; and (7) adult female-son ties. The nature of these seven classes of ties among a sample of living primates is probably adequate for this compact analysis of primate social structure.

The Nature of the Argument

Using a network approach in conjunction with current field data on Old World primates allows us to proceed and argue as follows: To the extent that early hominid social structure can be inferred from the bonding patterns among our closest primate relations, it might be reasonable to consider the restraints that age and sex class bonds initially placed upon those protohominids who moved from a wet, forested habitat (where the majority of primates are found), to a dryer woodland, bushland, or savanna-like environment (where the fossils of early hominids are *all* found). A paleoenvironmental change to an open habitat must have altered the ranging, dietary, and sleeping habits of early proto-hominids (for a discussion of hominid adaptive problems, see Foley 1984). Additionally, the predator populations known to have coexisted with Plio-Pleistocene hominids (see Maglio and Cooke 1978) must have made predator avoidance or resistance absolutely crucial for survival. Today, among open-country common baboons (*Papio*), a highly structured social order seemingly enhances individual fitness and reproductive success by deterring predators and lessening the chances of any one individual being chosen by a predator (Alexander 1974; Hamilton 1982; for a discussion of the regularities in baboon progressions, see Rhine, Boland, and Lodwick 1985). If we can assume that early hominids and baboons faced present-day or even more intense predation levels as the fossil record for the Plio-Pleistocene suggests, a rigorous formation of conspecifics seeking safety in sheer numbers would seem a plausible antipredator strategy for both baboons and hominids (see Anderson 1986).[6] However, it is likely that alterations in early hominid organization from an earlier forest existence were, to some degree, constrained by the already existing and phylogenetically driven pattern of social bonds among age and sex classes.

Thus, to the degree that we are willing to accept inferences about early hominid societies from relational data on our closest relatives—the African apes—we might (1) consider the nature of their social ties as influenced by mating and transfer systems; and then, (2) speculate on how their patterns of ties interacted under the ecological requirements of savanna-like conditions to produce the first hominid societies. This is the general theme. Now, to fill in some details, we will examine briefly the mating, transfer, and patterns of social ties among a few higher primates.[7]

MATING SYSTEMS, TRANSFER PATTERNS, AND SOCIAL TIES AMONG SELECTED PRIMATES

The primates for this analysis were selected on several criteria. First, an example of each major type of mating system is needed: (1) one male and female pair, (2) one male and multiple females, and (3) multiple males and multiple females. Since all species of gibbons (*Hylobates*) evidence the rare "monogamous" pair bond, these well-studied lesser apes are included for analysis. For the "polygynous" pattern, two monkey genera, gelada (*Theropithecus*) and patas (*Erythrocebus*), and one ape genera, gorilla (Gorilla), are discussed. For the transitory or multiple partner pattern, two monkey species, the baboon (*Papio anubis*) and macaque (*Macaca fuscata*), as well as one species of ape, the common chimpanzee (*Pan troglodytes*), are included. Second, because early hominids were Old World primates, only African and Asian primates are examined. These sampled species are well studied, making it possible to illustrate the variability in social relations associated with different mating and transfer systems. Third, because early hominids faced the adaptive problems of an open bushland or savanna-like habitat, African species who inhabit either dry woodlands or grasslands are especially well represented. Finally, the two forest-living African apes who are genetically closest to humans are included, the common chimpanzee and the gorilla. Among ape genera, then, only the semisolitary Asian orangutan is excluded since this Great Ape has few affiliative interactions and its stable groupings are limited to mother and dependent offspring.

Thus, our sample of species revealing different degrees of closeness to humans, different habitats, diverse patterns of mating, different transfer systems, and distinctive social ties, should provide a sufficient data base—at least for exploratory purposes. Since apes constitute only a handful of species none of whom lives permanently outside the forest, and we have many species of monkeys, this sample is representative. The next step is to compare the basic organizational arrangements of these selected primates.

One Male-One Female Primate Arrangement

Asian gibbons (Hylobates). All lesser apes are strictly arboreal, territorial, and organized into small isolated "family" units with an average and modal size of about four individuals (Ellefson 1974; Gittens 1980; Chivers 1984; Leighton 1987). Manifesting little or no sexual dimorphism, an adult male and female gibbon (and sometimes dependent offspring) fiercely protect a small stable territory from all conspecifics. This conjugated alliance may facilitate the formation of the strong heterosexual-pair bond, sometimes viewed as coming close to the monogamous ideal of "mating for life" (MacKinnon and MacKinnon 1984, p. 291). This fidelity may also facilitate male parental care and the formation of strong tie cliques within the nuclear unit. However, over time as offspring mature, ties between parents and offspring weaken until, at puberty, both sons and daughters leave the natal territory (Tilson 1981). This one male-one female organizational arrangement, with its strong heterosexual-pair bond, shared parental care, and transfer of offspring at puberty, is a consistent pattern among lesser apes and is connected to the bonding pattern outlined at the top of Table 1 (Carpenter 1940; Chivers 1974, 1984; Brockelman and Srikosamatara 1984; Tenaza 1975; Tilson 1981).

One Male-Multiple Female Primate Arrangement

A relatively stable sexual connection between one male and two or more females is a common primate mating pattern. In this alliance, dubbed the "harem" plan, males evidence considerable dimorphism over females. Reproductive units usually have one breeding male, although gorilla groups may contain several adult males.

African geladas (Theropithecus). Gelada monkeys are open-country primates who reproduce in one male-multiple female groups. While large herds of geladas congregate on the African savanna, embedded within these masses are socially detached "bachelor" groups and "bisexual" groups containing one

Table 1. Patterns of Social Ties in Reproductive Units as Conditioned by Mating and Transfer Patterns among Primates

| | Ties Among | | | | | | |
| | Adults | | | Adult-Offspring | | | |
	Male/Male	Female/Female	Male/Female	Father/Daughter	Father/Son	Mother/Daughter	Mother/Son
1. Gibbon/Siamang Apes	Absent tie	Absent tie	Strong tie	Strong tie (until puberty)	Strong tie (until puberty)	Strong tie (until puberty)	Strong tie (until puberty)
2. Gelada Monkeys	Absent to weak tie	Strong tie	Weak tie (to most harem females)	Absent tie	Absent tie	Strong tie	Strong tie (until puberty)
3. Patas Monkeys	Absent tie	Strong tie	Absent to weak tie (to most harem females)	Absent tie	Absent tie	Strong tie	Strong tie (until puberty)
4. Gorilla Apes	Weak tie	Absent to weak ties	Moderate ties among lead male and females with offspring, weak ties among all males and females without offspring	Unknown tie (most likely absent)	Unknown tie (most likely absent)	Strong tie (until puberty)	Strong tie (until puberty)
5. Japanese Macaque Monkeys	Absent to weak tie	Strong tie	Weak to moderate tie	Unknown tie (most likely absent)	Unknown tie (most likely absent)	Strong tie	Strong tie (until puberty)
6. Olive Baboon Monkeys	Absent to weak tie	Strong tie	Weak to moderate tie	Unknown tie (mosts likely absent)	Unknown tie (most likely absent)	Strong tie	Strong tie (until puberty)
7. Common Chimpanzee Apes	Moderate to strong	Absent to weak tie	Weak tie	Unknown tie (most likely absent)	Unknown tie (most likely absent)	Strong tie (until puberty)	Strong tie

male and up to ten mature females and their offspring (Crook 1966; Ohsawa 1979a; Mori and Kawai 1975; Dunbar 1984, pp. 11-39). Normally, a "harem-holder" has exclusive sexual rights to females in his harem, even though some groups have a second adult male. Thus, gelada males are less likely to compete for access to single females than they are for ownership rights to harems (Mori 1979a; Dunbar 1978).

Although the leader male is the focal point for sexual activity, he otherwise spends little time with his females (Dunbar 1979). Leader males also spend a negligible amount of time interacting with other mature males; even when a friendly relation does occasionally develop between two adult males in a bisexual group, antagonism intensifies if the subordinate abandons his passive sexual role (see Mori [1979d] for a discussion of the second male and his role in group fission). Interactions between a harem leader and immatures are also infrequent and ties are reported to be absent or weak. Typically, a leader male forms a close tie only with a single high-ranking female (Dunbar 1983a, 1984, p. 46; Bramblett 1970; Mori 1979b).

Unlike the detached male, harem females evince strong bonds with immatures and with particular females. Strong-tie cliques (believed to be made up of mother, daughter, and sister bonds) make up the stable core in each group. These matrifocal units endure over generations and seemingly inhibit social intercourse and female transfer between different groups. Only sons leave at puberty to become members of all male "bachelor units" while single females rarely desert their natal group (Ohsawa 1979b; Mori 1979c; Dunbar 1983b, 1984, p. 20; Mori and Kawai 1975).[8] Thus, membership changes usually result from males moving in or out, with female geladas forming matrilines and socializing primarily with blood relatives (Mori 1979c; Dunbar 1984, pp. 40-41). Females without living relatives are often socially detached, leading one scholar to argue that a female with a strong tie to a leader male is probably one without a kinship network (Dunbar 1983a).[9] The gelada mating arrangement, where one male has sexual rights to a harem, where males leave the natal unit at puberty, and where females interact almost exclusively with close relatives, is part of the social-ties pattern delineated at the top of Table 1.

African patas (Erythrocebus). Patas monkeys are open-country primates whose one-male groups may contain up to 12 adult females and their offspring (Hall 1965; Struhsaker and Gartlan 1970). Normally, each harem-holder has breeding rights over his females, although patas sexual relationships are reported to be "brief" and "business-like" (Chism, Rowell, and Olson 1984; Rowell and Hartwell 1978). In every other activity, a harem male is a peripheral figure who, at best, associates occasionally with one or two adult females (Rowell and Hartwell 1978), but who otherwise interacts very little with females and immatures (Harding and Olson 1986). Leader males evidence considerable "vigilant" behavior, however, most notably when rival males are nearby.

Moreover, even natal males are no longer tolerated after puberty, with the result that they transfer to all-male groups. Otherwise, aggression within reproductive units is rare, and except for the emigration of young males, patas groups are relatively stable in size and composition (Hall and Mayer 1967; Struhsaker and Gartlan 1970; Gutstein 1978).

In contrast to the peripheral adult male, adult females are highly social and cohesive. Where blood ties are known, adult females show a marked social preference for relatives (Chism, Rowell, and Olson 1984; Loy and Harnois 1988). Since male turnover may be as often as once a year, the group's internal coherence rests upon female bonds. Additionally, females are essential to the maintenance of spacing arrangements between groups (Struhsaker and Gartlan 1970; Chism, Rowell, and Olson 1984) and to the direction and timing of group movements, with one female sometimes serving as unit leader over her companions (Hall 1965, p. 80). Thus, the patas mating arrangement, with its aloof male, male-transfer pattern, female-controlled group, and affiliative female-female bonding pattern, converges to the pattern of social ties outlined near the top of Table 1 (Chism, Rowell, and Olson 1984; Struhsaker and Gartlan 1970; Hall 1965; Loy and Harnois 1988).

African gorilla (Gorilla). These large terrestrial apes inhabit secondary (regenerating) or montane forest (Watts 1985; Fossey 1976, 1982). With one leader "silverback" male and several adult females and their immatures making up the core of a gorilla group (Fossey 1982), gorillas are typically organized into loose harem units that average 12 individuals. Four or more gorilla groups and some single males normally share a home range, with occasional reports of such groups day-resting, traveling, and even bedding down together overnight (Schaller 1962, 1972; Dixson 1981, pp. 112-13; Fossey 1976; A. Goodall 1979; Yamagiwa 1983). In each gorilla group, a dominant silverback is most often the sexual partner for resident adult females, although gorillas reveal a flexible harem organization since up to four potentially breeding adult males may be present in a gorilla group (Weber and Vedder 1983; Harcourt 1978; Dixson 1981, p. 125; Yamagiwa 1983). At puberty, males and females both depart their natal unit. When males depart, they become either solitary or transient group visitors within their natal home range. When females depart, they normally transfer to another group or to a solitary male, usually transferring several times and often to a group in a neighboring range (Pusey and Packer 1987, p. 253; Harcourt, Fossey, Stewart, and Watts 1980; Harcourt, Stewart, and Fossey 1976). Within reproductive units, positive interactions normally prevail (Dixson 1981, p. 128). Familiar adult males are very tolerant of each other, although they engage in few overt interactions (Watts 1988; Yamagiwa 1983; Cousins 1978). Adult females are also tolerant of each other, although they rarely interact, in part because they are usually strangers from different natal groups (Harcourt 1979; Stewart and Harcourt 1987). Adult male and female relations vary depending upon the status of a male and the maternal cycle of a female. A female with young usually sits in close day proximity with the leader silverback (Stewart and Harcourt 1987). A female without dependents (or in the event of an immature's death) usually sits outside the "family" social circle, and such a peripheral female often leaves the group for another male partner. Whether a female forms a stable bond with a leader male is seemingly dependent upon her success in raising offspring and, perhaps for this reason, the leader male is normally involved in child-care assistance and even serves as "baby sitter" when a mother is involved in some other activity. In the case of an orphaned infant or juvenile, male leaders normally assume full parental care that includes the sharing of a nighttime bed (for discussions, see Stewart 1981; Harcourt 1979; Yamagiwa 1983; Stewart and Harcourt 1987). This arrangement, where both males and females depart their natal unit at puberty and where a silverback heads a gorilla group and assists resident mothers in raising offspring, is represented in the bonding pattern in row 4 of Table 1.

Multiple Male-Multiple Female Primate Arrangement

The absence of a stable heterosexual bond is the most common primate mating pattern. There is sexual dimorphism, but its prominence differs among species. Characteristic of this mating system is the continual presence of more than one breeding male in a reproductive unit and relatively open mating, with three important exceptions: (1) for many species, mother and son rarely mate; (2) for some species, brother-sister matings are less frequent than those between unrelated pairs; and (3) for many species, females when sexually receptive consort with one male, or mate with a serial number of males, or both (Itani 1972; Sade 1968; Tutin 1979; Demarest 1977; Pusey and Packer 1987).

Asian macaques (Macaca). Even though macaque monkeys live in a variety of habitats (including parts of Africa and Europe), most species reproduce in multiple male-multiple female groups. Among Japanese macaques (*Macaca fuscata*), discrete groups may number as many as 200 monkeys, with an average ratio of one adult male to four adult females (Fedigan 1982, p. 218). Normally, adult males are immigrants from other groups and are organized into a relatively stable dominance hierarchy of central adult males, peripheral adult males seeking to join a group, and finally, peripheral young males slowly drawing away from their natal group. Evidently, friendly interactions among males are infrequent, and they rarely form close social bonds (Grewal 1980; Fedigan 1982, p. 222). However, high status males are very involved in group activities and are reported to protect individuals from external threat, to lead group movements, to mediate in quarrels between group members, and to have a definite mating advantage over peripheral males (Grewal 1980; Fedigan 1976). Leader males are also reported to have close ties with particular adult females, although these bonds are reported to be unstable and changeable from year to year (Grewal 1980). Leader males may also form temporary close ties with particular immatures but, as yet, Japanese macaque males are not known to bias their "paternal" care in any way that would suggest a "father-offspring" bond (Gouzoules 1984; Fedigan 1982, p. 218).

With only sons typically departing at puberty, a macaque troop contains a number of matrifocal cliques (Fedigan 1976; Kurland 1977). Females may also form bonds with nonrelatives and with lead males, but group stability seemingly depends upon the mother-daughter bond and the strong ties that develop on the basis of blood ties. These mating and transfer patterns—where sexual relations are transitory, where males leave their natal unit at puberty, and where female-based kinship ties are prominent—are summarized in row 5 of Table 1.

African baboons (Papio).   While common baboons are found in both forest and savanna habitats, they are the dominant open-country monkey in Africa, with most species revealing the multiple male and multiple female breeding arrangement (Harding 1976; Richard 1985, p. 222). In open environments, olive baboons (Papio anubis) may number up to 200 monkeys although the more typical troop size is about 50 members (Richard 1985; Napier and Napier 1985, p. 135). In each baboon troop, immigrant males typically form a dominance hierarchy and only occasionally engage in friendly interactions (Harding 1980; Richard 1985, p. 315). In contrast, adult male and female interactions are very friendly, even when the female is not sexually active (Ransom 1981; Seyfarth 1978). Adult males also have social ties with some immatures, but whether these bonds include paternal care by the biological father is unknown. Adult females form the strongest bonds. For all common baboon species, a clear preference for kin over nonkin is evident, with maternal genealogies being very important (Nash 1978; Seyfarth 1977; Melnick and Pearl 1987, p. 128). This pattern apparently parallels that among the macaques, who form strong kin-based cliques. Since males rather than females are much more likely to leave their natal unit at puberty (Nash 1976; Packer 1979; Greenwood 1980), the stability and endurance of baboon society seemingly rest on the mother-daughter bond. This pattern of nonexclusive mating, where males typically transfer at puberty and where female bonds assure group continuity, is outlined in row 6 of Table 1.

African chimpanzees (Pan).   Chimpanzees are large apes that inhabit open canopy woodlands, forest-fringes, or forest habitats, spending their time both in trees and on the ground (Hill 1969; Clutton-Brock and Gillett 1979; Ghiglieri 1984). They mate in multiple male-multiple female social units. Yet, chimpanzee social structure varies dramatically from that of baboons and macaques. While adult males have status differences, dominance relations are not pronounced, in part because of the fellowship among natal males that is evidenced by frequent social grooming and other highly affiliative interactions

(Nishida and Hiraiwa-Hasegawa 1987; Goodall 1986, pp. 159ff; Tuttle 1986, pp. 266ff). Adult males also evidence great tolerance in mating, with aggressive sexual competition for females rare (Tuttle 1986, pp. 276ff). This relatively loose and relaxed hierarchy is associated with moderate to strong ties among males. For adult females, status differences are hard to detect, since females usually ignore each other, and it is clear that their ties are typically absent to very weak. In part, this weakness of ties is related to female emigration from their natal unit at puberty—either temporarily or permanently—and to the tendency for incoming females to shy away from each other (Wrangham and Smuts 1980; Goodall 1986, pp. 399ff; Takasaki 1985; Nishida 1970, 1979; Kawanaka 1984; Pusey 1980). Even the mother-daughter bond weakens at puberty, as females with dependent offspring have few affiliative interactions with anyone, spending most of their time alone accompanied only by dependent offspring (Nishida 1979; Wrangham and Smuts 1980). Male-female bonds are also weak. Unless sexually receptive, adult females spend little time interacting with adult males (Goodall 1986, p. 149; Nishida and Hiraiwa-Hasegawa 1987). In contrast, chimpanzee mother-son relations typically remain strong, in part because males are not burdened with dependents and are rarely reported to leave their natal home range. Mother and her son(s) are frequently seen feeding, traveling and grooming together (Goodall-Van Lawick 1975; Goodall 1986, p. 177). Father-offspring ties are, of course, unknown.

This rare primate pattern of female transfer in conjunction with multiple male-multiple female mating is associated in chimpanzees with a fluid regional population or "community" form of organization. In other words, chimpanzee organization is said to resemble human organization in that individuals socialize throughout the day in a varied number of temporary "parties" or groupings within a more inclusive regional population or "community" (Goodall 1986; Sugiyama 1968; Nishida 1968; Tutin, McGrew, and Baldwin 1983). That is, individuals may move about alone as they choose or freely join or leave a variety of temporary clusterings within a clearly defined spatial region, but the regional population itself (or those members who cooccupy a home range) is relatively stable over time. This pattern of social ties is delineated at the bottom of Table 1.

With this brief analysis of the mating, transfer, and social ties among these Old World primates, we can now consider the structural implications of the data summarized in Table 1 for the reconstruction of early hominid social structure.

IMPLICATIONS FOR RECONSTRUCTING EARLY HOMINID SOCIAL STRUCTURE

Mating and transfer patterns, as these affect the kinds of ties summarized for various primates in Table 1, offer clues about the social structure of early hominids. First, we can conclude that some classic nineteenth-century hypotheses on the origin of the family are structurally and phyletically improbable. For instance, since all studied primates regulate their mating to some degree, unrestricted promiscuity as the primordial basis for early hominid society can probably be set aside once and for all. Similarly, as polyandry does not occur among any known Old World primates and is extremely rare among New World primates (Terborgh and Wilson-Goldizen 1985; Sussman and Garber 1987), as well as among humans (Peter 1963), early evolutionary hypotheses about a polyandrous basis for society can also be dismissed.

Second, and more importantly, we can use these data to construct a plausible social structure for early hominids. In a number of African localities, early hominid and baboon fossils dating to the Plio-Pleistocene are found in association (Simon and Delson 1978). Given that both probably faced similar paleoenvironmental problems—that is, an adaptation to an open environment under conditions of predation and other selection pressures (e.g., food and its distribution, sleeping sites)—their social organizations probably underwent similar structural alterations. It could, therefore, be argued that early hominids adapted to an open environment in the manner of common baboons, with an often stiff male-dominance hierarchy and strongly tied matrifocal cliques. Yet, the relational data do not support this conclusion. Among baboons and macaques, and indeed among almost every monkey species, mother-and-daughter ties endure while mother-son ties usually diminish through male transfer at puberty (Greenwood 1980; Packer 1979; Pusey and Packer 1987). In contrast, among all hominoids—chimpanzees, gorillas, gibbons, and even among semisolitary orangutans (see Galdikas 1979, 1984, 1988 on Pongo) regardless of mating system or environment—mother-daughter ties are disrupted at puberty. In every living ape species, the pattern is for mother-and-daughter ties to lessen after puberty. Ape ties among mother and son are more problematic; they endure only among chimpanzees. But the central point is that matrifocal lineages can exist only when mothers and daughters (and sisters) remain in close spatial proximity. In living ape societies, this transgenerational continuity is disrupted by female dispersal. Further, this pattern of mother-daughter separation after puberty is not only typical of apes, it is also very common among humans. In most preindustrial societies, mothers and daughters are spatially separated because of the heavy bias toward a residence pattern of patrilocality (Murdock 1967; Ember 1978; Fox 1967). Since both ape and human daughters typically depart from their mothers after puberty, the likelihood that early hominid daughters also left their mothers is a valid hypothesis. Indeed, if the phyletic principle that a trait evident in two or more closely related species is likely to be an ancestral character retained from a common ancestor is correct, then this assumption about female-biased dispersal is even more plausible. In fact, if we argue that ape female transfer is not a conservative ancestral trait, we must then assume it evolved independently in five extant ape genera who live in very different habitats.

Hence, this hominoid pattern of daughter migration out of the natal unit after puberty would seemingly liberate early hominids from a baboon-type social structure, with matrifocal kinship networks as the central building blocks from which hominid society evolved.

So, regardless of the selection pressures operating when protohominids left the safety of the forest, it cannot be assumed that their social structure was transformed into one more typical of monkeys. Instead, it might serve us better to examine how mating, transfer, and social relations among African apes might provide an incipient social structure for the evolution of early hominids living under savanna-like conditions. Here, while both gorillas and chimpanzees will be discussed in the analysis to follow, chimpanzees have proven to be particularly useful for hominid models, as they are typically viewed as our closest living relative (Tanner 1987; Gibbons 1990). Chimpanzee organization with its "community" profile is also considered to resemble human organization more closely than any other ape. Of course, chimpanzees are the contemporary products of their own equally long ancestral line, but alterations in their social lifeways, from the time of the last shared ancestor with hominids, are viewed as remaining on the conservative side because chimpanzees have remained well within the tropical belt. Indeed, even fringe chimpanzees who inhabit forest-savanna mosaic or dry savanna invariably still rely upon a nearby forest for seasonal foods (Nishida and Hiraiwa-Hasegawa 1987; McGrew, Baldwin, and Tutin 1981; Kano 1972).

If we use a chimpanzee model for the protohominid condition, we begin with a "hang-loose" or fluid community lifestyle where single individuals move about on their own or join and then depart from transient subgroupings. In reviewing the patterning of chimpanzee ties that could serve as organizational building blocks for early hominid social structure, we have the following:

1. mother-son: strong ties;
2. adult female-adult female: absent to weak ties;
3. adult male-adult male: moderate to strong ties;
4. adult male-adult female: weak ties.

Turning first to tie (1), it is possible for mother and son to create lineal blood ties but, since they rarely mate with each other, this tie is a dead end, reproductively speaking. A social structure built on (2) is insuperably difficult since nonnatal females are often strangers and are unlikely to form strong ties or matrifocal units. The ties among males in (3) are moderate to strong; and, since chimpanzee males rarely transfer at puberty and behave as though they share a common fellowship or "sense of community" (Wrangham 1979; Teleki 1973), these ties are potential building blocks. Yet, shared sentiment alone cannot transform a loose aggregation of widely dispersed individuals into a more cohesive social structure. This is because patrifocal males are not structurally equivalent to matrilineal females, as strong-tie *patrilineal* connections cannot exist without male parental care and stable heterosexual bonds.

Finally, the weak relations in (4) between adult males and females have potential as a structural building block. Indeed, a strengthening of these weak male-female bonds seems, by far, the most parsimonious way that early hominids could initially reorganize more effectively in an open environment. Further, it is reasonable to surmise that these male-female bonds generated both monogamous and polygynous "families." A strict monogamous pattern, however, is unlikely for several reasons: (a) monogamous mating is a rare mating pattern among contemporary primates and, at least for gibbon apes, it requires the spatial isolation of each mated pair (and their immature offspring), the absence of ties among same-sexed adults, and an arboreal and otherwise very restricted environment; (b) monogamous primate species all evidence little or no sexual dimorphism, whereas there is evidence that early hominid fossils had a large sexual dimorphism (Johanson 1980; Wood 1985); and, (c) monogamy is not even today the exclusive pattern among humans, for it is polygyny that is the preferred form of marriage in the Middle East, Asia, and much of Africa (Plog and Bates 1980, p. 276). In Murdock's (1967) cross-cultural survey, one husband and multiple wives were found to be the favored mating arrangement for 70% of the world's societies.

Hence, an enduring male-female bond is probably a good choice for a building block for hominid social structure. Under the selection pressures created from open-range conditions where the elaboration rather than the diminution of structure would seem critical, selection would favor the strengthening of ties among adult males and females. But what would be the nature of this social structure?

If we assume that the existing protohominid ties placed some constraints on the kinds of structural changes that could be made in adapting to an open environment, it is likely that early hominids evidenced a rather peculiar pattern of organization for primates. For, a tightening of male-female bonds could not easily generate the typical one-male harem pattern found among monkeys where male transfer and strong female-female bonds exist, since this runs counter to the bonding and transfer patterns of all living hominoids.

For example, gorillas differ from chimpanzees in having more stable groupings, an adaptive strategy that seemingly reflects their terrestrial habitat in which predation from leopards and other predators abounds (Maryanski 1986). Additionally, both sexes disperse at puberty, although the gorilla male remains within his natal ranging area (recall, that several gorilla groups and some lone males equally share a ranging area), while the female often leaves her natal ranging area and becomes a group member in a neighboring ranging area (similar, it would seem, to chimpanzee females moving to another community). Both chimpanzee and gorilla females have absent to weak ties with their own sex, in part because they share a female dispersal pattern. Thus, despite greater group cohesion and stability, gorilla social structure is not at all similar to the high-density matrifocal monkey networks with a core structure of blood-related natal females (see bottom of Figure 1 for an illustration of a high density monkey network). Instead, gorilla groups, despite the spatial propinquity of their members, are low-density networks that resemble a star-shaped pattern such that females with young are attached to the leader male, although the females themselves are not attached to each other (see top of Figure 1 for an illustration of a low-density gorilla network). Further, male-female bonds form the core structure of a gorilla group, even though the basis of this bonding is seemingly dependent upon a female's ability to raise successful offspring (Stewart and Harcourt 1987).

Thus, given the female dispersal pattern common to all hominoids, it would seem in the case of chimpanzees to be an act of evolutionary gymnastics to convert a chimpanzee transfer pattern into the typical male monkey transfer pattern. That would require among chimpanzees fundamental changes in both male and female transfer patterns, a weakening of male-male bonds, and a strengthening of female-female bonds. What existing ties in chimpanzees might, therefore, be used to build social network ties for early hominids? It appears that the moderate to strong ties among adult male chimpanzees would not be contradicted by the strong mother-son ties, the absent to weak ties among females, or the transfer patterns of females out of the natal unit at puberty. So, to the extent that savanna living conditions generated selection pressures against lone individuals and temporary groupings while selecting for increased organizational structure, a trend toward the formation of a stable male-female bond and a form of "band" organization with an implicit *patrifocal* emphasis seems plausible. Such a system of dispersing the females at puberty, while keeping the males united for mutual aid and defense, has the great advantage of being the least disruptive arrangement. Further, a retention of good fellowship among adult males, oddly enough, may have also inadvertently laid the groundwork for a free and easy cooperation when hominid males began to hunt large game animals, as has been documented in the fossil record in the Upper Paleolithic (Olsen 1989).

In sum, chimpanzee-like social relations as conditioned by mating and transfer systems would be most likely to evolve into strengthened male-female ties with an implicit patrifocal emphasis, especially under selection pressures for increased structural stability. Such a system, permitting related males to remain together, offers a rigorous organizational structure for protection against predators. Moreover, strengthened male-female bonds allow for an efficient breakdown of a larger grouping into smaller heterosexual foraging parties during times of scarce or scattered resources. To band together as one large patrifocal group or to separate easily into smaller parties would seem advantageous for large mammals living in an open environment. Also, to the

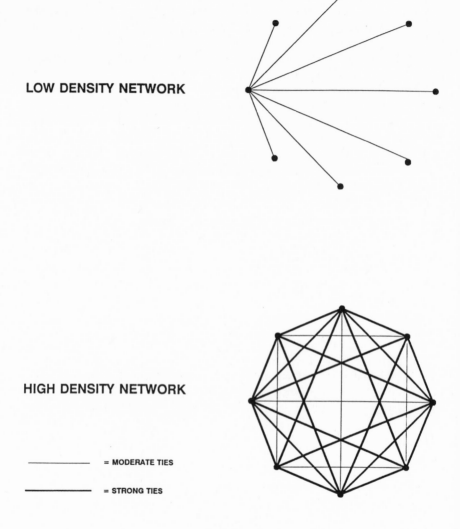

Figure 1.   Low and High Density Networks

extent that "patrilocal" residence in hunters and gatherers evolved from some more simple structural pattern, then strengthened female-male bonds and a patrifocal emphasis are good candidates.

IMPLICATIONS FOR HUMAN SOCIAL STRUCTURE

While the above reconstruction of "protohominid" society is of course speculative, it can provide us with some plausible generalizations on human social evolution. For example, since societies tend to build on the residential and ecological foundations that they inherit, an initial strengthening of early hominid male and female bonds would have facilitated stable sexual relations, while a residence bias of patrilocality and female-biased dispersal (to be later augmented by purely cultural rules for exogamy) would have eventually produced the nuclear family. In turn, with the family as the basic unit of production, the sexual division of labor as a key adaptive strategy would further strengthen ties and reinforce conjugal role relations through the creation of mutual dependencies. Although there is room here for variation, this conclusion lends further support to the classic residential hypothesis favored by Radcliffe-Brown (1930), Service (1962), Williams (1974), Fox (1967), Ember (1978), and Martin and Stewart (1982), that Pleistocene hunters and gatherers were predominantly patrilocal with female dispersal. It is also the case that contemporary human societies have also overwhelmingly favored patrilocal residence and female exogamy (Murdock 1967; Fox 1967; Ember 1978). To the extent that a patrilocal residence pattern eventually gave rise to a system of descent, it is probably not a coincidence that patrilineal kin groups combine almost inevitably with this residence rule (Murdock 1967).

Finally, while the intent of this paper has been largely exploratory, it may not be too much to say that many of the controversial issues of the present era dealing with the nature of humans might be illuminated by a consideration of primate social networks (see Maryanski 1992; Maryanski and Ishii-Kuntz 1991). For example, the human sociobiology debate rages on, yet theorists have little to say about the social-structural base of hominid ancestors. Without reasonable inferences (based on the only social data available) as to how early hominids organized themselves, a "missing supplement" to the fossil record on human organization exists. This paper has tried to help fill this gap by using primate networks as a kind of "distant mirror" to consider the ecological and structural boundaries of what was possible for protohominids in their adaptation to a Plio-Pleistocene savanna habitat.

ACKNOWLEDGMENT

The author thanks the Netherlands Institute for Advanced Study where this paper was originally drafted.

NOTES

1. The use of hominid here refers to any early taxa on the Homo lineage or sidebranch of this lineage after the divergence of Pan and Gorilla.

2. Vernon Reynold's (1968) paper, "Kinship and the Family in Monkeys, Apes and Man," is an insightful article that is responsible, in part, for the relational approach taken in this paper.

3. Although each of these indicators is somewhat independent of the other, they are probably intracorrelated.

4. In the words of T.T. Struhsaker (1969, pp. 113-114), "In considering the relation between ecology and society, it must be emphasized that each species brings a different phylogenetic heritage into a particular ecological scene. Consequently, one must consider not only ecology but also phylogeny in attempting to understand the evolution of primate social organization."

5. See Marsden and Lin (1982) and Wellman and Berkowitz (1988) for readings on social network theory and analysis. For similar strategies that emphasize primate social relationships, see Hinde (1983) and Carpenter (1955).

6. In her review of primate predation, Anderson (1986) found that the higher the rate of predation, the less likely are males to wander off alone, while the likelihood of females doing so is virtually nonexistent. Thus, with a high rate of predation, conspecifics are likely to mass close together as one spatially bounded group.

7. It is not possible in a limited space to provide detailed exceptions to the patterns discussed. What is reported here are the normative and well-documented age and sex class attachments for a given primate species and their structural implications.

8. Researchers had earlier suggested that both sexes transfer at puberty, but long-term data have established that typically only males leave. See Dunbar (1984, pp. 72-76).

9. Data collected by Kummer (1975) on a captive gelada population somewhat contradicts this conclusion (he argued that the frequencies with which harem females groomed a leader male correlated closely with their dominance rank). However, Dunbar suggests that the observed differences are due to Kummer's having a newly formed captive population that lacked familial ties, forcing females to turn to their next best alliance, the harem male. Dunbar's data on captive geladas where females had blood ties showed the normal strong tie matrilines (see Dunbar 1982, 1984, p. 46).

REFERENCES

Alexander, R. 1974. "The Evolution of Social Behaviors." *Annual Review of Ecology and Systematics* 5: 325-383.

Anderson, C. 1986. "Predation and Primate Evolution." *Primates* 27: 15-39.

Bachofen, J. J. 1861. *Das Mutterrecht* [*The Mother-Right*]. Basel, Switzerland: Benno Schwabe.

Bartholomew, G.A., and J.P. Birdsell. 1953. "Ecology and the Proto-Hominids." *American Anthropologist* 55: 481-498.

Blumenberg, B. 1985. "Population Characteristics of Extinct Hominid Endocranial Volume." *American Journal of Physical Anthropology* 68: 269-279.

Bramblett, C. 1970. "Coalitions Among Gelada Baboons." *Primates* 11: 327-33.

Brockelman, W.Y., and S. Srikosamatara. 1984. "Maintenance and Evolution of Social Structure in Gibbons." Pp. 267-81 in *The Lesser Apes*, edited by H. Prevschoft, D. Chivers, W. Brockelman, and N. Creel. Edinburgh, Scotland: Edinburgh University Press.

Campbell, B.G. 1988. *Humankind Emerging*. Boston, MA: Little, Brown.

Carpenter, R. 1940. "A Field Study in Siam of the Behaviour and Social Relationships of the Gibbon (Hylobates/Lar)." *Psychology Monograph* 16: 1-21.

_____. 1942. "Societies of Monkeys and Apes." *Biological Symposia* VIII: 177-204.

_____. 1955. "Tentative Generalizations on the Grouping Behavior of Non-Human Primates." Pp. 91-98 in *Non-Human Primates and Human Evolution*, edited by J. Gavan. Detroit: Wayne University Press.

Cheney, D.R., R. Seyfarth, and B. Smuts. 1986. "Social Relationships and Social Cognition in Nonhuman Primates." *Science* 234: 1361-1366.

Chism, J., T. Rowell, and D. Olson. 1984. "Life History Patterns of Female Patas Monkeys." Pp. 175-190 in *Female Primates. Studies by Women Primatologists*, edited by M. Small. New York: Alan Liss.

Chivers, D. 1974. *The Siamang in Malaya. Contributions to Primatology* 40. New York: S. Karger.

_____. 1984. "Feeding and Ranging in Gibbons: A Summary." Pp. 267-81 in *The Lesser Apes*, edited by H. Prevschoft, D. Chivers, W. Brockelman, and N. Creel. Edinburgh, Scotland: Edinburgh University Press.

Clark, J.D. 1985. "Leaving No Stone Unturned: Archaeological Advances and Behavioral Adaptations." Pp. 65-88 in *Hominid Evolution: Past, Present and Future*, edited by P. Tobias. New York: Alan Liss.

Clutton-Brock, T.H. 1974. "Primate Social Organization and Ecology." *Nature* 250: 539-542.

Clutton-Brock, T.H., and J.B. Gillett. 1979. "A Survey of Forest Composition in the Gombe National Park, Tanzania." *African Journal of Ecology* 17: 131-158.

Clutton-Brock, T.H., and P. Harvey. 1977. "Primate Ecology and Social Organization." *Journal of Zoology, London* 183: 1-39.

Cousins, D. 1978. "Aggressive Behavior in Gorillas." *Ratel* 5: 10-13.

Crook, J.H. 1966. "Gelada Baboon Herd Structure and Movement." *Symposia of the Zoological Society of London* 18: 237-258.

Demarest, W. 1977. "Incest Avoidance Among Human and Nonhuman Primates." Pp. 323-42 in *Primate Bio-Social Development: Biological, Social, and Ecological Determinants*, edited by S. Chevalier-Skolnikoff and F. Poirier. New York: Garland Publishing.

DeVore, I. 1964. "The Evolution of Social Life." Pp. 24-35 in *Horizons in Anthropology*, edited by S. Tax. Chicago: University Press.

DeVore, I., and S. L. Washburn. 1963. "Baboon Ecology and Human Evolution." In *African Ecology and Human Evolution. Viking Fund Publications in Anthropology* 36: 335-367.

Dixson, A. 1981. *The Natural History of the Gorilla*. New York: Columbia University Press.

Drickamer, L.C., and S. Vassey. 1973. "Group Changing in Free-Ranging Male Rhesus Monkeys." *Primates* 14: 359-368.

Dunbar, R.I.M. 1978. "Sexual Behaviour and Social Relationships among Gelada Baboons." *Animal Behaviour* 26: 167-178.

_____. 1979. "Structure of Gelada Baboon Reproductive Units, Stability of Social Relationships." *Behaviour* 69: 72-87.

_____. 1982. "Structure of Social Relationships in a Captive Gelada Group: A Test of Some Hypotheses Derived from Field Studies of a Wild Population." *Primates* 23: 89-94.

_____. 1983a. "Structure of Gelada Baboon Reproductive Units. III. The Male's Relationship with His Females." *Animal Behaviour* 31: 565-576.

_____. 1983b. "Structure of Gelada Baboon Reproductive Units. II. Social Relationships Between Reproductive Units." *Animal Behaviour* 556-564.

_____. 1984. *Reproductive Decisions: An Economic Analysis of Gelada Baboon Social Strategies*. Princeton, NJ: Princeton University Press.

Eisenberg. J., N.A. Muckenhirn, and R. Rudran. 1972. "The Relations Between Ecology and Social Structure in Primates." *Science* 176: 863-874.

Ellefson, S.O. 1974. "A Natural History of White-Handed Gibbons in the Malayian Peninsula." Pp. 1-136 in *Gibbon and Siamang*. Vol. 3, edited by D. Rumbaugh. Basel, Swizterland: Karger.

Ember, C. 1978. "Myths about Hunter-Gatherers." *Ethnology* 17: 439-448.

Engels, F. 1902. *The Origin of the Family, Private Property and the State.* Translated by E. Untermann. Chicago: C.H. Kerr & Company.

Fedigan, L.M. 1976. "A Study of Roles in the Anashiyama West Troop of Japanese Monkeys (Macaca fuscata)." *Contributions to Primatology* 9. Basel, Switzerland: S. Karger.

――――. 1982. *Primate Paradigms: Sex Roles and Social Bonds.* Canada: Eden Press.

Foley, R. 1984. *Hominid Evolutions and Community Ecology.* London: Academic Press.

Fossey, D. 1976. *The Behavior of the Mountain Gorilla.* Ph.D. dissertation, Department of Zoology, University of Cambridge, Madinghey, Cambridge.

――――. 1982. "Reproduction among Free-Living Mountain Gorillas." *American Journal of Primatology* (Supplement 1): 97-104.

Fox, R. 1967. *Kinship and Marriage.* Harmondsworth, England: Penguin Books.

Galdikas, B. 1979. "Orangutan Adaptation at Tanjung Puting Reserve: Mating and Ecology." Pp. 194-233 in *The Great Apes,* edited by D. Hamburg and E. McCown. Menlo Park, CA: Benjamin Cummings.

――――. 1984. "Adult Female Sociality Among Wild Orangutans at Tanjung Puting Reserve." Pp. 217-235 in *Female Primates: Studies by Women Primatologists,* edited by M. Small. New York: Alan Liss.

――――. 1988. "Orangutan Diet, Range, and Activity at Tanjung Puting, Central Borneo." *International Journal of Primatology* 9: 1-35.

Ghiglieri, M. 1984. *The Chimpanzees of Kibale Forest.* New York: Columbia University Press.

Gibbons, A. 1990. "Our Chimp Cousins Get That Much Closer." *Science* 250: 376.

Giraud-Teulon, A. 1884. *Les Origines du Marriage et La Famille [The Origins of Marriage and the Family].* Paris: E. Thorin.

Gittens, S.P. 1980. "Territorial Behavior in the Agile Gibbon." *International Journal of Primatology* 1: 381-399.

Goodall, A. 1979. *The Wandering Gorillas.* London: Collins.

Goodall-Van Lawick, J. 1975a. "The Behaviour of the Chimpanzee." Pp. 74-136 in *Hominisation and Behavior,* edited by G. Kurth and I. Eibl. Eibesfeldt. Stuttgart: Gustav Fischer Verlag.

Goodall, J. 1975b. "Continuities Between Chimpanzee and Human Behavior." Pp. 81-95 in *Perspectives on Human Evolution,* Vol. 3, edited by G. Isaac and E. McCown. Menlo Park, CA: Benjamin/Cummings.

――――. 1986. *The Chimpanzees of Gombe.* Cambridge: Belknap Press.

Goodall, J., and D. Hamburg. 1975. "Chimpanzee Behaviour as a Model for the Behaviour of Early Man." Pp. 14-43 in *America Handbook of Psychiatry,* Vol. 6, edited by D. Hamburg and K. H. Brodie. New York: Basic Books.

Gouzoules, S. 1984. "Primate Mating Systems, Kin Associations, and Cooperative Behavior: Evidence for Kin Recognition?" *Yearbook of Physical Anthropology* 27: 99-134.

Greenwood, P. 1980. "Mating Systems, Philopatry, and Dispersal in Birds and Mammals." *Animal Behaviour* 30: 1140-1162.

Grewal, B.S. 1980. "Social Relationships Between Adult Central Males and Kinship Groups of Japanese Monkeys at Arashiyama With Some Aspects of Troop Organization." *Primates* 21: 161-180.

Grine, F. 1988. *Evolutionary History of the "Robust" Australopithecines.* New York: Aldine de Gruyter.

Gutstein, J. 1978. "Behavioural Correlates of Male Dispersal in Patas Monkeys." Pp. 79-82 in *Recent Advances in Primatology,* Vol. 1, edited by D.J. Chivers and J. Herbert. London: Academic Press.

Hall, K.R.L. 1965. "Behaviour and Ecology of the Wild Patas Monkey (*Erythrocebus patas*). In Uganda." *Journal Zoology, London* 148: 15-87.

Hall, K.R.L., and B. Mayer. 1967. "Social Interactions in a Group of Captive Patas Monkeys

(*Erythrocebus patas*)." *Folia Primatologica* 5: 213-236.

Hamilton, W. 1982. "Baboon Sleeping Site Preferences and Relationships to Primate Grouping Patterns." *American Journal of Primatology* 3: 41-53.

Harcourt, A. 1978. "Strategies of Emigration and Transfer by Primates, With Particular Reference to Gorillas." *Tierpsychologie* 48: 401-420.

————. 1979. "Social Relationships Among Adult Female Mountain Gorillas." *Animal Behavior* 27: 251-264.

Harcourt, A., D. Fossey, K. Stewart, and D. Watts. 1980. "Reproduction in Wild Gorillas and Some Comparisons with Chimpanzees." *Journal of Reproduction and Fertility* 28(Supplement): 59-70.

Harcourt, A.H., K.S. Stewart, and D. Fossey. 1976. "Male Emigration and Female Transfer in Wild Mountain Gorilla." *Nature* 263: 226-227.

Harding, R. 1976. "Ranging Patterns of Baboons (Papio anubis) in Kenya." *Folia Primatologica* 25: 143-185.

————. 1980. "Agonism, Ranking and the Social Behavior of Adult Male Baboons." *American Journal of Physical Anthropology* 53: 203-216.

Harding, R., and D. Olson. 1986. "Patterns of Mating Among Male Patas Monkeys." *American Journal of Primatology* 11: 343-358.

Hill, W.C.O. 1969. "The Nomenclature, Taxonomy and Distribution of Chimpanzees." *The Chimpanzee* 1: 22-49.

Hinde, R.A. 1979. "The Nature of Social Structure." Pp. 295-315 in *The Great Apes*, edited by D. Hamburg and E. McCown. Menlo Park, CA: Benjamin/Cummings.

————. 1983. *Primate Social Relationships: An Integrated Approach*. Sunderland, MA: Sinauer Associates.

Hooton, E. 1955. "The Importance of Primate Studies in Anthropology." Pp. 1-10 in *Non-Human Primates and Human Evolution*, edited by J. Gaven. Detroit, MI: Wayne University Press.

Isaac, G., and E. McCown. 1975. *Human Origins: Louis Leakey and the East African Evidence*. Menlo Park, CA: Benjamin/Cummings.

Itani, I. 1972. "A Preliminary Essay on the Relationship Between Social Organization and Incest Avoidance in Non-Human Primates." Pp. 165-172 in *Primate Socialization*, edited by F. Poirier. New York: London House.

Johanson, D.C. 1980. "Early African Hominid Phylogenesis: A Re-Evaluation." Pp. 31-69 in *Current Argument on Early Man*, edited by L. K. Konigsson. Oxford, England: Pergamon Press.

————. 1985. "The Most Primitive Australopithecus." Pp. 203-12 in *Hominid Evolution: Past, Present and Future*, edited by P. Tobias. New York: Alan Liss.

Johanson, D.C., and T.D. White. 1979. "A Systematic Assessment of Early African Hominids." *Science* 203: 321-330.

Jolly, A. 1985. *The Evolution of Primate Behavior*. New York: Macmillan.

Jolly, C. 1970. "The Seed-Eaters: A New Model of Hominid Differentiation Based on a Baboon Analogy." *Man* 5: 5-26.

————. 1978. *Early Hominids of Africa*. London: Duckworth.

————. 1985. *The Evolution of Primate Behavior*. New York: Macmillan.

Kano, T. 1972. "Distribution and Adaptation of the Chimpanzee on the Eastern Shore of Lake Tanganyika." *Kyoto University African Studies* 7: 37-129.

Kawanaka, K. 1984. "Association, Ranging, and the Social Unit in Chimpanzees of the Mahale Mountains, Tanzania." *International Journal of Primatology* 5: 411-34.

Kinzey, W. 1987. *The Evolution of Human Behavior: Primate Models*. Albany, NY: State University of New York Press.

Kortlandt, A. 1972. *New Perspectives on Ape and Human Evolution*. Amsterdam: University of Amsterdam.

238   A.R. MARYANSKI

Kummer, H. 1975. "Rules of Dyad and Group Formation Among Captive Gelada Baboons (*Theropithecus Gelada*)." Pp. 129-59 in *Proceedings from the Symposia of the 5th Congress of the International Primatological Society*, edited by S. Kondo, M. Kawai, A. Ehara, and S. Kawamura. Tokyo: Japan Science Press.

Kurland, J.A. 1977. *Kin Selection in the Japanese Monkey*. Basel, Switzerland: S. Karger.

Lancaster, J. 1968. "On the Evolution of Tool-Using Behavior." *American Anthropologist* 70: 56-66.

Leakey, M., and R. Hay. 1979. "Pliocene Footprints in Lae Tolil Beds at Lae Toli, Northern Tanzania." *Nature* 278: 317-323.

Leakey, R., and R. Lewin. 1977. *Origins*. New York: Dutton.

Leighton, D. 1987. "Gibbons: Territoriality and Monogamy." Pp. 135-45 in *Primate Societies*, edited by B. Smuts, D. Cheney, R. Seyfarth, R. Wrangham, and T. Struhsaker. Chicago: University of Chicago Press.

Lewin, R. 1987a. *Bones of Contention: Controversies in the Search for Human Origins*. New York: Simon & Schuster.

_____. 1987b. "The Earliest "Humans" Were More Like Apes." *Science* 236: 1061-1063.

Lovejoy, C.O. 1981. "The Origin of Man." *Science* 211: 341-350.

Loy, J., and M. Harnois. 1988. "An Assessment of Dominance and Kinship Among Patas Monkeys." *Primates* 29: 331-342.

Lubbock, J. 1889. *The Origin of Civilization and the Primitive Condition of Man: Mental and Social Condition of Savages*. London: Longmans Green.

Lucas, P.W., R.T. Corlett and D.A. Luke. 1985. "Plio-Pleistocene Hominid Diets: An Approach Combining Masticatory and Ecological Analysis." *Journal of Human Evolution* 14: 187-202.

MacKinnon, J., and S. MacKinnon. 1984. "Territoriality, Monogamy and Song in Gibbons and Tarsiers." Pp. 267-81 in *The Lesser Apes*, edited by H. Prevschoft, D. Chivers, W. Brockelman, and N. Creel. Edinburgh, Scotland: Edinburgh University Press.

Maglio, V., and H.B.S. Cooke. 1978. *Evolution of African Mammals*. Cambridge, MA: Harvard University Press.

Maine, Sir Henry. 1874. *Ancient Law*. London: John Murray.

Marsden, P., and N. Lin. 1982. *Social Structure and Network Analysis*. Beverly Hills, CA: Sage.

Martin, J., and Donald Stewart. 1982. "A Demographic Basis for Patrilineal Hordes." *American Anthropologist* 84: 79-96.

Maryanski, A. 1986. *African Ape Social Structure: A Comparative Analysis*. Ph.D. dissertation, School of Social Science, University of California, Irvine.

_____. 1992. "The Last Ancestor: A Network-Ecological Model on the Origins of Human Sociality." *Advances in Human Ecology*, 1: 1-32.

Maryanski, A., and M. Ishii-Kuntz. 1992. "A Cross-Species Application of Bott's Hypothesis on Role Segregation and Social Networks." *Sociological Perspectives* 34: 403-425.

McGrew, W.C.P. 1981. "The Female Chimpanzee as a Human Evolutionary Prototype." Pp. 35-73 in *Woman the Gatherer*, edited by F. Dahlbeng. New Haven, CT: Yale University Press.

McGrew, W.C.P., J. Baldwin, and C.E.G. Tutin. 1981. "Chimpanzees in a Hot, Dry and Open Habitat: Mt. Assirik, Senegal, West Africa." *Journal of Human Evolution* 10: 227-244.

McLennan, J. 1865. *Primitive Marriage. Edinburgh: Adam and Charles Black*.

Melnick, D., and M. Pearl. 1987. "Cercopithecines in Multimale Groups: Genetic Diversity and Population Structure." Pp. 121-34 in Primate Societies, edited by B. Smuts, D. Cheney, R. Seyfarth, R. Wrangham, and T. Struhsaker. Chicago: University of Chicago Press.

Morgan, L.H. 1870. *Systems of Consanguinity and Affinity of the Human Family*. Washington, DC: Smithsonian Institution.

_____. 1877. *Ancient Society*. London: Macmillan.

Mori, U. 1979a. "Social Structure of Gelada Baboons." Pp. 244-47 in *Ecological and Sociological Studies of Gelada Baboons*, edited by M. Kawai. Basel: S. Karger.

_____. 1979b. "Individual Relationships Within a Unit." Pp. 94-122 in *Ecological and Sociological Studies of Gelada Baboons*, edited by M. Kawai. Basel, Switzerland: S. Karger.

_____. 1979c. "Development of Sociability and Social Status." Pp. 125-152 in *Ecological and Sociological Studies*, edited by M. Kawai. Basel, Switzerland: S. Karger.

_____. 1979d. "Individual Relationships Within a Unit." Pp. 155-81 in *Ecological and Sociological Studies of Gelada Baboons*, edited by M. Kawai. Basel, Switzerland: S. Karger.

Mori, U., and M. Kawai. 1975. "Social Relations and Behavior of Gelada Baboons." Pp. 470-474 in *Contemporary Primatology, 5th International Congress of Primatology*, Nayoga 1974. Basel, Switzerland: S. Karger.

Murdock, G. 1967. *Ethnographical Atlas*. Pittsburgh, PA: University of Pittsburgh Press.

Napier, J. R. and P. H. Napier. 1985. *The Natural History of the Primates*. Cambridge, MA: MIT Press.

Nash, L. 1976. "Troop Fission in Free-Ranging Baboons in the Gombe National Park, Tanzania." *American Journal of Physical Anthropology* 44: 63-78.

_____. 1978. "Kin Preference in the Behavior of Young Baboons." Pp. 71-73 in *Recent Advances in Primatology* Vol. 1, edited by D.J. Chivers, and J. Herbert. London: Academic Press.

Nishida, T. 1968. "The Social Group of Wild Chimpanzees in the Mahale Mountains." *Primates* 9: 167-224.

_____. 1970. "Social Behavior and Relationship among Wild Chimpanzees of the Mahali Mountains." *Primates* 11: 47-87.

_____. 1979. "The Social Structure of Chimpanzees of the Mahäle Mountains." Pp. 73-121 in *The Great Apes*, edited by D. Hamburg, and E. McCown. Menlo Park, CA: Benjamin/Cummings.

Nishida, T., and M. Hiraiwa-Hasegawa. 1987. "Chimpanzees and Bonobos: Cooperative Relationships Among Males." Pp. 165-180 in *Primate Societies*, edited by B. Smuts, D. Cheney, R. Seyfarth, R. Wrangham, and T. Struhsaker. Chicago: University of Chicago Press.

Ohsawa, H. 1979a. "Herd Dynamics." Pp. 47-75 in *Ecological and Sociological Studies of Gelada Baboons*, edited by M. Kawai. Basel, Switzerland: S. Karger.

_____. 1979b. "The Local Gelada Population and Environment of the Gish Area." Pp. 4-44 in *Ecological and Sociological Studies of Gelada Baboons*, edited by M. Kawai. Basel, Switzerland: S. Karger.

Olsen, S. 1989. "Solutre: A Theoretical Approach to the Reconstruction of Upper Paleolithic Hunting Strategies." *Journal of Human Evolution* 18: 295-327.

Packer, C. 1979. "Inter-troop Transfer and Inbreeding Avoidance in Papio Anubis." *Animal Behavior* 27: 1-36.

Peter, Prince of Greece and Denmark. 1963. A Study of Polyandry. The Hague, Netherlands: Mouton.

Plog, F., and D. Bates. 1980. *Cultural Anthropology*. New York: Alfred Knopf.

Post, A.H. 1875. *Die Geschlechts Genossenschaft der Urzeit und die Entstehung der Ehe* [*Primitive Sexual Relations and the Origin of the Family*]. Oldenburg, Germany: Schulzesche.

Pusey, A.E. 1980. "Inbreeding Avoidance in Chimpanzees." *Animal Behavior* 28: 543-552.

Pusey, A., and C. Packer. 1987. "Dispersal and Philopatry." Pp. 250-66 in *Primate Societies*, edited by B. Smuts, D. Cheney, R. Seyfarth, R. Wrangham and T. Struhsaker. Chicago: University of Chicago Press.

Radcliffe-Brown, A.R. 1930. "The Social Organization of the Australian Tribes." *Oceana* 1: 1-63, 206-246.

Rak, Y. 1983. *The Australopithecine Face*. New York: Academic Press.

Ransom, T. 1981. *Beach Troop of the Gombe*. London: Bucknell University Press.

Rapp, G., and C. Vonda. 1981. *Hominid Sites: Their Geologic Settings*. Boulder, CO: Westview Press.

Reynolds, V. 1966. "Open Groups and Hominid Evolution." *Man* 1: 441-452.

―――――. 1968. "Kinship and the Family in Monkeys, Apes, and Man." *Man* 3: 209-223.

Rhine, R. J., P. Boland, and L. Lodwick. 1985. "Progressions of Adult Male Chacma Baboons (*Papio ursinus*) in the Moremi Wild Life Reserve." *International Journal of Primatology* 6: 116-122.

Richard, A. 1985. *Primates in Nature*. New York: W.H. Freeman.

Rowell, T., and K. Hartwell. 1978. "The Interactions of Behavior and Reproductive Cycles in Patas Monkeys." *Behavioral Biology* 24: 141-61.

Sade, D.S. 1968. "Inhibition of Son-Mother Matings Among Free-Ranging Rhesus Monkeys." *Science and Phychoanalysis*. 12: 18-38.

Schaller, G. 1962. "The Ecology and Behavior of the Mountain Gorilla." Ph.D. dissertation, University of Wisconsin.

―――――. 1972. "The Behavior of the Mountain Gorilla." Pp. 85-123 in *Primate Patterns*, edited by P. Dolhinow. New York: Holt, Rinehart, and Winston.

Service, E. 1962. *Primitive Social Organization*. New York: Random House.

Seyfarth, R. 1977. "A Model of Social Grooming Among Adult Female Monkeys." *Journal of Theoretical Biology* 65: 671-698.

―――――. 1978. "Social Relationships Among Adult Male and Female Baboons, II. Behaviour Throughout the Female Reproductive Cycle." *Behaviour* 64: 227-247.

Simon, E.L., and E. Delson. 1978. "Cercopithecidae and Parapithecidae." Pp. 100-117 in *Evolution of African Mammals*, edited by V. Magio and H.B.S. Cooke. Cambridge, MA: Harvard University Press.

Southwick, C., and M.F. Siddiqi. 1974. "Contrasts in Primate Social Behavior." *Bioscience* 24: 398-406.

Stewart, K. 1981. "Social Development of Wild Mountain Gorillas." Ph.D. dissertation, Department of Zoology, University of Cambridge. Madingley, Cambridge, England.

Stewart, K., and A. Harcourt. 1987. "Gorillas: Variation in Female Relationships." Pp. 155-64 in *Primate Societies*, edited by B. Smuts, D. Cheney, R. Seyfarth, R. Wrangham, and T. Struhsaker. Chicago: University of Chicago Press.

Stringer, C. 1984. "Human Evolution and Biological Adaptation in the Pleistocene." Pp. 55-83 in *Hominid Evolution and Community Ecology*, edited by R. Toley. London: Academic Press.

Struhsaker, T.T. 1969. "Correlates of Ecology and Social Organization Among African Cercopithecines." *Folia Primatology* 11: 80-118.

Struhsaker, T., and S. Gartlan. 1970. "Observations on the Behaviour and Ecology of the Patas Monkey (*Erythnocebus Patas*) in the Waza Reserve, Cameroon." *Journal of Zoology*, London 161: 49-63.

Strum, S. 1987. "Baboon Models and Muddles." Pp. 87-104 in *The Evolution of Human Behavior: Primate Models*, edited by W. Kinzey. Albany, NY: State University of New York Press.

Sugiyama, Y. 1968. "Social Organization of Chimpanzees in the Budongo Forest, Uganda." *Primates* 9: 225-58.

Sussman, R.W., and P.A. Garber. 1987. "A New Interpretation of the Social Organization and Mating System of the Callitrichidae." *Internaltional Journal of Primatology* 8: 73-92.

Takasaki, H. 1985. "Female Life History and Mating Patterns Among the M Group Chimpanzees of the Mahale National Park, Tanzania." *Primates* 26: 121-129.

Tanner, N. 1987. "The Chimpanzee Model Revisited and the Gathering Hypothesis." Pp. 3-27 in *The Evolution of Human Behavior: Primate Models*, edited by W. Kinzey. Albany, NY: State University of New York Press.

Teleki, G. 1973. *The Predatory Behavior of Wild Chimpanzee.* Lewisburg, PA: Bucknell University Press.

Tenaza, R.R. 1975. "Territory and Monogamy amaong Kloss' Gibbons (*Hylobates klossii*) in Siberut Island, Indonesia." *Folia Primatology* 24: 60-80.

Terborgh, J., and A. Wilson-Goldizan. 1985. "On the Mating System of Cooperatively Breeding Saddle-Backed Tamarin (*Saquinus fuscicollis*)." *Behavioral Ecology and Sociobiology* 16: 293-299.

Tilson, R. L. 1981. "Family Formation Strategies of Kloss's Gibbons." *Folia Primatology* 35: 259-287.

Tobias, P. 1985. *Hominid Evolution: Past, Present and Future.* New York: Alan Liss.

Tutin, C.E.G. 1979. "Mating Patterns and Reproductive Strategies in a Community of Wild Chimpanzees, Pan Troglodytes Schweinfurthii." *Behavioral Ecology Sociobiology* 6: 29-38.

Tutin, C.E.G., W.C. McGrew, and P.J. Baldwin. 1983. "Social Organization of Savanna-Dwelling Chimpanzees, Pan Troglodytes Verus, at Mt. Assirik, Senegal." *Primates* 24: 154-173.

Tuttle, R. 1986. *Apes of the World: Their Social Behavior Communication, Mentality, and Ecology.* Park Ridge, NJ: Noyes Publication.

Washburn, S.L. 1963. "Behavior and Human Evolution." Pp. 190-203 in *Classification and Human Evolution*, edited by S.L. Washburn. Chicago: Aldine.

Washburn, S.L., and I. DeVore. 1961. "Social Behavior of Baboons and Early Man." Pp. 91-105 in *Social Life of Early Man*, edited by S.L. Washburn. Chicago: Aldine.

Watts, D. 1985. "Relations Between Group Size and Composition and Feeding Competition in Mountain Gorilla Groups." *Animal Behavior* 33: 72-85.

_____. 1988. "Environmental Influences on Mountain Gorilla Time Budgets." *American Journal of Primatology* 15: 195-211.

Weber, A.W., and A. Vedder. 1983. "Population Dynamics of the Gorillas: 1959-1978." *Biological Conservation* 26: 341-366.

Wellman, B., and S.D. Berkowitz. 1988. *Social Structures: A Network Approach.* Cambridge: Cambridge University Press.

Westermarck, E. 1891. *The History of Human Marriage.* London: Macmillan.

Williams, B.J. 1974. "A Model of Band Society." *American Antiquity* 39, Pt. 2, Memoir 29.

Wolpoff, M.H. 1976. "Some Aspects of the Evolution of Early Hominid Sexual Dimorphism." *Current Anthropology* 17: 579-606.

_____. 1978. "Analogies and Interpretations in Paleoanthropology." Pp. 461-503 in *Early Hominids of Africa*, edited by C. Jolly. London: Duckworth.

Wood, B. 1985. "Sexual Dimorphism in the Hominid Fossil Record." Pp. 105-123 in *Human Sexual Dimorphism*, edited by J. Ghesquiere, R.D. Martin, and F. Newcombe. London: Taylor and Francis.

Wrangham, R.W. 1979. "On the Evolution of Ape Social Systems." *Social Science Information* 18: 335-368.

_____. 1987. "The Significance of African Apes for Reconstructing Human Social Evolution." Pp. 51-71 in *The Evolution of Human Behavior: Primate Models*, edited by W. Kinzey. New York: State University of New York Press.

Wrangham, R.W., and B. Smuts. 1980. "Sex Differences in the Behavioural Ecology of Chimpanzees in the Gombe National Park, Tanzania." *Journal Reproductive Fertility* 28(Supplement): 13-31.

Yamagiwa, J. 1983. "Diachronic Changes in Two Eastern Lowland Gorilla Groups (Gorilla gorilla graueri) in the Mt. Kahuzi Region, Zaire." *Primates* 25: 174-183.

Zihlman, A.L., and J.M. Lowenstein. 1983. "Ramapithecus and Pan Paniscus: Significance for Human Origins." Pp. 677-94 in *New Interpretations of Ape and Human Ancestry*, edited by R. Ciochon and R. Corruccin. New York: Plenum Press.

Advances in Human Ecology

Edited by **Lee Freese,** *Washington State University*

Volume 1, 1992, 234 pp. $73.25
ISBN 1-55938-091-8

CONTENTS: **Preface,** *Lee Freese.* **The Last Ancestor: An Ecological Network Model on the Origins of Human Sociality,** *Alexandra Maryanski.* **The Evolution of Macrosociety: Why Are Large Societies Rare?,** *Richard Machalek.* **Separation Versus Unification in Sociological Human Ecology,** *William R. Catton, Jr.* **The Natural Ecology of Human Ecology,** *Jeffrey S. Wicken.* **Between the Atom and the Void: Hierarchy in Human Ecology,** *Gerald L. Young.* **From Entropy to Economy: A Thorny Path,** *C. Dyke.* **The Ethical Foundations of Sustainable Economic Development,** *R. Kerry Turner and David W. Pearce.* **The Energy Consumption Turnaround and Socioeconomic Well-Being in Industrial Societies in the 1980s,** *Marvin E. Olsen.*

JAI PRESS INC.

55 Old Post Road - No. 2   P.O. Box 1678
Greenwich, Connecticut 06836-1678
Tel: (203) 661-7602   Fax: (203)661-0792